ASYLUM SEEKERS AND T

# Asylum Seekers and the State

## The Politics of Protection in a Security-Conscious World

CLAUDIA TAZREITER
*University of New South Wales, Australia*

ASHGATE

Published by
Ashgate Publishing Limited
Gower House
Croft Road
Aldershot
Hants GU11 3HR
England

Ashgate Publishing Company
Suite 420
101 Cherry Street
Burlington, VT 05401-4405
USA

Ashgate website: http://www.ashgate.com

**British Library Cataloguing in Publication Data**
Tazreiter, Claudia
Asylum seekers and the state : the politics of protection in a security-conscious world
1.Asylum, Right of - Germany 2.Asylum, Right of - Australia 3.Refugees - Government policy - Germany 4.Refugees - Government policy - Australia 5.Germany - Emigration and immigration 6.Australia - Emigration and immigration
I.Title
323.6'31

**Library of Congress Cataloging-in-Publication Data**
Tazreiter, Claudia.
Asylum seekers and the State : the politics of protection in a security-conscious world / by Claudia Tazreiter.
p. cm.
Includes bibliographical references and index.
ISBN 0-7546-4069-8
1. Refugees--Government policy. 2. Refugees--Government policy--Germany. 3. Refugees--Government policy--Australia. 4. Refugees--Legal status, laws, etc. 5. Asylum, Right of. I. Title.

JV6346.T39 2004
362.87'56--dc22

2004006897

ISBN 0 7546 4069 8
ISBN 978-0-7546-4069-1

Reprinted 2006

Printed in Great Britain by Antony Rowe Ltd, Chippenham, Wiltshire

# Contents

## PART II: HISTORICAL AND CULTURAL DEVELOPMENTS IN IMMIGRATION AND PROTECTION: THE CASE STUDIES



## PART III: THE POLITICS OF EXCLUSION

# List of Tables

# Acknowledgements

My deep gratitude goes to the many non-government organisations and advocates for asylum seekers in both Germany and Australia who gave generously of their time and expertise and contributed to this research by taking part in interviews and making documents available to me. Many of the Germany NGOs were also gracious and generous hosts at a time when I was far away from home.

Maria Markus provided guidance, encouragement and displayed her generous humanity throughout the process of writing this book. Michael Pusey, Michael Humphrey, Clive Kessler, Jocelyn Pixley and Paul Jones from the School of Sociology and Anthropology at the University of New South Wales, offered collegiality, support and encouragement. Klaus Bade, Director of the Institute for Migration and Intercultural Studies (IMIS), at the University of Osanbrück was a gracious host during a research visit to Germany. The German Academic Exchange Fellowship (DAAD) assisted the research with a grant which enabled me to stay in Germany for an extended period. Diarmuid Maguire in the Department of Government and International Relations at University of Sydney, supported the early stages of my research.

Finally, my family have been a source of steadfast support and encouragement through the process of research and writing.

# List of Abbreviations

| | |
|---|---|
| **ACM** | Australasian Correctional Management |
| **ACSJC** | Australian Catholic Social Justice Council |
| **AI** | Amnesty International |
| **APS** | Australian Protective Service |
| **AUST** | *The Australian* |
| **CAT** | Convention Against Torture |
| **CDU** | Christlich-Demokratische Union |
| **CEDAW** | Convention on the Elimination of All Forms of Discrimination Against Women 1981 |
| **CROC** | Convention on the Rights of the Child 1989 |
| **CSU** | Christlich-Soziale Union |
| **DIMA** | Department of Immigration and Multicultural Affairs (1996-2001) |
| **DIMIA** | Department of Immigration, Multicultural and Indigenous Affairs (2001-) |
| **DRK** | Deutsches Rotes Kreuz (German Red Cross) |
| **ECRE** | European Council on Refugees and Exiles |
| **EU** | European Union |
| **FAZ** | *Frankfurter Allgemeine Zeitung* |
| **FDP** | Freie Demokratische Partei |
| **FR** | *Frankfurter Rundschau* |
| **HREOC** | Human Rights and Equal Opportunity Commission |
| **HRW** | Human Rights Watch |
| **ICCPR** | International Covenant on Civil and Political Rights |
| **IOM** | International Organization for Migration |
| **JRS** | Jesuit Refugee Service |
| **RCOA** | Refugee Council of Australia |
| **RRT** | Refugee Review Tribunal |
| **SIS** | Schengen Information System |
| **SMH** | *Sydney Morning Herald* |
| **SPD** | Sozialdemokratische Partei Deutschlands |
| **STARTTS** | Service for the Treatment and Rehabilitation of Torture and Trauma Survivors |
| **SZ** | *Süddeutsche Zeitung* |
| **TAZ** | *Die Tageszeitung* |
| **TPV** | Temporary Protection Visa |
| **UDHR** | Universal Declaration of Human Rights 1948 |
| **UN** | United Nations |
| **UNHCR** | United Nations High Commission for Refugees |
| **VFST** | Victorian Foundation for the Survivors of Torture |
| **WCC** | World Council of Churches |

# Chapter 1

# Introduction: ambivalence and the outsider

Media outlets around the world are saturated with stories focused on security, war and terrorism. From many vantage points, East and West, in economically developed and less developed countries, fear and suspicion of outsiders has intensified into visceral hatred expressed in overt and covert acts of violence. Some acts of violence against outsiders are carried out by individuals, others are the actions of states using coercive force in both symbolic and in tangible ways to exclude certain groups and individuals. Some of these actions may well be justified. Many are not.

Individuals express opinions, and states carry out actions premised on a complex interplay of social, economic and political anxieties. Caught in the web of these anxieties are refugees and asylum seekers. Those individuals seeking protection have faced an increasingly hostile reception in the countries in which they seek asylum in the period since the end of Communism in Europe. Hostility toward refugees and asylum seekers has intensified since 2001. In no small measure, such sentiment rests on a fear of terrorism. The human rights of the most threatened and marginalised people in the world; those at risk of severe forms of persecution, torture, or loss of life – have been put at greater risk by the new emphasis on security in the developed world since the September 11, 2001 terrorist attacks on New York and Washington.

This book seeks to deal with an aspect of the global dilemma of people moving across borders in search of protection and safety. The way in which such people are received and treated in countries which are signatories to International Human Rights Conventions is significant in a number of ways. With a world that is increasingly interconnected in economic, political and in cultural ways, harsh and exclusionary measures by one state are likely to have negative knock-on effects for neighbouring states. To be sure, the root-causes of refugee flows need to be identified, and real solutions found to the violence which causes flight. At the same time, the obligations placed on states who are signatories to the 1951 United Nations Refugee Convention (hereafter, *Refugee Convention*) are fundamental to ensuring those in need of protection are not placed in danger by being sent back to the source of their persecution – *refouled.* Indeed the test of a state's commitment to human rights principles and the spirit of the *Refugee Convention,* is in the treatment of asylum seekers who will almost always of necessity enter a country in a clandestine fashion in order to ask for protection. This book examines the dilemma which asylum seekers present to states they enter through the case studies of Germany and Australia.

## Protection: a background

In 1999, the National Gallery of Great Britain held an exhibition of work by the Brazilian artist Ana Maria Pacheco. The subject matter of the paintings and sculptures draws on Christian images of trial, tribulation, sacrifice and pain such as the martyrdom of Saint Sebastian and the temptation of Saint Anthony. The artist's interpretations evoke some of the most harrowing excesses of the twentieth century: the torture and death of innocent martyrs on the altar of modern cruelty. A large triptych in the exhibition, *Luz Eterna,* is evocative of the experience of exile. On the left, an exhausted figure is dragged away by two men, a surveillance camera taking in the scene. The central panel shows a mass of frightened exiles attempting to flee, at the same time transfixed by a horde of helicopters hovering above them. Pacheco says that one of the inspirations for this central panel was a photograph of refugees in Jordan in 1990 along with a strikingly similar image of huddled masses from 1897, depicting victims of religious strife in Brazil. The last panel depicts a writhing martyr, drawing on Saint Anthony, fleeing the menacing clutches of two Sphinxes. In the background, burnt-out, bombed remains of a city suggest the decimated cities of Europe after World War II. The added spectre of a concentration camp is suggested on the horizon, where rings of barbed wire are suggestive of this twentieth century form of mass cruelty.

Visual representations of the human condition can have the power to synthesise the complexity of persecution and degradation, freezing a moment, an emotion, a cry, and communicating it with energy and clarity which can escape the written form. Images of exile and of punishment, whether in painted or photographic form, give us a view into an expansive world of displacement and homelessness: themes which seem to traverse historical epochs.

The persecution of individuals and groups on political religious or cultural grounds has persisted in various waves throughout human history. While the reasons for persecution have varied greatly, so has the preparedness of host countries to receive those fleeing persecution. This book explores the reception asylum seekers face in the late twentieth century. In particular, the developments in Germany and Australia since 1989 are explored. The approach of this book, as a comparative study, indicates the response of two particular liberal democracies to problems at their borders and the tensions of arbitrating between national political, economic and social interests and transnational obligations pertaining to human rights. Secondly, the structure of the book, focusing on the issue of asylum seekers through the vehicle of NGOs, highlights the way in which non-state actors are of increased significance as representatives of groups and individuals rendered mute or powerless by violence, coercion and political upheaval.

The year 2001 marked the 50th anniversary of *Refugee Convention*, which most directly articulates the grounds of protection that should be offered those fleeing persecution. The majority of countries in the world do have real obligations to people who claim to be refugees, as signatories to the *Refugee Convention* and its Protocol of 1967.[1] In the fifty-year period since the establishment of the *Refugee Convention*, the idea of (some) rights being universal, and thereby applicable to all of humanity rather than the members of a particular state, has been given political efficacy through the vehicle of human rights. Rights, such as those embodied in the *Universal Declaration of Human Rights* of 1948 privilege no particular concept of human life, of cultural traits, beliefs or practices. Moreover, the rise in the international efficacy of human rights as principles of broad value to all people has been enabled, at least in part, through the proliferation of non-government organisations (NGOs) since the end of the Second World War, who have advocated for the extension of such rights in many forums: locally, nationally and internationally, with governments, business and citizen groups. NGOs such as Amnesty International and Human Rights Watch, are only the most prominent of hundreds of organisations which advocate for human rights in situations where they see such rights being abused. NGOs have increasingly spoken out for the marginalised and the voiceless around the world in an 'advocacy revolution' (Ignatieff 2001; 8). The proliferation of such activity has not only occurred in economically developing countries and in 'emergent' democracies, but also in the affluent democracies of the West.

We see that the consolidation of human rights has gathered momentum in the later half of the twentieth century through the proliferation of human rights institutions and the efficacy of the idea that protecting such rights is of intrinsic value across and between cultures and nations. The central pillars of human rights, including the *Refugee Convention,* continue to be important instruments for ensuring the protection of people in vulnerable, life-threatening circumstances. Yet at the same time, the persecution of individuals and groups has continued around the world, testing the practical efficacy of the universal norms embodied in the obligations of 'transnational' justice. The grounds for persecution of particular individuals or groups continue to relate to those characteristics which differentiate people, such as race, religion, nationality, gender and particular political affiliations. Those very distinctions are what should be irrelevant, or at least suspended, if more than lip service is paid to the normative framework of human rights.

While we may agree that the penetration of human rights as valued principles have proliferated during the late twentieth century, geopolitical shifts in the balance of political order from the early 1990s have resulted in an increase in localised conflicts and in humanitarian crises in many parts of the world. The dissolution of the Soviet Union ruptured the Cold War stand-off which had

1 134 countries are Party to the Refugee Convention and to the Protocol of 1967 (see UNHCR 2000).

maintained a false sense of certainty with the political polarisation of the world around the camps of two superpowers, the Soviet Union and the United States of America. The effects of decolonisation in Africa and Asia also continued to be felt into the 1990s with regional and local conflict in the African continent and in many parts of Asia.

A brief overview of developments in the last decade, related to the processes resulting in people becoming refugees, begins the story from which I formulate the central problem addressed in this book. I ask: how can we best ensure a balance between the protection obligations which those claiming asylum seek to engage, and the local needs and interests within societies which are asylum destinations? Moreover, what are some of the recent models which address this question?

Before elaborating the various questions and dilemmas which flow from this problem, I will briefly sketch the context. In 1989 there were 15 million 'persons of concern' according to the UNHCR.[2] In 1995 there were more than 27 million; in the year 2000 over 22 million. The UNHCR warns that such figures should only be used as a 'snapshot', as data is collected haphazardly – even by industrialised nations – and in areas of war and conflict, hazard and inaccessibility can make the collation of accurate statistics impossible. This would suggest that the true numbers of 'people of concern' could well be much higher. New 'push factors' forcing people to flee their homes surface in different parts of the world every few months, sometimes every few weeks. In 1992, the world witnessed a mass exodus from Somalia. A few years later Rwanda erupted in hatred and violence, in the form of 'ethnic cleansing'; a phenomenon we also witnessed with horror in the former Yugoslavia. Violence spread through the Balkans during the late 1990s in Kosovo and further east, in Chechnya. In 2001, the United States of America instigated a 'war on terrorism', following the September 11 attacks on the World Trade Centre in New York and on the Pentagon in Washington. This 'war on terrorism' has resulted in a renewed exodus and displacement of people in Afghanistan, and more recently, Iraq. In many other locations, disaster, violence and persecution have led to individuals and groups fleeing their homes in search of safety and peace. Though there are many 'root causes' of the social, political and economic problems that create the mass displacements of populations, durable solutions are not easily found.

Paradoxically, it is the countries which themselves safeguard democratic principles, uphold the rule of law, and are the most vocal defenders of human rights around the globe which have felt the need to increase mechanisms of

[2] 'Persons of concern' include refugees as persons recognised under the 1951 UN Refugee Convention, the 1969 OAU Refugee Convention, persons granted humanitarian status, and those granted temporary protection; asylum seekers, as persons whose application for refugee status is pending; returned refugees who have returned to their place of origin but remain of concern to UNHCR for a maximum period of two years; and Internally displaced persons (IDPs) who have been displaced within their country and returned IDPs, who remain of concern to UNHCR for a maximum period of two years.

immigration control over the last decade. Western democracies, which have in the past benefited from immigration, whether through guest worker programmes, or other planned immigration intakes, are increasingly concerned to guard their borders from the movement of people, including those claiming protection under the *Refugee Convention*, with the result that migration has become increasingly clandestine, with people-smugglers profiting from the trade in human cargo.

Herein lies a dilemma for the defenders of human rights as a universal ideal: the ongoing and incommensurable nature of such rights and the question of how they are to be defended and articulated as obligations alongside the legitimate needs and priorities within sovereign states. Of course, if we are only talking of human rights as 'negative rights', as neoliberals might – stopping short of causing harm to others – the dilemma remains narrowly contained. However, if human rights are to be substantiated through the dispensation of 'positive' rights, we have a more substantive dilemma. The idea of 'positive' rights, applicable across borders even in a minimal sense, requires some form of cosmopolitan institutional and legal framework with coercive powers (Habermas 1998; 319). Moreover, a human rights framework, as outlined in the Universal Declaration of Human Rights of 1948 (UDHR), differentiates between civil and political rights, and social and economic rights.[3] While most attention within human rights discourse in the post Second World War period, has been on civil and political rights, economic and social rights have increasingly been raised by various parties and organisations in the late twentieth century as important rights to facilitate full human development. With the issue of 'positive rights', human needs and the thorny issue of resources and their distribution become central.

The 1951 *Refugee Convention* promises non-refoulement; that those with genuine fears of persecution will not be returned to the source of their persecution. With this promise, receiver societies also bear the consequence (burden), of providing for the needs of such new arrivals. It would follow that addressing the 'root causes' of flight would be in the long-term interest of receiver societies, ensuring that the numbers of unanticipated arrivals claiming protection are reduced. However, through the 1990s we have seen efforts on the part of Western states directed at deterring such 'irregular' arrivals, and measures aimed at their removal, rather than initiatives seeking the resolution of refugee-causing conflict and violence. Monetary aid to economically developing countries has been in decline in many countries of the West, and what development assistance is given is often in the form of 'tied aid', focusing on particular projects with an economic or other benefit to the donor country. Certainly diplomatic, development and

[3] This distinction, articulated by T.H. Marshall (1950), embodied a complete vision of human development supported by a rights framework which went beyond narrow 'negative' rights. Marshall's approach is a 'thick' vision, comprising the quality and conditions of life, as well as ideals and aspirations. These rights were later affirmed by the United Nations International Covenant on Civil and Political Rights of 1966 and the United Nations International Covenant on Economic, Social and Cultural Rights of 1966.

democratic institution-building efforts in refugee-producing states continue to take place. At the same time though, measures aimed at deterring the arrival of asylum seekers have become a priority for states of the West, with an infusion of significant resources to fund internal and external measures to detect, detain, deport and in other ways discourage 'irregular' or 'illegal' immigrants, or 'aliens', including those with protection claims.

The response to those who have fled their homes and seek protection elsewhere requires careful and detailed differentiation, highlighting the needs and the rights of the resident as well as the newcomer. It is this tension between the 'needs of strangers' and the needs of citizens which both state and non-state actors reflect in their arguments for admission or expulsion (rejection) of asylum seekers. Michael Ignatieff (1984) reminds us that understanding human needs and their fulfilment is a process open to politicisation and manipulation, as it is a process based upon a presumption that someone knows the needs of another, or indeed that we truly understand our own needs. Ignatieff asks the penetration question: 'when is it right to speak for the needs of strangers? Politics is not only the art of representing the needs of strangers; it is also the perilous business of speaking on behalf of needs which strangers have had no chance to articulate on their own' (ibid.; 12). Ignatieff's invocation reminds us that the issue of representation is by no means clear-cut.

## On obligation and the stranger: theoretical perspectives

How then shall we consider an obligation to be held across borders in the form of transnational justice? Moreover, how should we think about an obligation to a stranger who may be either near or distant? The idea of an obligation to an 'other' raises the issue of justice and what boundaries demarcate it, as well as the persons to whom just conduct should be extended. In other words, how do we decide the extent to which we are obliged to act in a just manner? The literature conceptualising and debating the definitions and boundaries of justice and of obligations is vast and wide-ranging, emerging from the social contract tradition of the seventeenth and eighteenth centuries and beyond. In the late twentieth century the seminal work on justice, *A Theory of Justice,* by John Rawls, has been the trigger for a vigorous debate on the limits of justice, more particularly in view of the conditions of modern life. The polarities of this debate lie between cosmopolitans, holding the view that justice must have a transnational character in order to be consistent with the idea that all people share 'basic rights'; and at the other end of the spectrum, communitarians, who hold that duties are in the main held to members of the same community, defined according to descent or to culture, and the bonds of common citizenship (O'Neill 2000; 187).

Rights, in the form of human rights, must be given substance through detailing to whom obligations lie and what the basis of such obligations is. In this regard the moral standing of a person, or how we see others, will help to answer the question of obligation, indicating where and how a claim can be made. In our daily lives we make countless assumptions about others which guide our own actions and choices. Such assumptions may be unconscious or part of a routine action repertoire; taken-for-granted ways of judging, thinking and acting. However, does action towards distant strangers carry the same 'regularity' or ease, which action toward those closer at hand can exhibit? Is nearness or distance a sufficient guiding principle for determining who remains within the domain of moral concern and who is excluded from it? On what basis is such a concept of distance grounded; physical distance, cultural distance? Rights, in isolation from the question of obligation, make it difficult to define where a claim can be lodged and which institutional mechanisms can fulfil or guarantee a right:

> Since action at a distance is usually institutionally and technologically mediated action, it is hard and often impossible to determine just which individual's action harms or injures which others, and hence hard to discern who might have rights of redress against whom (O'Neill 2000: 199).

The obligation that holds specifically for those seeking protection requires a state to properly consider a protection application. The refugee policy of a state reveals much more than just the most evident, superficial administrative and strategic techniques and priorities of a particular government. Refugee policy also reveals aspects of the core values of a state, which immigration policy *per se* does not reveal. Immigration policy is broadly understood as an aspect of 'nation-building', utilised to balance economic and social deficits at particular points in time. On the other hand, a state which has acceded to international human rights conventions, has 'special' obligations towards an individual who may be a refugee, no matter his/her mode of entry. Such 'special' obligations relate to the protection which a refugee requires while the origin of his/her persecution continues and moreover, these are obligations which do not extend to immigrants generally. However, it is the process of establishing to whom such obligations extend which remains the crucible testing all the parties to the agreement and is a process which can be physically and psychologically testing for genuine claimants. Those claiming protection are subject to an enormous variety of conditions and entitlements while 'living through' a determination period.

## Living with strangers

The profile of 'stranger' remains central to the global disorder which distinguishes 'late modernity'. Fluid and disjunctive arrangements and priorities press on the institutions people rely on; institutions which increasingly are faced with an incommensurability between the demands put on them and the resource capability to meet such demands. The concept of globalisation, while remaining a much contested concept with no singular definition, is a phenomenon which explains the compression of distance and the erosion of physical and socio-economic borders which have accelerated over the last decade and more (Held and McGrew 2000; 3). With the rapid, instantaneous nature of communication and the capacity to be able to transact and negotiate with people, institutions and states right around the globe, the world has become at once smaller and yet simultaneously too large to properly engage with – except perhaps in the economic realm. I follow here the distinction drawn by Ulrich Beck between *globalisation* and *globalism*. *Globalisation* is seen as dissolving and fragmenting the certainties and control mechanisms within individual states, where transnational actors engage in networks which cut through and undermine the sovereignty of states by contesting various forms of power, identities and so on. *Globalism* on the other hand relates to the view that the world market eliminates or takes over the need for political action: '. . . the ideology of rule by the world market . . . proceeds monocausally and economistically, reducing the multi-dimensionality of globalisation to a single, economic dimension that is itself conceived in a linear fashion. If it mentions at all the other dimensions of globalisation – ecology, culture, politics, civil society – it does so only by placing them under the sway of the world-market system' (Beck 2000; 100). From this perspective we can begin to comprehend the gravity of the task an individual state faces in maintaining internal coherence in meeting the needs of members and balancing obligations which are transnational.

While the phenomenon of *globalisation* and the economically focused *globalism* continue in an 'uneven' trajectory across the globe, the locally felt impact of this multifarious phenomenon regularly manifests itself in some form of defensive mechanism or strategy. The effects of globalisation are not necessarily linear or felt in the same way in all locations. Indeed the effects of global interactions may have opposing effects at different sites (Bohmann and Lutz-Bachman 1997; 11, Appadurai 1990). A certain *disjuncture* occurs both from the differential impact of global forces and the variety of cultural expressions which continue and evolve alongside, or in spite of, the homogenisation that results under global forces.

We may think here of the stranger, or *other* in contemporary societies as the ever-present figure who inadvertently makes uneasy those who are 'at home' or who belong. The stranger is a counterpoint to what is homogenous and predictable, yet necessary to the very conditions which modernity or the 'second modernity' we are living through hold as central: '. . . universalist rationality, emotional detachment, the priority given to intellectual life and money' (Beck in Tabonni 1995; 21). Whereas in colonial or imperialist times, the stranger could either be excluded or assimilated (Bauman 1995; 2), in late modernity a different manifestation of the stranger is relevant. The uncertainty or 'disembeddedness' which are consequences of contemporary life, mean that the stranger is now a regular part of a generalised uncertainty. The stranger is indeed here today and with us tomorrow, yet it is not so much the presence of the stranger which continues to confound or annoy, but the *ambivalence* which characterises both the category of stranger and the distance between the stranger and those who are at home. When the certainties of life, of one's place in it, of a sense of belonging to place or to a culture are increasingly uncertain and contested, *ambivalence as existence* can become the prevailing 'feeling'. In such a scenario, the presence of the stranger, perhaps because she/he is by now a permanent feature of modern societies, is increasingly unnerving; a regular reminder of one's own frailty (Beck 1996; 384).

It is unnerving to consider that the stranger who does not fit the ' . . . cognitive, moral, or aesthetic map of the world' (Bauman 1995; 1), is in a constant process of change, with different groups and individuals moving in and out of categories of insider and outsider. It is the way we live with strangers today that is at issue; what rights are conferred on the stranger and on what basis obligations toward the stranger are met. A degree of social distance is a given in mass societies, with the urban individual a stranger to most of his/her neighbours and certainly to those encountered in the daily transactions of life. We may actively engage with only a tiny percentage of those that daily appear on our horizons - on trains, in bank queues, in a park or a cafe. Moreover, we give special treatment to those we are intimately connected with, who sustain us socially (Hollinger 2001; 238). The perception of 'others' is mostly filtered through some third party - often an institution such as mass media, or an arm of bureaucracy. It is in this light that we see evidence of the incommensurability between what we *ought* to do, *can* do, or indeed *want* to do. To extrapolate from Kantian ethics, the *ought* is guided by a judgement which would hold many of the differences which render a person as a stranger or 'other' to be morally irrelevant. Yet the instrumentalisation of much of our combined will through institutional means, puts our judgement and actions at arms length from those upon whom it has an impact. Some of the dilemmas which arise from the distance created by modern institutions are discussed in later chapters. At this most general level though, a widespread predisposition toward ambivalence which from the sum total of the pressures, complexities and layering of contemporary life, and the uncertainty which accompanies it. I take ambivalence to be an unintended by-product of universalism and of the cosmopolitan ideals which are complementary to it; in this sense, a product of modernity itself. First, the very universality of human rights causes a degree of ambivalence even where there is an agreement to the value of such rights, because of the problem of situating obligations. Second, ambivalence is a product of self-defence in the face of the complexities and uncertainties of modern life.

Though in the case of asylum seekers, obligations do exist, they are not as easily articulated or transparent as obligations to fellow citizens. Rather, obligations to asylum seekers require an additional dose of impartiality to the more straightforward obligations we have to fellow citizens. Moreover, the obligations relevant to 'protection' mechanisms are readily able to be politicised. The way in which political leaders communicate about such obligations can have a transformative impact to public opinion and social attitudes. We are more likely to be ambivalent in our judgement when we are not personally touched by an event, even more so when an event occurs to a stranger. It is particularly on an issue such as territorial sovereignty, which uninvited asylum seekers breach, that the so-called 'zero-sum game' view of rights emerges in the reactions of receiver societies. This false, though nevertheless potent view, imagines that conferring rights on one group will detract from, or negate the rights conferred on the rest.

Keeping in mind the discussion so far, a two-pronged hypothesis emerges from the dilemmas articulated earlier in relation to the sorts of obligations which hold toward a stranger. First, I contend that asylum flows cannot be fully controlled at national borders without an erosion of the foundations upon which justice and human rights are based. Second, the reaction to asylum seekers is one significant aspect of a politics of *social distance* which is not only a reaction to asylum seekers, but to all 'strangers' Accordingly, the politics of *social distance* can be imposed on members of a polity who are judged as less worthy or deserving, just as they can on strangers and non-members. The transnational forces described earlier (globalisation and globalism), impact on local neighbourhoods around the globe in often opaque and multi-layered processes that are not readily understood. Transnational cultural and political networks and globalising economies, lead to sporadic outbursts of anxiety, expressed at times in violence towards foreigners, at other times at the ballot box in support for nationalist and protectionist policies. The psychological yearning for social space defined and able to be controlled within a nation-state *for* members, fosters antagonism toward the stranger who would encroach possibilities for certainty, or the comfort of cultural traditions; a yearning for an idealised past. Those most visible as having encroached valuable social distance are likely to become the target of policy initiatives aimed at national security and 'sealing' measures flowing in the opposite direction to economic and political initiatives of co-operation toward transnational, global initiatives. Asylum seekers within the borders of a state, and particularly where they have entered in a clandestine fashion, are a likely target of such measures.

It is precisely this tension in representing others and the dilemmas which arise from such actions; knowing when to act, how far to articulate a needs hierarchy for others, and taking some account of the often unintended consequences of action, which I address in relation to asylum seekers who have made their way to Western states. How can a balance be struck between the protection obligations which those claiming asylum seek to engage, and the local needs and interests within societies which are asylum destinations? The way in which Western countries deal with asylum seekers who have a strong moral claim to (some) resources of that society, fall into both predictable and unpredictable camps. Paradoxically, it is the internal arrangements of Western societies, founded on principles of individual rights, liberty and democratic institutions, which bestow the potential extension of rights to those seeking protection in the first place. Under conditions where such rights and the institutions which safeguard them are seen as finite, even fragile, the introduction of harsh and increasingly restrictive measures in dealing with asylum seekers should not surprise us.

There are numerous vantage points from which to shed light on the asylum discourse in national and international contexts. In this book I investigate the work of non-state actors who advocate for those claiming to be refugees as the prism through which to understand the relationship between states and unwanted, uninvited arrivals who are claiming protection. I make no claim that asylum seekers are more worthy of attention than any of the groups designated as 'people of concern' by the UNHCR. Certainly it can be argued that other categories of people, such as IDPs (internally displaced people) are in equally hazardous situations to asylum seekers, and through the last decade have been more numerous than asylum seekers who have managed to enter an asylum country. However, my objective is to account for the reaction in particular host countries, as well as the intervention of NGOs to policies aimed at asylum seekers. My intention is to better understand host societies and the processes which impact on the reception and treatment of those claiming protection.

The reception of those seeking protection in host countries is addressed explicitly in following chapters, with the root causes of exile addressed only where the context requires. The admission or rejection of an asylum seeker in a host country is a process which leaves an imprint first and foremost on the individual asking for protection, followed by the host country, as well as having knock-on effects for future arrivals who wish to claim protection. In addition, neighbouring countries and the international and national organisations which respond to the arrival of asylum seekers respond in a variety of ways to the dilemma asylum seekers pose. Due to the complexity and intermeshing of these relationships, I undertake a comparison of two countries which are significant countries of asylum. I compare the treatment of asylum seekers in Germany and Australia and the role of NGOs in this process. The time-frame under consideration is the period from 1989 to 2003.

The central questions of the book are:

1. How can the abstract obligations which hold for asylum seekers be reconciled with the quantitative and social limits of needs fulfilment of an individual state (the 'national interest')?
2. As NGOs emerge and proliferate, what impact can we expect from their action within and across states?
3. Is it possible to identify certain forms of action or of communication most appropriate or effective in advocacy for asylum seekers as non-members of the society in which they seek protection?
4. What burden can citizens be expected to bear in meeting the needs of asylum seekers?

The book outlines the context within which the so-called 'world refugee problem' can be considered. Though the following two chapters focus upon presenting the theoretical dilemmas relevant to the problem at hand, these discussions are interspersed with some data and evidence of both the treatment of asylum seekers and the impact they have on receiver societies. How have the German and the Australian state responded to the arrival of refugees and asylum seekers? In turn, how have refugee NGOs acted and reacted to these responses in both states? Through the middle sections of the book (chapters four to seven), the theoretical framework discussed in the opening chapters is set against the national discourses on the reception of refugees and asylum seekers. Is there a correlation between (political) perceptions of refugees and asylum seekers, the administrative logic applied to such perceptions, and the reality of the impact which these arrivals have? How should we consider any dissonance between these developments?

Chapter two explores state sovereignty, the integration of newcomers and the concepts of obligations and rights within and beyond the state. Moreover, this chapter distinguishes refugee from migrant, outlining the distinction that ought to be made between the two groups. The political culture of a given state can have as potent a bearing on the path through which an individual claiming asylum negotiates, as the legal framework which establishes the limits of claims. This chapter builds the theoretical framework for considering how asylum seekers are dealt with.

Chapter three outlines a framework for deciphering the action of non-governmental actors. Such action is considered both at the elite level of policy formation and on the 'ground level' of everyday practice and engagement. NGOs are also considered in the broader *field* of civil society where other forms of action and dissent occur. Chapters four and five deal with Germany and Australia respectively, outlining the history of immigration and the situation of refugees and asylum seekers, amidst the broader grouping of outsiders – newcomer/stranger/foreigner.

Chapters six and seven continue to explore the case studies and to test the hypothesis of NGO action outlined in chapter three through specific points of tension in the refugee discourse in both countries such as refugee policy development, detention and deportation as well as the ongoing debates over resource allocation in meeting the basic needs of asylum seekers.

Chapter eight reviews the major arguments made in this book, as well as making some recommendations both for the activities of NGOs and states in dealing with asylum seekers.

## The comparison of Germany and Australia

As I suggested at the outset, those seeking protection warrant, in fact demand a response, first by their mere presence and second, under the transnational obligations flowing from a human rights framework. Even silence in the face of the question, 'will you protect me, offer me refuge' is a response of a kind - pointing to rejection. If someone knocks at our door and we do not answer, the message is all too clear – you are not welcome, not even for a respite. No doubt the arrival of people seeking protection at the back door (without invitation or documentation) has exacerbated the fear and distrust with which such individuals are met. Justifiable claims for a transnational system of belonging (transnational citizenship) and justice for all people (a cosmopolitan order), continue to be argued for in various forums. However, certainly for the movement of people across borders, the nation-state remains *the* significant broker of residence, formal as well as informal belonging, and for the allocation of resources. Comparative research of the response to protection claims provides valuable data for shedding light on the interplay between international and national asylum systems, highlighting different responses to the same phenomenon, as well as a variety of local interpretations of international laws. As Aleinikoff (1995) shows, the *Refugee Convention* as an instrument of International law, fails to establish any duty of states to admit refugees – merely not to *refoul*[4] them. This indeed proves to be a conundrum when played out on individual lives. Adequate reporting and monitoring devices are not in place in many areas of the world to ensure that states comply with the guarantee of *non-refoulement.*[5]

In the early 1980s increasingly restrictive asylum practices were introduced in many industrialised states relating to the admission and entitlements of people wanting to claim refugee status (UNHCR 1997; 191). Such developments coincided with an increase in the numbers of people seeking protection from new areas of the world. During the 1950s and 1960s those seeking protection in Western European countries came predominantly from the Communist countries of Europe, but by the late 1970s and early 1980s asylum seekers from Latin American, South America and Asian countries entered Western Europe, North America and Australia in increasing numbers. At the same time we have seen the development of national as well as regional policies to deter the arrival of those seeking protection. Deterrence measures have, over time, become more sophisticated, as well as co-ordinated between countries. Governments have deliberatively co-ordinated their policies and bureaucratic practices to unify measures aimed at deterring asylum seekers from entering their territory and for rejecting their claims if they do manage to enter. Strategies adopted by member states of the European Union, by the United States, Canada and Australia have converged in the use of external and internal controls. We must also bear in mind that migration movements have caused fissures within receiving countries as the demands of newcomers meet with resistance. Newcomers do not only highlight the tensions around the allocation of national resources, but expose the more or less stable identities to new influences and transformations.

There are cogent arguments to defend the actions of a state in ensuring its sovereignty is not threatened, and the economic and social well-being of its citizens is safeguarded. This does not, however, relieve the state of obligations to non citizens in their territory. It is reasonable and 'just' for a state to place a general immigration intake within a domestic policy agenda. This is most clearly indicated in classic countries of immigration such as Australia, where quotas of

---

[4] The return to the country of persecution.

[5] This is a role that NGOs have increasingly taken on, though with limited resources they often only highlight the most dramatic cases.

immigrants are directly related to domestic needs and fluctuations as well as to political considerations changing over time.

The countries under consideration were chosen as they are representative of 'most different' models of asylum host countries. Germany has been the key destination of asylum seekers in Europe for the past decade and moreover it has received significant numbers of immigrants of other categories in the post World War II period. Nevertheless, Germany has not had a proactive immigration system in place to deal with newcomers. The development of 'asylum politics' (Asylpolitik) in Germany has had a symbolic significance for other countries in the European Union, as well as for the global discussion of forced migration, resettlement and repatriation. In contemporary German society a number of factors have led to a heightened introspection of German identity and national belonging. The unification of East and West Germany is the most obvious as well as dramatic example. The question of foreigners living in Germany is a factor with a long history, but one with particular relevance in the 1990s. Just as Germany goes through the process of social unification (which many commentators argue will take at least one more generation), an opportunity remains open to recast the position of foreigners in Germany, thereby challenging the meaning of what it is to be a German. These factors compose the immigration terrain which an asylum seeker entering Germany faces. There are a number of different 'types' of foreigners living in Germany with distinct legal definitions and a variety of rights and entitlements. However, such differences are not apparent in the streets of cities and towns. Rather, the fact that another stranger is living 'among us' is the reality of everyday life. The lack of legal and social inclusion of second and third-generation guestworkers for instance, extends the total number of people registered as foreigners. Asylum seekers add to this number, creating an impression of being overburdened, flooded and so on.

By the mid 1990s the Federal Republic of Germany had become the second largest recipient of immigrants in the post-World War II period, after the United States. Since the mid 1980s refugees have made up a significant proportion of this immigration, with Germany being the most significant destination for refugees and asylum seekers in Europe by the early 1990s.[6] However, over and above sheer numbers, Germany is a particularly significant case study for research on the integration or indeed exclusion of refugees in Western countries, due to its distinct relationship to the concept of political persecution in the aftermath of World War II. Partly as atonement for actions under National Socialism, Germany has until recently had the most liberal constitution of Western countries in relation to refugees. These developments are detailed in chapter four.

Australia, in distinction from Germany, has a well established 'control system' of refugee resettlement within a broader 'quota' immigration system. This is

---

[6] Germany received more asylum seekers than the sum total of all other EU states during the early 1990s. By the late 1990s this situation had changed, with Great Britain being the recipient of the largest number of asylum seekers and illegal arrivals in 1999.

manifest in a 'humanitarian programme' as one component of a yearly immigration quota, whereby Australian immigration officials in overseas posts select 'off-shore' applicants who have met the refugee criteria, for resettlement in Australia. Applicants for resettlement places are usually selected in refugee camps and are permitted to permanently settle in Australia. In distinction, 'irregular immigrants', who arrive and subsequently seek to invoke Australia's protection obligations under the *Refugee Convention,* are termed 'on-shore' arrivals. On-shore arrivals constitute two groups; those who arrive with a visa for entry to Australia and those who do not. The former remain in the Australian community while their application for protection is assessed, the later have been subject to mandatory and non-reviewable detention since 1989. Such 'unauthorised arrivals' are detained until such time as a protection claim is accepted, or they are deported. Initially, we see immigration *per se* playing a distinctly different role in Germany and Australia in terms of 'nation-building'; in Australia immigration is an essential ingredient in the political and economic processes of 'nation-building; in Germany this is not the case. How then do such differences influence refugee policy and the treatment of asylum seekers? Is a country of immigration such as Australia, more open and receptive to asylum seekers as a result of a long-standing, institutionalised immigration system? Is there a greater resolve in the Australian community toward an understanding and acceptance of people from refugee backgrounds than is the case in Germany?

In addition, questions remain with us from the paradox between universal values and ethics which appear so central to how we formulate our lives on the one hand, and the reality of spatially bounded polities privileging their members *even* as it harms others. More than half a century ago, Hannah Arendt gave a pessimistic assessment of universal human rights as incapable of granting concrete protection in the face of inward looking states (Arendt 1973; 294). Her assessment remains relevant today in the face of an international protection system fracturing at the point where individual states are required to dispense their duties to those who need protection. Striking a balance between local needs and interests and those which are held universally remains the challenge for those who regard the 'community of persons' to extend beyond a predictable circle of loyalty – family, kin, nation.

While it is true that the 1990s has been a period of increased introspection about the arrival of refugees and asylum seekers in countries of the West, the term 'crisis', often used by government representatives, by international bodies, as well as in the media, mostly overplays the reality. The facts indicate that the majority of refugees are housed, fed and cared for in less developed countries, often bordering or close to a refugee's country of origin, albeit with international aid contributions. A relatively small percentage of potential refugees are able to make a claim for protection in countries of the West. This means that in the case of countries of the West, the 'crisis' in relation to refugees, is largely a matter of perception, and of how the arrival of asylum seekers is communicated to the members of the host country. For advocacy NGOs, it is a matter of engaging the *gentle art of persuasion*, of winning the *hearts and minds* of citizens and their representatives to maintain an open attitude to the arrival of refugees and asylum seekers, rather than leaving unchallenged the tendency toward reactive policy and administrative approaches which are themselves fuelled by political leaders attunded to a 'reactive' population, and at times playing on xenophobic attitudes and orientations.

In order to understand the reception outsiders face, one must first engage with those characteristics and factors which differentiate nations, peoples and cultures. Can we expect a similar reception and reaction to refugees in all places and situations? The comparative structure of the case studies allows this question to be addressed from the perspective of two countries with similar political structures, reflected in democratic institutions and the rule of law, yet diverging cultural legacies and understandings of nation. Moreover, geographical specificities vary enormously between Germany and Australia; Germany in the middle of Europe, is more susceptible to clandestine movement across its borders; Australia, in distinction, is relatively isolated as an island in the Asia Pacific region. Both countries share certain characteristics including a free press and vigourous civil society and a federation of states. They are both signatories to the 1951 *Refugee Convention* and the 1967 *Protocol*. However, they also differ in many other respects; culturally, historically and in terms of the formal and informal processes of identity formation. In addition, the relationship between civil society and the state differ between Germany and Australia, as does the role of the major churches.

One of the aims of this book will be to consider the effectiveness of NGO activity in these different national locations and cultural settings and to gauge the efficacy of universal norms over local and regional particularities. In short, to what extent are the principles that inform advocacy for refugees and asylum seekers able to be enacted in different local settings given the plethora of competing claims for resources and recognition by groups within a nation, before any consideration is given to newcomers?

## Non-government action

Earlier, I argued that NGOs have been pivotal in the proliferation and efficacy of the universalisation of human rights. In addition, it seems that NGOs are well placed to capture and interpret the detail and nuances of issues surrounding refugees and asylum seekers and to advocate for them as a result of the practical, grass roots and front line aspect of their work. Moreover, the growth of collaboration between national and international NGOs, as well as the relative independence of NGOs both from political influence and the dictates of the market, add to the efficacy of their work. A hypothesis which emerged through the research process was that NGOs have the potential, not always realised, of closing the gap between international norms held through human rights standards and the logic of 'national' sovereignty, as collective action can challenge the logic of state action in ways in which individuals rarely can.

If we accept that it is often the 'local' situation within a country of asylum which impacts on the prospects of those individuals seeking the protection of a particular state, we begin to grasp the fragility of the mechanisms in question. The local political culture; the efficacy of democratic institutions; and not least the degree to which local people will engage in political action on behalf of others, all contribute to the variety of local responses to asylum seekers. Universally held covenants and treaties are laid bare and held up for judgement with each person who faces the test of credibility in substantiating a refugee claim. The country of asylum which tests such a claim is undergoing a trial of a different sort in terms of the process entered into, in each individual case being brought to a just conclusion. The question of how an individual who is a stranger is treated until a just determination can be made is also of significance. Here, the interventions of non-government groups at local, regional and national levels emerge as advocates for asylum seekers. Non-government groups and actors are among the important markers, perhaps even moral maps, of the limits of tolerance of a society. In complex modern societies the state is an abstract structure, removed from everyday contact with ordinary citizens. Non-government groups are often able to gauge and stay in touch with local sentiment and reality in a more concrete fashion due to their grass-roots orientation.

## Some methodological considerations

I begin from the basic premise that unannounced refugee arrivals (asylum seekers), present receiving states with significant dilemmas in applying international norms to local contexts. Much of the first-hand information on refugees and asylum seekers is gathered and generated by NGOs, as the front-line organisations who work directly with such individuals in local, regional and in international contexts. Therefore, apart from the analysis of existing data, I have identified NGOs and their action and interaction with the state as a key point for generating empirical material for this study, as well enabling insights into social and political dilemmas that result from the arrival of asylum seekers. Furthermore, the hypothesis I approached the research with, was that NGOs may reveal a logic in relation to the problems that arise from the arrival of asylum seekers which may be distinct from the logic evident in the actions of the state. In other words, the state might view asylum seekers primarily in terms of a legal and an administrative rationale, while NGOs may have a wider range of possibilities, from a focus on universal moral principles such as human rights, to a focus on the individual through various types of service delivery.

The issues addressed in this book are increasingly important in the international system of states. Dealing with asylum seekers justly, and the broader questions of the integration of immigrants, citizenship and the increasing porousness of nation-state boundaries, are also of growing theoretical interest.

I conducted thirty interviews in Germany during 1996 and 1997 with a variety of non-government organisations (see Appendix: Interviews). Many of the interviewees invited me to various meetings and public events, and introduced me to various centres and organisations where I could collect data for my research. Through the networks of these NGOs I was able to visit detention facilities in Berlin and at the Frankfurt Airport. I concentrated on the cities of Berlin, Frankfurt and Munich, all of which have significant numbers of NGOs working for immigrant groups and asylum seekers. In addition, I conducted interviews in Bonn, Stuttgart and Freiburg. I was also able to interview a small selection of politicians involved in the immigration and asylum issue.

In Australia, I conducted twenty-three interviews during 1998 in Sydney, Melbourne and Canberra, and also attended numerous meetings, conferences and forums on refugees and asylum seekers. Through NGO networks, I regularly visited the Villawood detention centre in Sydney. In Australia interviews were limited primarily to NGOs, and some senior bureaucrats of the Department of Immigration, Multicultural and Indigenous Affairs (DIMIA). I interviewed representatives of the UNHCR in both Germany and Australia.

Though the work of NGOs and social movements involves volunteers, the majority of the interviews I conducted were with paid staff. This reflects the fact that in the senior ranks of NGOs, workers are often highly qualified professionals who choose to work on specific issues such as human rights, often over a lifetime of work. Therefore, on an issue such as asylum seekers, the key players in the non-state arena are well known and in many cases have a high public profile in the media.

Through the open-ended, in-depth interviews I conducted, a pattern of central problems was able to be identified. The qualitative interview process can lead to a 'richness' of information which cannot be anticipated by the researcher. The interaction between the interviewer and interviewee has some influence on the data gathered (Bourdieu 1999; 609). Nevertheless, as this study is comparative, but issue specific, data gathering has to be systematic, reliable, and fairly amenable to replication as Almond and Verba suggest (1989, 43). In addition to the highly valuable interview material which I analyse as primary data, I also draw on an analysis of secondary data through newspapers, periodicals and the significant body of written material which NGOs generate including annual reports, newsletters, position papers, and press releases; so-called 'grey material'.[7] For the

---

[7] NGOs in western countries who work in the area of refugee and asylum seeker advocacy as well as 'development' NGOs working in other parts of the world, gather vast amounts of information often in the form of reports, minutes of meetings, pamphlets and press release materials. The Refugee Studies Centre at Oxford University has, since 1998, been the central gathering point for such 'grey' material.

German case study, the newspapers I drew on included, *Die Süddeutsche Zeitung, Die Tageszeitung, Frankfurter Rundschau, Frankfurter Allgemeine Zeitung,* and *Der Spiegel.* For the Australian case study I drew on *The Sydney Morning Herald, The Australian, ABC* Radio and Television, and *SBS* Broadcasting.

Several theoretical frames are harnessed in order to interpret the empirical data gathered. First, aspects of the significant debates regarding the role of the state in shaping immigration, and the relationship between state and the non-state sector are developed. Second, and emerging from the first debate, the issue of rights and obligations which dominates the politico/legal framework of democratic polities is discussed. Annexed to this second theoretical frame is the challenge of democratic practice and human rights which is increasingly relevant transnationally as well as within states. These theoretical frames are significant to the immigration debates to which refugee discourse is often directly connected. Although many human rights organisations, and international advocates continue to argue that refugees are distinct from other migrants, and therefore should be regarded separately in legal and policy domains, the distinctions are rarely articulated in the public sphere of a particular state, where issues are debated as part of the political process of opinion and will formation. The boundaries of citizenship and thereby the social, political and economic entitlements that accompany formal and informal belonging to a nation-state, impact on the resettlement prospects of migrants, including refugees. A number of writers on the nature of citizenship in modern nation-states, engage in the problematics immigration poses to citizenship and democracy (Soysal 1994, Beck 1998, Rubio-Marin 2000, Bauböck 1994). These discussions explore the challenge that transnational understandings of citizenship pose to the lives of individuals; discussions which cut across such issues as the rights of movement across borders and the integration of immigrants to receiver societies.

In what follows in chapter two, I begin the task of contextualising asylum as a historical phenomenon, rather than a purely modern 'problem'. In order to understand the complexity of responses to those seeking asylum, I turn to some central concepts of social and political theory, sketching a framework to guide analysis through the subsequent chapters.

# PART I
# THEORETICAL CONCEPTS

# Chapter 2

# Locating the obligation to protect

> The peoples of the earth have . . . entered in varying degrees into a universal community, and it has developed to the point where a violation of laws in *one* part of the World is felt *everywhere*. The idea of a cosmopolitan law is therefore not fantastic and overstrained: it is a necessary complement to the unwritten code of political and international law, transforming it into a universal law of humanity.
>
> Immanuel Kant, *Toward Perpetual Peace*

> Bertrand Russell argued that when reading the newspaper each day, we ought routinely to substitute the names of alternative countries to the reported actions in order to test whether our response to the event arises from a moral assessment of the action or instead from a set of prejudices about the country (Scarry 1999; 292).

This chapter will elaborate the foundations upon which obligations to others are grounded within and across societies. Obligations are taken seriously in those societies where individual liberty is guarded by democratic principles, institutionalised and guided by the balancing strength of the rule of law and the separation of powers. The appeal which human rights have as moral concepts which cut across borders, cultures, political and social systems, maintaining that every person *ought* to be extended basic assistance as a right when in dire need, gain substance only when this *right* is able to be lodged as a claim – substantiated through some form of obligation (O'Neill 2000; 199). Herein begins the difficulty of grounded justice; working out who did what to whom and how the harm done is best addressed.

The concept of the social contract, understood as a metaphor for joining together in a community of mutual benefit (in Lockean terms, a 'Commonwealth'), is a useful starting point in formulating my argument here. Locke had already begun the substitution of 'contract' with 'consent' (1960; 332), which continues to be the basis of obligation in the modern state. We consent to reason, in that it is *reasonable* to live with, or alongside others in cooperative arrangements of mutual benefit. According to Pateman, modern political systems have not resolved the problem of obligation, particularly at times of social and political change (1985; 4). Moreover, obligation is tested by the practical application of the distribution and redistribution of resources. Along with resources and their distribution, the question of boundaries arises. Which boundaries matter and are legitimate between people? Moreover, what sorts of identities and modes of belonging may lay a claim to resources? These questions lead to a discussion of the nation-state and citizenship in order to contextualise the specific rights of those claiming protection and the obligations that ought to be extended to them.

The idea of the bounded, sovereign 'nation-state' remains the institutionalised from of organising territory, members and resources through defining where and to whom obligations lie. However, the boundaries that denote the modern nation-state, whether spatial or psychic (an 'imagined community') are historically arbitrary. Moreover, the morally arbitrary circumstance of which nation-state we happen to be born in determines our life chances to a significant degree (Carens 1987, Joppke 1997). The Treaty of Westphalia, confirming that sovereignty should pertain not just to a 'sovereign' but to a territory, was signed in 1648, ending the Thirty Years War and marking the beginning of the nation-state system.[1]

Today, the nation-state system presents us with contradictory phenomena. On the one hand, the collapse of the Cold War order has seen a proliferation of new states as a result of both violent and non-violent independence movements. At the same time, the power and reach of the nation-state has decreased with transnational capital, and international organisations embracing economic and political activity previously the domain of individual nation-states. Immigration control though, remains largely the domain of nation-states, arbitrating both those within a given territory as well as over those wishing to enter. A nation-state has the sovereign right to administer, manage and direct members and non-members who are within a given territory, including various forms of coercion and at times even the utilisation of violent means in defence of 'national interest'.

In the public 'management' of an issue such as the reception and treatment of asylum seekers, the differing logics and tools of 'nation' and of 'state' are utilised to achieve distinctly different outcomes. For the most part the discussion of immigration and refugee policy revolves around the logic of the administrative state, adjusting policy and resource allocation in accordance with political, economic and social circumstances. As well as the domains of the administrative state, the logic emanating from the 'identity nation' or the 'imagined community' (Anderson 1991), which define belonging, sentiment and historical character, emerge as powerful ordering mechanisms for dealing with outsiders – strangers. Politicisation of the refugee issue is an example of the instrumentalisation of

[1] Since 1945 the creation of new nation-states increased with post-colonial independence struggles of various kinds, with the imposition of territorial borders over older borders, or indeed where none had previously existed. While such events were often focused on the creation of new 'homelands' of safety and familiarity for ethnic, cultural and/or political groups, the exclusion of non-members has been a consequence of nation formation – even if at times unintended.

national identity. Those seeking protection may be portrayed as violating sovereignty through incursions to territory, to resources and even to 'sacred' symbols.

## Violence and the modern state

The modern state is in significant ways a security state, guarding what is held as valuable by members. Even more basic to the state than mechanisms of security is the use of force and violence. Max Weber, in defining the activity of 'politics,' situates the modern state at the centre of sources of violence - indeed as having the *monopoly of legitimate physical violence*. The state has at its disposal the coercive means of the military, overt and covert forms of surveillance and not least an established politico/legal order with which to govern a given territory.

Despite the expansion of various globalising processes, the state and its representatives still maintain control over the dimensions of territory and membership. Indeed it is in this area where many states have chosen to exercise force in validating and displaying control. It is the 'security state' with which newcomers, and particularly those who enter a territory unlawfully, first make contact. Border patrols, police, army and navy, are the physical embodiments of the security state, enforcing the integrity of the nation. Security forces are only the most visible manifestations of violence a state will carry out towards a perceived threat. Modern legal systems of *positive law,* view violence as a product of history, judging all evolving law only in as much as it is critical of the means utilised (Benjamin 1978; 278). We can further extrapolate that the modern state, having institutionalised in various ways positive law, utilises violence in the pursuit of 'just' ends. So long as it can legitimate the method (means) employed, the authority of the state is reinforced through the use of force. That is, violence can not be seen to be used for its own sake, but is valid so long as it is employed for specific purposes. In antithesis it follows that ' . . . law sees violence in the hands of individuals as a danger undermining the legal system' (ibid.; 280). A legal institution exists through the residual understanding (consciousness) that violence is a latent presence of contractual arrangements in that the state will employ sanctions and even force to ensure that certain rules are adhered to. This brings us again to a Weberian understanding of a 'political community', where such non-arbitrary and institutionalised uses of violence and of coercion, and the memory of it, undergird the institutions of law.

What then are the consequences for the subject in relation to state violence and its embededness in law? Strategies of coercion are marked by 'unrefusable offers'. In other words coercive acts, whether they employ direct violence or not, communicate to the victim the compliance required and the impossibility of non-compliance.

> Unrefusable 'offers' work because they link choice of any but the compliant option to residual options which the particular agent cannot survive or sustain. The coercers' skill is to identify how to tailor 'offers' to the incapacities of particular victims, how to make non-compliant action not merely less preferred but unsustainable, so that their victims are driven to compliance. An unrefusable 'offer' is not, indeed, one where non-compliance is made logically or physically impossible for all victims; it is one that a particular victim cannot refuse without deep damage to sense of self or identity (O'Neill 2000; 91).

Let us not forget that coercive means and strategies take different forms, the less direct of which are often difficult to demarcate and to quantify. Benjamin already alerted us to the role of language as a sphere of activity which appears to be non-violent inasmuch as it is largely inaccessible to modes of violence. Yet language does have a role as an ostracising or stigmatising mechanism in contemporary societies; we may think of the political regulation of language or the psychological exercise of violence (Honneth 1995; 297), whereby images and words can be powerful means of rocking a sense of stability, certainty, or comfort. Here again we encounter the figure of the stranger and the role of cultural difference in everyday exchanges. The use of stereotypes in building enemy pictures (Beck 1996; 392) is but one way in which language is employed in what could perhaps be termed 'soft' coercion. This form of coercion in the less direct and opaque methods employed can be likened to 'symbolic violence'.

Durkheim reminds us of the importance of symbolic systems which lie underneath the reality we see in the social world (1965). Similarly, Bourdieu's theory of symbolic power provides a nuanced series of instruments with which to gauge social and political processes. Such symbolic instruments are: *structuring structures,* as the instruments with which we know and construct the objective world (the *modus operandi*); *structured structures*, as the means of communication; and *instruments of domination*, as the forms of power exerted in the competition for production of what come to be seen as legitimate goods (Bourdieu 1991; 165). In this tripartite schema, 'symbolic violence' is a result of the sum total of the instruments utilised, representing a type of orthodoxy. Violence is manifest in the codifications that communicate one set of values and dispositions as superior to others. Alternatives may not be totally excluded, yet orthodoxy causes a slippage in hierarchies to occur. Various political manifestations of the violence of symbolic systems occur through domination:

> . . . the power to impose (or even to inculcate) the arbitrary instruments of knowledge and expression (taxonomies) of social reality – but instruments whose arbitrary nature is not realised as such (Bourdieu 1991; 168).

Aside from the uses of symbolic systems relevant to particular cultures or political spaces (nation-states), the coercive potential of symbolic violence is produced under conditions of variable autonomy. Bourdieu, just as Foucault and Weber, differentiates between such symbolic production by *specialists* as opposed to a 'group'. As the 'group' is often dispossessed of the instruments by which symbolic production takes place, domination by elites or specialists reorganises the symbolic system, establishing an order which appears straightforward (orthodox), perhaps rational, as new rites are performed and repeated. Violence comes to be the end result of systems of symbolic power which are held in place most effectively through covert means, rather than tangible acts of force. Misrecognition of the loss of autonomy at the very outset of the processes by which symbolic systems are formed, result in the naturalisation of orthodoxies that hold one 'system' in place over another (Bourdieu 1991;169). The idea of misrecognition describes the false deduction that orthodoxy already carries or embodies diversity; that is an 'open' position inherently interested in the 'other'. Before discussing in more detail the idea of recognition and the role of culture as norm producing and reinforcing phenomenon, I return now to the concept of obligation, considering how it is that rights are given substance.

## On obligation

The 'universal community' of persons remains for the most part only thinly held and secondary to the priorities and needs of exclusive groupings based on national belonging. The nation-state system, as the prevalent form of organising political and social needs of a defined group of people within a particular territory, has a structuring and ordering effect on members, potential members as well as negotiating partners in the international arena (Habermas 1996; 502). Nonetheless, values and perhaps virtues held transnationally, such as universal human rights, underpin the rights enshrined in citizenship and in a constitution (Scarry 1999; 302). There may be moments when citizens of a democratic nation-state may have call to international conventions (of human rights) to uphold some fundamental right. The contradictions and spaces between a universal community and a plethora of national communities emerge at various points in the hierarchies of human needs. These contradictions are evident in phenomena such as the movement of people across national borders. Immigration sets into motion a series of bureaucratic and administrative processes, connected to the communicative apparatuses of the political public sphere of mass media and of political parties, and unleashes a series of anxieties, fears and defence mechanisms in the receiver society. Were asylum seekers to remain 'international people' there would be no cause for concern. We know, though, that the idea of 'international people' is at best an abstract notion. As soon as the abstraction *international,* is overlaid against a human needs thesis, such as 'basic rights', the uncomfortable reality of a person with the need for food, shelter and clothing and the right to dignity in the fulfilment of human potential like education and work is evident. This tension in part defines the anxiety expressed by states confronted with those seeking protection, and is part of the rationale which stimulates the commonly used linguistic pairing; refugee 'problem', or indeed asylum seeker 'crisis'. In abstract terms, those seeking protection are an indeterminate group, adrift on a sea of international concern, and sympathy at a distance; dislocated from the necessary resources to find a resolution. I shall now continue the discussion of the theoretical foundations of justice and to whom obligations are due, before turning to the more practical aspects of 'mapping' borders which encompass both people and territory, though differentially, in the operationalising of such obligations.

In defining the question of obligation, as distinct from rights, the Kantian focus on the *ought* is as good a starting point as any: 'What ought to be done'? We can then deliberate about negative duties; that is, not to harm others as opposed to positive duties which require resources and action. The idea of justice as articulated by Rawls equates obligation with 'fairness'.[2] The principle of fairness answers all the requirements of obligations as distinct from 'natural' duties (Rawls 1972; 111). When a number of people enter a venture that is mutually advantageous, such as the *social contract*, they do so in the knowledge that they restrict some of their individual liberty for the advantage of the venture as a whole. What is of course implicit in this suspension of parts of individual liberty is the reciprocal benefit at some future point. If arrangements are just, then each person will receive a 'fair' share of benefits (ibid.; 112). In his more recent work, Rawls aligns 'justice as fairness' more specifically to international law, focusing on *people* not *states* (1999; 23). The dilemma which remains with us is reconciling the claims of 'peoples' anywhere with those of specific (domestic) groups. How is a balance between claims to be established and maintained?

Justice in immigration is exemplified in the selection processes of who may and may not remain in a given territory, in the application of impartial law and in the

[2] It is noteworthy that under duties and obligations, Rawls lists justifications for civil disobedience and conscientious refusal (1972; chapter 6). For Habermas evidence of at least some, civil disobedience is a litmus test for democracy.

way quotas are set, while decent conduct and decency in institutions is evident in the everyday interactions between institutions and people. Most commonly immigrants, and particularly those without substantial economic means are seen as a burden on the state and, as a corollary, on the citizens of that state. Rubio-Marin, in defence of the contributions immigrants make to a receiver society, borrows the concept of 'free rider' from social movement theory, to argue that the exclusion of migrants from comprehensive rights, especially political rights, skews the economic benefit in favour of citizens. That is, as migrants continue to contribute to the social and economic well being of a society even while they are excluded from full participation for often significant periods of time, citizens become 'free riders' on the efforts of others who do not gain the full benefits of membership (Rubio-Marin 2000; 59).

In order to substantiate obligation, the moral standing of a person or a people must be articulated. Here we see the stand-off that continues between cosmopolitans and communitarians; between drawing no distinction in moral standing premised on distance or 'strangeness' on the one hand, and on the other, holding a marked distinction between compatriots and others (O'Neill 2000; 191, Tamir 1993, Sandel 1998, Goodin 1988, Pogge 1992). O'Neill provides a useful circuit-breaker in assessments of moral standing by arguing for a practical approach, taking into account those who feel the result of our actions and choices:

> 'To whom are we (or am I) committed to according moral standing in acting or in living in this way'? In posing this question we ask *what assumptions are we already building into our action, habits, practices and institutions.* If in acting we already assume that others are agents and subjects, then we can hardly deny this in the next breath. This conclusion holds even if our conceptions of what it is to be an agent or a subject are metaphysically primitive and leave many cases undetermined . . . A practical approach to moral standing claims only that what we assume in acting, we cannot selectively revoke in reaching ethical judgements (2000; 191-2).

This brings us back to the wider question of arrangements between people, socially, and between cultural, ethnic and political groups. How will justice take place between groups and individuals following divergent versions of the 'good life'? The sort of guarantee which the concept of a social contract between persons gives, relates to the impartiality that comes from imagining oneself prior to the arbitrary allocation of features and attributes of our contingent lives. In other words, we imagine ourselves in Rawls' *original position* (1972; 21). It is in such an idealised place that a general agreement can be reached as all the parties to an agreement choose principles as if they could apply to themselves just as to anyone else. Rawls also utilises the metaphoric tool of the *veil of ignorance* in order to imagine how we come to general agreements to live together without using people as means to an end. With the veil of ignorance drawn; ' . . . no one knows his place in society, his class position or social status; nor does he know his fortune in the distribution of natural assets and abilities' (ibid.; 137). This momentary stripping away or suspension of knowledge of our situated selves, allows a rotation of possibilities as yet unknown to us, it momentarily dislodges our loyalties and affinities, as we could be the 'other' beneath the veil.

What is important to obligation in the abstract is the voluntary nature of meeting such arrangements, either by individual action or through institutions. However, political obligation remains inherently problematic in reaching agreement with regard to just when a consensus is reached. The autonomous actions of political obligations are in reality often replaced by political obedience (Pateman 1985; 3). Liberal philosophy has an unresolved dilemma between the ideal of the autonomy of the individual and social responsibility for others in the fulfilment of obligations.

In considering obligation then, how we conceive of it and to whom it falls, leads us to the question of obligation within, between, and over territorial borders. I have so far discussed difficulties in locating substantive obligation in abstract liberal theory as well as in transnational justice. I now turn to a consideration of obligations to immigrants as expressed in the porousness or otherwise of borders.

### *(a) Open and closed borders*

Processes of integration or of expulsion of outsiders in a given society are both a constitutive part of a society and simultaneously reshape identity and institutions through these processes; often as unintended consequences of action. I argue that this takes places both at a formal and informal level. Namely, the administrative processes which shape the public will, and conversely the 'self constituted' public which in turn shapes political and administrative processes. The nation-state remains the significant 'power broker' which affects the chances of outsiders. As already pointed out, the particular group of outsiders which is at the forefront of my analysis, are refugees and those claiming to be refugees (asylum seekers). The duty to refugees and those who may prove to be a refugee is twofold: first that their application be given due consideration, and second that they be treated humanely while their applications are being considered. However, the various local understandings of 'refugee' vary with place and over time. Refugee arrivals present liberal democratic societies with a number of dilemmas. The particular manifestations of admission or rejection of refugees reveal the character of the nation-state to the observer - its moral foundations and the political manifestations of national interests overlaid with international pressure of an economic, political or indeed ethical nature.

In what way is it 'just' for borders to be closed, or open? What sort of duties or obligations do we owe to people outside our political community? On what basis do we defer the grant of good will and substantive goods (through distributive justice for instance), that we extend to those in our circle of loyalty, to others outside it? Do such demarcations rely on physical distance, or cultural, religious or ethnic difference?

It is neither a historical nor a philosophical given, that the borders of a nation should be impenetrable – a *cordon sanitaire*. Rather, there are a number of authors arguing a case for open borders. Joseph Carens (1987, 1997) has developed perhaps the most consistent and compelling case. He outlines a model of an open border society, arguing that under principles of justice read in the broadest sense of our common humanity, denying someone physical entry to a territory is without justification – with the minor exception of some restrictions being possible where 'harm' can be proven to the members of a particular territory if no border constraints were in place.

The interaction between the demarcation of borders and the question of justice leads inevitably to the arena of distributive justice. Distributive justice is an elastic concept, reshaped depending on which view of membership and loyalty is subscribed to. First, distributive justice principles can apply exclusively to members of a particular bounded political community – usually bounded by territorial borders. Individuals outside those borders can have no claim according to this version of distributive justice, to the resources of that territory. Moreover, in this first version of distributive justice:

> . . . outsiders are excluded from resources insiders can legitimately claim; therefore, whether one can have a claim to those resources will depend on whether one has access to the borders. Immigration policy determines which outsiders can become insiders; distributive justice then determines the rights of insiders. The principles of distributive justice determine particular entitlements, but do not themselves entail a particular immigration policy (Coleman and Harding 1995; 36).

An alternate theoretical approach to distributive justice views the global arena as the location both of individuals and of resources. In other words, political boundaries (territories) in this view are not initially significant. Rather, the important question relates to the allocation of global resources to individuals. It is true that the second approach does not pay heed to national immigration policies, as it initially views boundaries and membership of political communities as secondary to distributive justice. This second approach is akin to a transnational or extra-territorial citizenship with cosmopolitan values – with 'justice as a larger loyalty' (Rorty 1998; 47). Most commonly we think of loyalty as an affective quality which we grant to those closest to us - family, friends, kin. Justice on the other hand is related to an obligation with a universal and abstract quality - when the circle of those familiar expands too much, there is a requirement for general principles and laws that guide action, which override instinct and sentiment.

Taken from the perspective of liberal principles, where individual rights prevail over groups rights, there can be little legitimacy in the restriction of liberty of movement between societies, as within them. The moral claim of this argument rests upon the view that the challenge to national borders should have the strongest claim from people of the third world moving to the first world. This claim centres on the inherited privilege and status of citizenship in western liberal democracies - a matter of chance which has the ability of greatly enhancing the life chances of an individual; 'like feudal birthright privileges restrictive citizenship is hard to justify when one thinks about it closely' (Carens 1987; 252). The accumulated advantage of citizenship in wealthy liberal democracies is left unchallenged by the nation-state system, even under the forces of globalisation.

> . . . in global perspective, the very institution of citizenship, tying particular persons to particular states by virtue of the morally arbitrary accidents of birth, serves as a powerful instrument of social closure and a profoundly illiberal determinant of life chances. True, states are open at the margins to citizens of other states – but only at the margins. Seen from the outside, the prosperous and peaceful states of the world remain powerfully exclusionary (Brubaker 1994; 230).

The contrary positions to cosmopolitan arguments are articulated by communitarians, focusing on local and neighbourhood communities, which remain resilient only so long as the state safeguards them through relatively closed borders. While entry to people claiming protection is possible from a communitarian perspective, the emphasis is on mutual aid or 'good samaritanism', rather than a deeply-held obligation founded on common humanity. From a communitarian perspective, decisions on entry tend to be ad-hoc, driven by circumstance and perhaps sentiment, as opposed to the 'disinterested' justice principles which would apply from a cosmopolitan understanding.

Moreover, deliberations about entry depend on what model of the state is used; the minimal state, or the interventionist state. The minimal state, following Nozick, allows us to escape the uncertainty and vagaries of the state of nature, and enshrines individual property rights. Further, though this minimal state gives priority to the liberty of individuals, not necessarily citizens, it may interfere in exchanges between individuals, be they citizens or not, only if someone else's rights are violated. If we apply this view to immigration, it follows that entry to a state with a 'minimal' mode in operation, cannot be prevented by government unless the rights of other individuals are violated by such entry – otherwise the entry should not be the state's concern. There is then :

> . . . no basis for the state to exclude aliens and no basis for individuals to exclude aliens that could not be used to exclude citizens as well. Poor aliens could not afford to live in affluent suburbs (except in the servants' quarters), but that would be true of poor citizens too. Individual property owners could refuse to hire aliens, to rent them houses, to sell them food, and so on, but . . . they could do the same things to their fellow citizens. In other words, individuals may do what they like with their own personal property. They may normally exclude whomever they want from land they own. But they have this right to exclude as individuals, not as members of a collective. They cannot prevent other individuals from acting differently (hiring aliens, renting them houses, etc) (Carens 1987:254).

While Carens' argument provides a powerful logic for an open, tolerant approach to the arrival of 'aliens', such as those seeking protection, he chooses to overlook the conditions of liberal democratic societies, in which poverty is not tolerated beyond a certain point without the alleviation of it by various forms of state-assisted welfare. The entry of asylum seekers, many of whom do not have adequate resources of their own, expands the stratum of people in need of assistance. However, in more recent analysis, Carens has gone beyond his earlier arguments, conceding that the obligation to admit others, even those in desperate need, may change as number increase (1997; 8). I do, however, agree with Carens' qualification, that no matter the shifting 'practical obligations' in particular contexts, the underlying moral legitimacy of an applicant's request for protection does not change (ibid.).

Taken from the view of an interventionist or activist state, the restriction on immigration would operate under a different premise. Such a state has a firmer foundation of social welfare, or resource distribution, based upon justice principles. Principles to guide action in such a system are determined behind the 'veil of ignorance', an imaginary place, where gender, age, ethnicity, and other personal attributes, inherited or chosen are set aside for impartiality of judgement. As previously discussed, the 'veil of ignorance' is a tool of liberal philosophy, which neutralises natural and social contingencies: the things which set people apart and result in inequalities within and between nations. In this ideal *original position,* differences should not affect 'the choice of principles of justice' (Rawls in Carens 1987; 256). If we hold such general principles of equal treatment and equality before the law as important and agree that global inequalities which result in vast differentials in life chances and outcomes, it would follow that a global, rather than a narrow national application of the principle of the original position would be just.

If we were to apply the veil of ignorance in the *original position* to the issue of restrictions on freedom as in restrictions on movement of people across borders, it would follow that the parties would agree that no restrictions should be in place. Each of the parties would be unsure if such a restriction would encroach on his/her own wishes or needs to move home at some point in the future. The vast differences evident in actually-exisiting democracies, between such principles and the deliberations on those trying to enter a territory to find refuge could be justified if public order or security within a nation were under threat. However, restrictions would be justified only if there were a 'reasonable expectation' that unlimited immigration would damage the public order and this expectation would have to be based on 'evidence and ways of reasoning acceptable to all' (Rawls in Carens 1987; 259).

### *(b) Recognition and the significance of culture(s)*

Among the consequences of immigration is the formation of ethnic minority groups within a receiver society (Castles and Miller 1993). In recent years a proliferation of literature has appeared around the topic of minority rights, at times addressing the issue as 'group rights' versus the well established liberal concept of 'individual rights' (Kymlicka 1995, Waldron 1996). As will be discussed later in this chapter, the inadequate allocation and extension of political group rights to newcomers, in addition to economic and social rights, may result in a resentful, non-integrated minority group with little emotional connection to a receiver society. Such developments have long-term consequences for the social and economic well-being of the people who make up minority groups as well as less openly acknowledged consequences for the receiver society. The discourse around the 'politics of recognition' (Taylor 1994) is another aspect or consequence of immigration and the minority groups which may form as a direct result. The idea of recognition has a double meaning in the way it is proposed by Taylor (ibid; 25). In the first and perhaps most obvious way, recognition relates to the need a minority or 'subaltern' group has for recognition – an acknowledgement by others that the distinctions and differences of a group exist. Second, recognition relates to the understanding by a majority group of the situation of the minority which seeks recognition. In this second sense, recognition would go beyond a 'cool' toleration to a situation of affinity with the minority group and the fundamental characteristics of their humanity.

Forms of recognition, structured and negotiated socially, affirm as well as challenge particular identities, or various aspects of them. Hegel was already deeply concerned with the relationship which mutual recognition plays in structuring ethical life. Once we acknowledge the process of mutual recognition, it is evident that the relationships between subjects constantly alternate at various points between reconciliation and conflict (Honneth 1992; 209). In moral development the subject moves through various stages of recognition as individuality increases. In the relationship between parents and children the first form of reciprocal recognition takes place. In later life social relationships are transformed into more universal, contractual arrangements across society. By now persons recognise each other as having the freedom to pursue their own interests. And finally, it is in social conflicts that we recognise that we are dependent on each other socially, whilst remaining 'individuated persons' (ibid.; 209-11). The fully developed individual then, having gone through the developmental stages of mutual recognition, has at hand the social mechanisms for re-establishing affective relationships of solidarity which are bracketed off from mere legal/contractual relationships.

Just as mutual recognition follows a path of social development which affirms identity and culture, the opposite takes place in the form of misrecognition. *Mis*recognition occurs, causing damage and distortion to the minority group, as they see in the responses of the people around them a 'demeaning or contemptible picture of themselves' (Taylor 1994; 25). To extrapolate a practical application, the potential for misrecognition exists in the way receiver societies accept those seeking protection: in the many relationships and points of contact in the passage from becoming an exile and finding a place of resettlement which acknowledges (recognises) one's status. Misrecognition can result in knock-on effects at the everyday social level of interaction with others, and also accumulates over time in reactions which can become institutionalised in the form of policy, funding allocation and in the way institutions of communication such as the mass media portray particular groups. These relationships are discussed in some detail in chapters five and six.

My interest in the concept of recognition here is based on two factors: (1) that it is a valuable way of (re)focusing on the role of culture and the social development of the individual; and (2) the final stage of mutual recognition affirms the establishment of links of solidarity between people. We can then return to considering the points of engagement between national polities and transnational spaces, engagement in which processes of recognition are debated as vigourously as they are within nations.

In relation to the processes which apply to refugees, 'recognition' has a legal applicability, where a form of 'misrecognition' is also present. The process of legal 'recognition' is the life line between an asylum seeker who lacks any status which can grant her a measure of security in being able to stay in a specific territory and refugee status which can ensure the right to remain in a receiver society for temporary or permanent periods.

It is evident that an impasse exists in the exchange between transnational and national political engagement. How are the rights of individuals to be safeguarded when such rights oscillate across states? If, for argument's sake, we imagine transnational exchanges as vertical and national exchanges as horizontal, what mechanism brings the two closer together? Advocates for cosmopolitan democracy point to examples such as the European Union as democratic, transnational forms of organising economic, political and social institutions (Beck 1999; 53). What role do NGOs have in opening exchanges from local and national to transnational ones? These questions are addressed in chapter two. Let us now turn to consider the relationship between immigration and citizenship.

## Citizenship and belonging

Immigration is possible *because* of nation-states: nation-states who manage and administer borders and passports as well as shaping the more intangible notion of national belonging – the 'imagined community' of sentiments and traditions which remains a potent wellspring of opinion and the all too regular rationale for a nationalistic call to arms with violent intentions targeted at outsiders. At the same time immigration generates certain problems and tensions for the nation-state system. Citizenship and belonging in a cultural as well as in a politico/economic sense remains, in the post-Westphalian order of nation-states, the dominant tool for categorising people, as well as rationalising the way in which resources are allocated: citizens having a right to social, political and economic resources or 'goods' that non citizens have no, or little right to. Some argue for broadening the understanding of citizenship beyond national borders (Carens 1989, 1997, Bauböck 1994, Rubio-Marin 2000, Soysal 1994). Transnational citizenship remains, however, an illusory abstraction for most people.[3]

The reception of newcomers in a host society intersects with the issues of citizenship and what rights and obligations pertain to which groups within a particular society. The majority of literature on reception issues focuses on the medium to long-term impact of integration policy on the host society. Questions

---

[3] It could be argued that something resembling the status of transnational citizenship already exists for the very rich, the top echelon of transnational company employees, some international NGO workers, and some intellectuals.

about the economic, social and even environmental impact of immigration are prominent in this regard (Adelman et. al. 1994). Particularly in recent years, the demographic impact of immigration has been related to the ageing population base in many Western countries, as well as to declining birth rates, leading to anxiety about shrinking populations of people of working age able to sustain an economy. A select and growing literature deals with the arrival of refugees, asylum seekers and 'illegals' as an integral part of this newcomer group. Some of this literature draws links between reception policy which unfavourably targets groups of immigrants, or fails to effectively communicate with the host population about the effects of reception policy and the rise of ultra nationalist movements, xenophobia and violent acts against foreigners (Collins and Henry 1994).

Debates about the extent of immigrant integration and the attendant allocation of rights of membership of a particular country tend to oscillate between 'nationally exclusive' and 'postnationally inclusive' perspectives (Joppke 1999). These debates include such issues as the limits of tolerance towards newcomers and a variety of expectations regarding the life and behaviour of newcomers in a receiver society. It is certainly true that membership rights and issues of integration are generally long-term endeavours which do not concern the immediate needs or entitlements that are relevant to those seeking protection. Nevertheless, while the concept of citizenship and the rights and entitlements arguments that accompany it remain significant to one's 'life chances' and general well-being, it also remains an important factor in the development of refugee policy. I would maintain that this is so in at least two ways that relate directly to those seeking protection. First, to have membership in a Western democracy with all the attendant rights that flow from such membership is a significant advantage to one's 'life chances'. Second, while such advantage accumulates over time, enhancing membership, the passage of time renders the advantage 'natural' or taken for granted. Nevertheless, obligations to outsiders are not strong except where 'special' circumstances pertain: the need for protection is such a circumstance. Is it reasonable therefore to expect Western countries to exhibit a 'strengthened' obligation to those seeking protection?

The distinction between categories of newcomers can be a distraction. No doubt it is valid and important to make and keep distinctions in certain circumstances, but it is equally valid to think of refugees as the furthest extension of a population movement continuum. Particularly in the last three decades, the reasons for flight from a country of origin have blurred with other push factors not traditionally thought of as refugee-generating impulses or problems. In the area of refugee and asylum policy, perhaps more than in other areas of immigration policy, the need for not only consistency but also flexibility of the bureaucracy and administrative arms of government in dealing with what are often highly complex and changing circumstances is necessary both to ensure that genuine refugees are not mistreated or refouled, as well as maintaining the integrity of a state's immigration system.

Modern citizenship gives everyone the same status as 'equals' in the political public (Young 1998; 263). However, the link between citizenship for everyone, and being treated *the same*, is problematic in that the ideal is far removed from lived reality. Soysal (1994) argues that citizenship is not the most crucial criterion of migrant/guest worker integration and participation in a society, but rather the question of the extent to which norms and regulations fostering integration have been institutionalised. This differentiated focus is most useful, as it shifts from an introspection of the migrant/guest worker (or asylum seeker), as *the* problem, and instead focuses on the wider society which must justify inclusion or exclusion of these newcomers. From such a perspective on formal citizenship versus the substantive forms of belonging and inclusion, we can also further extrapolate that social, economic and political forms of inclusion, aside from citizenship, are needed to enhance the life chances of not only new immigrants but other marginalised groups.

In order to adequately address the response to the arrival of those seeking protection, a number of considerable dilemmas must be addressed, most of which relate in some way to the question of whether immigration policy is proactive or merely reactive. Either way, the outcomes of immigration policy are felt both locally as well as having knock-on effects in neighbouring countries and in the international arena of nation-states. First we see that the interaction between immigration and citizenship highlights rights of members in distinction from the lack of rights of non-members or newcomers. Individuals living in Western democracies, in relatively peaceful situations, enjoy both local as well as universal personhoods. They are subject to the rules and laws and have rights to the benefits of a particular territory (nation). In addition such 'national persons' have access to the international instruments that embody human rights which enliven universal personhood, giving it substance beyond a utopian idea. Though most individuals do not have call to invoke the instruments which give life to the idea of universal personhood in substantive terms, these instruments nevertheless act as a reminder and safeguard to national lawmakers, that certain limits to their behaviour and actions exist in the international arena, though these limits may well be mostly on a moral level or confined to diplomatic encounters.[4] Human rights, interfacing with national concerns, call into question by association the vibrancy and extent of democratic reflexivity present in a particular state. Liberal democratic states can

[4] In the case of Australia appeals to international bodies of the United Nations, most notably by Australian Indigenous groups, have reminded us in recent times that universal personhood is no fiction.

absorb only limited non-democratic or anti-democratic acts within their own territory without eroding the very same democratic ideals and the institutions which further such ideals. I will return to the question of the development in human rights debates later in this chapter.

My argument has so far developed around the idea that a receiver society is in some state of turmoil as a result of the 'irregular' (uninvited) arrival of asylum seekers. From this claim it follows that the institutions of a society will be tested in some way by the pressure applied by the arrival of asylum seekers. These institutions (both of the state and of civil society) and the citizens who uphold them through popular consent, are tested and even modified in interaction with others. As it is, the task of assessing the level of institutionalisation of societal norms and values in relation to the place of migrants and other 'strangers', is not my primary purpose here. Nevertheless, it is a secondary outcome of the structure of the study. The way in which public debate is conducted and framed will have a bearing on the reconfiguring of societal values.

## The needs of citizens versus needs of the 'other'

The fulfilment of human need is commonly envisioned as being negotiated and satisfied within a bounded nation. The sense of obligation and responsibility for others and a sharing or distribution of at least some resources is most familiar as being a national task - delegated to the state and consequently regulated through the institutionalised mechanisms such as welfare. Rarely are human needs in their temporal, immediate context envisioned in an extra-territorial way. International organisations do fulfil this task to some extent, as does international aid and the transfer of goods, money and other forms of assistance from affluent states to poor states. However, the work of international organisations, particularly relief and development organisations, is often built upon a charity model, premised on the values and beliefs of the donor, rather than upon principles of the basic rights all persons have to some resources. Resource allocation is not only shaped by competing interests, but is influenced by the extent of representation and lobbying that occurs from, or on behalf of, different interest groups.

In this context a *need* hypothesis can be read in a number of ways: the needs within a nation, the competing needs of those outside the nation who have a thinner claim, and the needs of refugees. In addition a needs thesis is the possibility of self-limitation strategies on the part of those whose needs are largely fulfilled. Claus Offe argues that social systems differ in the extent to which members have self-discipline and self-control manifest in the ability to limit their wants and desires. In the absence of such self-control, legal coercion and monetary incentives have to be applied to achieve this form of discipline (Offe 1992; 78). Such a development could be said to be oriented towards an 'ethic of responsibility', in an acknowledgement, for instance, of the connections between humanity across geographic and political territory, not just one's kin, national or ethnic group.[5] Heller (1999; 90) reminds us of the sense of urgency which drives needs fulfilment under conditions of modernity: urgency which is illogical, as needs have no limits from this view. The coveting of wealth, of power and fame for their own sake, rather than as qualitative ends, is a disposition of the modern world. At the same time such boundless needs are the engine room of modern economies, which aim for exponential growth, transnationally. Competing needs hierarchies both within and between countries are part of the conditions which those who advocate for asylum seekers face, consciously or unconsciously.

### *(a) The 'other'*

The granting of asylum or refuge has consequences in three distinct ways: first, in the life of the person granted asylum; second, for the host country; and third, for the country fled. Though all of these are important, it is the host country that is the focus of this study. The concepts of identity and nationhood are already well established in such host countries, and these concepts are fundamental in informing the reception or rejection of refugees as well as other newcomers. As I have already argued, the close association between migrants and refugees both in policy terms and also in societal attitudes toward 'foreigners' as a conflated category of 'other', influences the 'field' within which refugee advocates operate to mediate between refugees and asylum seekers and the host state.

A refugee is both a reflection of, and a problem for, the international system of states (Aleinikoff 1995). The existence of refugees in the late twentieth and early twenty-first centuries is a reminder that many states continue to persecute their citizens, placing them in often life-threatening situations. However, as will be detailed in chapter two, refugee movements emerge not only from persecution by the state of which a refugee is a member. In many instances occupation by another

---

[5] In addition to the relevance of various theories of need, the idea of the gift (Mauss 1990, Godbout 2000) remind us that market-driven reciprocity ensures little more than a 'thin' expression of 'fellow feeling' with others, be it a sense of solidarity or sympathy. In contrast, the idea of the gift embodies the expression of the self through spontaneity, and the act of donation, or giving where the return is not expected to be of 'equivalence' value.

state,[6] civil war and persecution by non-state actors results in movements of forced or involuntary migration. The legal instruments used to determine who qualifies as a refugee have very distinct criteria in mind, though disqualifying many who may be in substantive need of protection. Moreover, the application into domestic law of international instruments such as the *Refugee Convention* is highly differentiated between states, adding to the complexity of which individual may qualify as a refugee.

In the case of 'irregular' arrivals, the *right* to claim asylum sits alongside the *right* of a sovereign state to guard its borders and its resources. These two sets of rights are not fundamentally opposing rights. Nevertheless, the apparent scarcity of resources, or at least their differential distribution, potentially puts them into conflict. Modern peoples and their representatives (governments) most commonly understand rights and the allocation of resources within a bounded territory. Human rights have a currency and public understanding that defies borders, states and national demarcations in the contemporary world. Human rights in practice can appear antagonistic to the rights of members of a bounded territory.

If we keep in mind that the rights of refugees and those seeking asylum are broadly universal rights, located in the international arena, we must also remember that such rights can, in the most part, only be granted and given substance by a specific country in the form of temporary or permanent protection. The exception is the temporary protection afforded in refugee camps, and in 'safe havens' which are the domain of the United Nations. The right to asylum is essentially a moral question. Yet in concrete terms, this right contradicts territorial sovereignty, especially in the case of asylum seekers who most often enter a country in a clandestine fashion and subsequently attempt to invoke protection obligations. The obligation to grant protection can be given substance by the administrative decisions of a state. To what extent are the principles of protection supported through legislative, bureaucratic and funding decisions, as well as in the often intangible *public will* of a particular state? The principle of protection is exemplified by continuing support of the 1951 *Refugee Convention* and the 1967 Protocol in particular, International Human Rights Instruments, and the domestic law which complements international law. Most significant among the factors which distinguish immigration categories, is that asylum warrants a degree of special care due to the potential that people's lives are at stake in these decisions in ways that do not apply to general immigration decisions. This relates to the issue of

---

[6] As in the case of the creation of the state of Israel in 1948, resulting in the displacement of Palestinians who became stateless.

refoulement - the sending back of people from the country from which they sought asylum while a real fear of persecution still exists.

The principle of non-refoulement is central to granting protection under the Refugee Convention. The promise of non-refoulement which signatory states to the Convention make has the consequence of illuminating the source of human rights violations. The movement of refugees signals to the world the location of such problems. Moreover, the burden which non-refouling receiver societies who offer protection bear also generate incentives for taking steps to stop such human rights violations in the first place (Neuman 1993; 505).

A sovereign state has the right to control entry across its borders and a duty to its citizens to ensure a degree of territorial integrity though there are diverging views on how these duties should be dispensed, as previously discussed. The way in which such sovereignty is manifest in administrative procedures is open to a great deal of variation. A right to minimise or stop entry may be invoked particularly if the entry of migrants is likely to jeopardise the welfare of citizens already resident in the territory (Carens 1997). However, according to international law the right to place restrictions on entry does not extend to people who may be refugees - where turning such a person away constitutes *refoulement*: sending an individual who falls within the definition of the *Refugee Convention* to their country of origin while the source of their persecution still exists contravenes international law, putting that individual at risk. The problem that countries face is the dual requirement to make decisions quickly, yet with justice: quickly to minimise the period of uncertainty, to keep the cost down and maintain public support, and with justice to satisfy domestic and international obligations.

Sovereignty is expressed through state authority in that the state maintains legitimacy through the exercise of force in carrying out the mandate given by members. In relation to refugees and asylum seekers, this means screening and control over entry both extra-territorially; at national borders; within a state; and subsequently control over place of residence, of work, and of any benefits paid. The various legal manifestations of the principle of sovereignty can result in the detention the deportation of those seeking protection. Certainly the state should, indeed must uphold the principle of sovereignty in protecting the interests and security of members. At issue is achieving a balance between the national interest, embodied in sovereignty, and the observance of international norms which were set in place specifically to protect the needs of marginalised and persecuted peoples against the actions of individual states.

Rejecting asylum seekers at the border, not allowing them access to legal processes, putting time limits on their applications, or sending them back to a country of origin for non-compliance with certain laws or regulations, are strategies adopted by governments to maintain their sovereignty. To what extent some of these actions and strategies remain within the range of *reasonableness* in relation to the rights of those attempting to claim asylum is the issue here. Sovereignty in relation to immigration is, at its core, the right to choose who shall and who shall not enter a state.

The strength and transparency of claims put by individuals in their requests for protection can vary enormously. Yet the differentiation between 'forced migrants' who may have claims with differing moral weight should remain distinct from voluntary migrants:

> At one end of the continuum of refugee claimants are the pure economic migrants; at the other end are people personally targeted for torture and death by an oppressive government. In between are most of the claimants, facing various kinds of threats with varying degrees of severity and risk. It is an illusion to suppose that there are any sharp moral lines separating one claimant from the next closest along the continuum. (Carens 1997,11).

As Carens' typology of the migration continuum suggests, the distinction between people at the extreme ends of the continuum is relatively straightforward. The obscuring and slippage occurs with claimants who are closest to each other on the continuum. This slippage, however, should not deflect the moral urgency with which those seeking protection present us. We cannot respond to such persons as if they were voluntary migrants and expect to maintain the essence of the principles the *Refugee Convention* require.

If there is a scarcity of resources available to offer people such 'goods' as adequate resettlement services, there is an added impetus for a country to scrutinise individual claims judiciously to ensure that those with legitimate claims are protected. However, evidence from many Western countries of asylum suggests that the overwhelming emphasis in the last decade has been to exclude unauthorised arrivals as a group primarily *because* of their mode of arrival. The voracity of individual claims which make up the group become secondary to the stigma which attaches to the way an individual enters a country.

Even in differentiating between refugees it is important to be mindful of the legitimacy of many persons in 'refugee-like' situations who will not be offered substantive protection by a third state. It is outside the scope of this research to detail the impact, or the variety of responses to migration movements stemming from economic crises, or natural disaster, for instance. However, it is acknowledged by many researchers that indeed a grey area does exist between the categories migrants are placed in and how this correlates to their need for protection. In the main, this research focuses on those causes of flight which emerge from the *Refugee Convention* - issues of persecution due to political affiliation or membership of a particular religious, social or ethnic group, or membership of a particular political party or movement.

## Immigration policy as a political process

The international migration of people between states is conditioned and controlled by individual states in a number of ways. Labour shortages at regular intervals since the post-World War II period as well as the 'nation building' needs of settler societies such as Australia, Canada and the United States have been among the major 'pull factors' leading to the influx of significant numbers of immigrants to some states. The active recruitment of immigrants has involved incentive schemes for those who could fulfil specific criteria. In contrast, people who have left their country of origin with some level of urgency are said to leave due to 'push factors', denoting either economic, social or political breakdown or some kind of internal conflict. International migration in turn impacts on the political systems of those states which receive newcomers. The mode of arrival of newcomers, whether legal or illegal, and the reception they receive both formally and informally, will shape not only the immediate life circumstances of the newcomers, but leave a longer imprint on the social and political 'field' of the receiver society (Castles and Miller 1993, Soysal 1994, Joppke 1999).

Immigration embodies aspects of the substantive activities of the economic, the political and social spheres of a society. Whatever the intention of planning and control mechanisms utilised by a state, the arrival of immigrants places similar demands on any receiver society, particularly in the first years of settlement in a new country. However, the way in which a state approaches immigration varies enormously, shaping the settlement experience of migrants as well as the receptiveness of the local population to the newcomers. I will outline later in this chapter the way in which refugee arrivals differ from other immigrants and argue a case for the 'special needs' of this group. Notwithstanding this, the immigration experience as a whole is the context which shapes the experience of refugees in a receiver society. Moreover, as migration is an international process, the immigration policy of any one state cannot be sealed off or made immune to external migratory pressures (Hollifield 2000, Faist 1998, Castles and Miller 1993). Moreover, the legislative and administrative decisions taken on immigration in one state have repercussions for neighbouring states, the region and global migration processes and movements.

Outside academic discourses, immigration is defined and debated and reflected in policies and administrative techniques, in relatively rigid terms. As already outlined, nations of immigration, such as Australia, Canada and the United States, have recruited immigrants to assist in 'nation building' and a new, larger labour force. Recruited immigrants, as well as those who arrive uninvited, have been, and continue to be, a significant factor in the building of the 'identity nation'. On the whole, I maintain that it is the state which remains the major influence shaping the material and non-material conditions newcomers face in their settlement experiences. Through the legal and the social institutions of a society, the various indices of inclusion or of exclusion of newcomers are engaged in and communicated about not only to the newcomers but also to the wider population of citizens – fostering an environment conducive to either inclusion or to exclusion.

Newcomers, be they recruited immigrants or uninvited ('illegal') arrivals, do impact on a receiver society in a number of significant ways: economically, culturally, politically and socially. Accounting for the degree of impact is by no means straightforward. Moreover, the way in which the issue of newcomers enter a political discourse is not a neutral, nor a predictable process. This is expressed for instance, in the ongoing balance required in democratic systems between the political process and law. The quantity of politics cannot overburden lawmaking without violating democratic procedure (Habermas 1996; 428).

## 'Asylum' and the refugee regime in historical perspective

The revocation of the *Edict of Nantes* in 1685 forced 250,000 French Protestants to flee their country and marked the beginning of the modern tradition of asylum in Europe. Subsequently the Marquis of Brandenburg issued the *Edict of Potsdam,* allowing the settlement of Huguenots in his territory. After the French Revolution, the category of *refugee* fleeing political rather than religious persecution began gained legitimacy. Although the first recorded use of the term 'The Right of Asylum' occurred as early as 1725, asylum continued to be viewed more as a prerogative of the Sovereign rather than as an individual right to protection up until the early years of the 20th century, when the concept of human rights was first developed comprehensively with an institutionalisation of some universal norms at an international level (UNHCR 1993).

Though refuge and asylum have been recurring phenomena throughout human history, what is relatively new is the stigmatising of refugees as pariahs – outcasts and liabilities to those societies who host them (Loescher 1993; 32). Internationally co-ordinated refugee regimes began after WW1. In Europe at the beginning of the twentieth century, it was Russian refugees, escaping from the Soviet Union, who triggered a search for solutions by voluntary agencies (Loescher 1993; 36-7). By the 1930s, totalitarian fascist regimes in Europe generated large refugees flows out of Europe. The earliest precursor of the contemporary refugee regime was in evidence through the establishment of the first unilateral co-ordinating mechanism for refugees – the High Commissioner for Refugees, with the first Commissioner, Fridtjof Nansen appointed in 1921 by the League of Nations. During the inter-war period the refugee regime however, proved to be ineffective in responding to the developing refugee crisis in Europe. In 1950 the current Office of the United Nations High Commission for Refugees (UNHCR) was established. Loescher contends that the office reflected the; '. . . political and strategic interests of the European powers and, specifically, the United States' (Loescher 1994; 357).

### *(a) Historical change in the perception of refugees*

In the post-Cold War era, the characterisation of refugees and people in refugee-like situations by prospective host countries underwent another transformation. Individuals who moved across borders without visas, passports or other forms of identification came to be seen as 'illegals', associated with criminality by their mode of entry. In earlier decades, particularly in the aftermath of World War II, but also through the period of the Cold War, refugees were welcomed into Western European countries, as well as to Australia and the United States, as especially deserving of protection and assistance to resume a new life after violence and conflict. This was not though a universal act of charity, of benevolence, extended to anyone seeking asylum. The strongest impetus for such reception was the abhorrence with which the regimes they fled were viewed - the communist regimes of Eastern European countries, and totalitarian regimes in some Latin American, Asian and African countries. The end of the Cold War has however, been marked by a significant cooling of regard for the needs of refugees and asylum seekers.

There is no doubt that there has been an increase in the numbers of refugees and asylum seekers around the globe, particularly from the mid 1980s. While in 1980, the UNHCR assessed there to be 5.7 million refugees around the world, by 1985 the figure was 10.5 million and in 1990 the figure had reached 14.9 million (1995; 248).[7]

Table 2.1, below, shows the numbers of asylum applicants in Germany and Australia from 1990-2001. The table which follows, Table 2.2, indicates the per capita intake of asylum seekers in Germany, Australia and some other Western

[7] As the UNHCR makes clear, the accuracy of statistical information varies depending on the context of a refugee-generating issue and the level of institutional infrastructure and transparency in a host country.

countries in the period 1998-99. This table highlights the disproportional 'burden' placed on different countries. Both Britain and Germany received around three times as many asylum seekers as Australia, while Canada received twice as many.

**Table 2.1 Asylum applications 1990-2001**

| Germany | Asylum applications | Recognition rates |
|---|---|---|
| 1990 | 193,100 | 4.4 |
| 1991 | 256,100 | 6.9 |
| 1992 | 438,200 | 4.2 |
| 1993 | 322,600 | 3.2 |
| 1994 | 127,200 | 7.5 |
| 1995 | 127,900 | 13.5 |
| 1996 | 116,400 | 13.5 |
| 1997 | 104,400 | 12.3 |
| 1998 | 98,600 | 9.4 |
| 1999 | 95,100 | 9.1 |
| 2000 | 78,764 | – |
| 2001 | 88,363 | – |
| TOTAL | 2,046,727 | |

| Australia | Asylum applications | Recognition rate | Resettlement |
|---|---|---|---|
| 1990 | 12,100 | 31.8 | 12,000 |
| 1991 | 16,700 | 11.4 | 7,800 |
| 1992 | 6,100 | 5.8 | 7,200 |
| 1993 | 7,200 | 9.9 | 10,900 |
| 1994 | 6,300 | 13.3 | 11,400 |
| 1995 | 7,600 | 9.1 | 13,600 |
| 1996 | 9,800 | 18.1 | 11,300 |
| 1997 | 9,300 | 6.6 | 8,000 |
| 1998 | 8,200 | 23.8 | 11,100 |
| 1999 | 9,500 | 26.4 | 8.300 |
| 2000 | 12,936 | – | – |
| 2001 | 11,570 | – | |
| TOTAL | 117,306 | | |

Source: UNHCR, *The State of the World's Refugees* (2000; 321) and http://www.unhcr

**Table 2.2 Estimated number of 'persons of concern' to the UNHCR, 2001**

| Region | Number |
|---|---|
| Asia | 8,450,000 |
| Africa | 6,072,900 |
| Europe | 5,571,700 |
| North America | 1,047,100 |
| Latin America | 575,600 |
| Oceania | 76,000 |
| TOTAL | 21,793,300 |

**Table 2.3 Per Capita Intake of Asylum seekers 1998-99**

| Country | Onshore Asylum Seekers 1998-1999 | Asylum Seekers Per Capita of Population |
|---|---|---|
| Switzerland | 41,100 | 1 per 156 residents |
| Netherlands | 45,200 | 1 per 395 |
| Britain | 91,000 | 1 per 604 |
| Germany | 98,644 | 1 per 760 |
| Sweden | 12,800 | 1 per 781 |
| Canada | 24,937 | 1 per 980 |
| Australia | 8,257 | 1 per 1,961 |
| United States | 79,800 | 1 per 3,172 |

Source: UNHCR

## Refugees, asylum seekers and 'illegals': legal and popular definitions

While there are millions of people around the world who are displaced, only a relatively small number are afforded the substantive protection of refugee status. As public sympathy for those seeking protection has eroded in the last decade, the UN refugee agency, the UNHCR, has searched for new approaches to assisting 'people of concern'. The emphasis of the UNHCR has shifted to repatriation and temporary protection, responding to increased anxiety by states about the arrival of 'irregular' migrants in their territory, particularly by governments of the West.

The 1951 UN Convention Relating to the Status of Refugees remains the central mechanisms of international refugee protection, with one amending Protocol, adopted in 1967. The Refugee Convention defines a refugee as a person who:

> . . . owing to a well founded fear of being persecuted for reasons of race, religion, nationality, membership of a particular social group or political opinion, is outside the country of his nationality and is unable or, owing to such fear, is unwilling to avail himself of the protection of that country; or who, not having a nationality and being outside the country of his former habitual residence as a result of such events, is unable or, owing to such fear, is unwilling to return to it (Article 1A (2) of the *Refugee Convention*).

The contemporary refugee regime - which includes the office of the United Nations High Commissioner for Refugees (UNHCR), is a result of refugee pressures in Europe particularly after World War II (Ferris 1993, Loescher 1993, Zolberg 1989, Harris & Weinfeld 1994). Many contemporary commentators have pointed to the inability of this refugee regime to cope with the contemporary refugee situation (for a useful summary see Goodwin-Gill 2001).

The literature which examines the shortcomings of the *Refugee Convention* documents the shortfall of protecting people in vulnerable situations. The existing *Refugee Convention* is seen as failing in that 'new' refugee producing situations are not easily accommodated within the existing definition: ethnic violence and gender-based persecution are examples (Goodwin Gill 2001; 1). A recurring argument in favour of keeping the current Convention untouched is that the narrow definition of refugee limits the number of people who qualify, and therefore leaves the system within tolerable limits for Western governments and societies. A further problem with the current refugee regime and those countries who are signatories to it, is that in principle there is no upward limit to the number of refugees a state should recognise, if asked. No doubt political considerations become relevant in this context. Second, there are different obligations on the refugee continuum. In later chapters some arguments about the limits of the current *Refugee Convention* will be explored, with particular reference to the obligation of non-refoulement and the so-called 'safe country' and 'first country' policies, as well as forms of persecution particular to women, which are inadequately addressed in the present system of refugee determination.

The period from the late 1980s has seen the UNHCR and those individuals and organisations involved in international human rights law struggle with appropriate responses to people fleeing their country of origin. In the face of stiff resistance by Western countries to the arrival of those seeking some form of protection, the UNHCR has generated ever more complex formulas of 'types' of flight. 'People of concern' is a term which is now used to include people who do not fit the narrow definition of refugee as outlined in the *Refugee Convention*, but who nevertheless cannot safely return to their country of origin. This group are also commonly called '*de facto* refugees'.

The provisions of international law, including the *Refugee Convention* as well as the UN Convention on Human Rights, indicate a contradiction in that the right to leave is provided with no complementary right to admission anywhere else. This contradiction has, particularly since the mid-1980s when refugee numbers began to grow significantly, resulted in the prevalence of 'statelessness' and the phenomenon of 'refugees in orbit' as states have increased administrative measures aimed at deterring all irregular arrivals.

Though the majority of asylum seekers in Europe since 1989 have been European, predominantly East European, the fall of the Berlin Wall caused not only a mass movement of people within Europe, but also resulted in a hierarchy of asylum seekers - with Third World, and particularly African asylum seekers often being an (unstated) last priority. Since the early 1990s the recognition rates of asylum determination processes have declined in many Western states.[8]

The processes of 'harmonisation' evident in European countries means that the responses and changes in asylum administration in one country can have knock-on effects in another, termed by some writers a 'downward harmonisation' (Carens 1997; 26) or a 'race to the bottom'. Concrete measures such as fingerprinting of asylum seekers at borders, the co-ordination of security intelligence between states and the instituting of 'third country' and 'safe country' policies may have domestic harmony in mind at the national level, but undoubtedly also add to the mental picture of those seeking protection as being people not to be trusted; even criminal individuals transiting in search of entry points.[9]

While according to international law, embodied in the *Refugee Convention*, a person is a refugee at the point at which s/he meets the definition of refugee, the problem many individuals face in seeking the protection of a state other than their own, is *living through* the period that lapses between the events which transformed

---

[8] The issue of racism in refugee policy has become the focus of recent research, with claims that certain individuals do not gain fair hearings of protection claims due to their ethnicity, rather than the substance of their claims.

[9] Dummet gives the example of claims by Sri Lankan asylum seekers during 1996; Canada allowed 82 per cent of claims for protection by Sri Lankans, while in Britain only 0.2 per cent were accepted. Dummet argues that as the criteria used in both countries are the same, the disparity in recognition rates for people fleeing the same state suggests a different *spirit* of subjective judgements by the immigration officials who decide such claims (2001; 37). Racism in refugee policy in the Australian system has been under renewed scrutiny in the late 1990s particularly due to the issue of mandatory detention of illegal arrivals. These developments are analysed in chapter six. The issues of racism and xenophobia in the treatment of asylum seekers are considered in chapters six and seven.

her into a refugee, and substantive protection which affirms refugee status, thereby granting such things as residency rights, the right to work, to education, to language training. Furthermore, if that protection is itself increasingly seen as a resource rather than as a right, it would follow that refugees can expect no assurance of protection in a third country - particularly when individuals arrive as asylum seekers. If we see evidence of such a link between resources and the level of protection which is forthcoming, it can well be argued that the obligation to protection is not taken seriously. To be sure, it is true that when arrival is 'illegal' or unauthorised, the process of formal recognition can be difficult and lengthy and costly to the state but this in no way diminishes the obligation to protection on the receiving state. If this obligation is indeed taken seriously, it is not dispensed until such time as an individual is found not to be a refugee, rather than the reverse, where a person is assumed as non-genuine for a variety of contingent reasons, including mode of arrival, or even ethnicity, rather than being received impartially.

**Human rights**

The 1948 Universal Declaration of Human Rights is perhaps the most well known and comprehensive human rights standard, outlining the right of each human being to equal dignity (Article 1), security (Article 3) the right to free movement (Article 13), and numerous other rights outlined in the 30 Articles of this Declaration. In sum, the 1948 Declaration on Human Rights remains a highly aspirational document. Nevertheless, the concept of human rights has become intrinsic to values which are held globally, not only in the West. The Declaration of Human Rights is highly relevant to the situation of refugees and those seeking protection. It codifies the general principles of equality and dignity of all human beings, emphasising that among other things, people should not be subjected to torture, or to cruel, inhuman or degrading treatment or punishment (Article 5); that all people have the right to freedom of movement and residence within the border of each state, and similarly, the right to leave any country, including his own, and to return to his country (Article 13); that all people have the right to seek and to enjoy in other countries asylum from persecution (Article 14). These articles are of particular relevance to those seeking protection. Such human rights principles grant rights to individuals, whereas prior to World War II, states had primary rights under international law to decide to whom rights would be extended. With the Universal Declaration, individuals are uniquely granted rights by which they can challenge unjust state laws or oppressive customary practice, and do so regardless of race, creed, gender, age or any other status (Ignatieff 2001; 5).

Apart from international human rights instruments, the European Union has a distinct human rights mechanism to which the residents of member states, including Germany, have recourse if they feel their human rights have been contravened by the state they are a member of. The European Union relies in such instances on the Court of Human Rights and the European Court of Justice. For Australia there is no such regional mechanism, and in the absence of a Bill of Rights, Australians have recourse only to the UN human rights mechanisms as an outside arbiter.

Discrepancies in the application of human rights by individual states are scrutinised by national and international human rights groups and organisations such as Amnesty International and Human Rights Watch, to name only the most prominent such organisations, in order to elicit stricter compliance and standards of states. These groups follow policy developments and legislative changes and the impact they have on those seeking protection, and utilise such data in lobbying governments, international bodies as well as the media and individuals around the world as members and supporters of such organisations.

As I have discussed earlier in this chapter, there are certain standards of conduct in relation to universal human rights principles which are expected from democratic governments, and for the lack of which renegade nations are punished through such means as economic sanctions or political exclusion. Much discussion has taken place in relation to the cultural universality or otherwise of human rights norms. Non-European perspectives as well as perspectives from a non-Christian tradition have long claimed that human rights norms have a Western bias (Ignatieff 1999, Beetham 1999, Parekh 1999). Reaching a consensus on human rights, across cultures and ethnic groups, is no doubt difficult. Some of this discussion comes to light in later chapters when the substance of NGO advocacy on behalf of those seeking protection is discussed in detail.

## Resources for whom?

The ability of an individual to develop his/her human potential, is possible only when at least *basic needs* are met and *basic rights* are available through various of institutionalised processes. Human needs and their articulation and codification into rights are relevant for national and international policy development and the allocation of resources within, as well as between states. However, in the international system of states, the allocation of resources and the guarantee of rights has primarily been in the domain of a specific nation-state, and extended to the members born into, or integrated into the jurisdiction of that nation-state through immigration. In the dichotomy between local and global priorities, a state is concerned with internal and external control of particularly those areas where a significant degree of autonomy remains. As I have discussed, immigration control is one such area over which a state may exercise discretionary power over borders, and indeed will go to some lengths to gain such control.

I argue that protection has indeed become a scarce resource for refugees and potential refugees. Such a claim must be judged from the perspective of the hierarchy of human needs and interests. If human needs are general, and at least in part - such as in terms of basic rights - universally applicable, it follows that their fulfilment through allocation of resources could also be expected to be general - universally applicable. Such a broad schema, however, collides in the real world with the needs and interests internal to a nation-state, which is also where the need for protection of a refugee must be met. The politics of home and of nation have several concrete manifestations with regard to those seeking protection, including:

1. Increased *external deterrence* in the form of pre-entry controls in foreign ports, and the sharing of intelligence and security information between nations.
2. *Deterrence at entry*, through more stringent control at either land border, airports or sea ports.
3. *Internal deterrence*, including the withdrawal or limiting of social and economic rights, including work permits, reduced legal support and the use of detention.
4. *Legislative deterrence:* changes to laws and to administrative procedures which make the granting of substantive protections more difficult.
5. *Communicative deterrence:* the modes of communication utilised by political leaders and in the media, painting a negative stereotype of asylum seekers, with a potential impact on their chances of a fair hearing and successful settlement once protection is granted.

These forms of deterrence, particularly when and where they accumulate, are barriers in two ways: 1) they are a barrier to asylum seekers themselves; 2) they are barriers to NGOs who advocate for asylum seekers. The continuing dilemma which is relevant to these barriers of deterrence is between the in-principle agreement to protection that signatories to the *Refugee Convention* and Protocol give, and the reality of granting protection in the broader social, economic and cultural context of a given country. The administration and management of the international protection system is challenged and called into question by the everyday realities of the physical, legal and psychological needs of asylum seekers during the determination process. What role is there for NGOs in this process?

What forms of exchange and communication are appropriate in meeting such needs?

As I have previously discussed, there is a marked increase in the number and impact of measures, both legislative and administrative, across Western countries, which aim to control the numbers of people entering a territory and asking for asylum. In addition, an increase in measures which limit the support asylum seekers are entitled to while their claim is being processed is also evident. Much of the effort of individual countries, and the co-operation between them, through inter-governmental forums on asylum and border control, for instance, is premised upon a judgement that a large proportion of those seeking asylum do not have substantive claims, and are not 'genuine' refugees. How should the priorities between the rights of the individual and the right of a nation-state be balanced? As national sovereignty is synonymous *with* the modern state, any challenge to it is likely to meet stiff resistance by its guardians (Hollifield 2000; 141, Halliday 1999; 11). These two distinct rights; of the nation-state to maintain sovereignty; and of an individual to be able to ask for protection and due process in making such a claim, in the end collide. Both parties have in principle a just cause to have their 'rights' upheld and protected. How should questions over the impasse on priorities be resolved? To what extent does the 'politics of migration' impinge on the development of refugee and asylum policy? These questions form the core of what is discussed and analysed in later chapters.

As already stated, the language of refugee protection places the principle of non-refoulement in a central position; asserting that those who have a genuine case of persecution cannot be sent back to the origin of that persecution. This principle is the central pillar of the *Refugee Convention,* without any attendant obligatory mechanism which can be engaged to require states to take in those seeking asylum. In the tightening of asylum law and administration measures aimed at deterring and limiting the rights of those who may seek asylum, evident across Europe, North America and Australia in the past decade, anecdotal evidence of refoulement by Western states has increased. Such evidence is gathered primarily through transnational NGO networks between receiving countries and countries of origin. What is impossible to quantify is the number of individuals who have been 'turned around' at a border, airport or indeed on the high seas, without having been 'counted in' as a potential refugee.

Moreover, both in European countries and in Australia, the route of entry often determines access to an asylum process, with those arriving 'illegally' being excluded even before their case is heard. Asylum is (or perhaps more correctly, has come to be) a resource because of the nexus between ethical principles - urging us to give protection to those with a just claim, and political pragmatism (a realist perspective) exemplifies as the ability to pay for the process, both in monetary terms and in 'keeping faith' with public opinion. In other words, as an increasing number of asylum seekers have sought protection in Western democracies, the cost of this process is regularly called into question. In part this has been due to the relatively large percentage of failed applicants - those determined as not having met the criteria of the *Refugee Convention*, who are often subsequently seen as abusing the asylum system through 'manifestly unfounded' claims – or 'abuse' of the asylum system.

## 'Special' rights of refugees

The state has perfected, in domestic and local settings, the bureaucratic administration of persons (Arendt 1951; 287-298). The state is adamant that the demarcation between insiders and outsiders should be maintained in order that the integrity of the nation is not called into question. The management of borders and of the status of those within its territory remains of great importance to the integrity of the state.

If a pattern appears that indicates liberal democratic states are not acting justly toward refugees, the actions and interventions of other actors (non-state or international) can be expected to be of increased significance. A refugee, and particularly an asylum seeker, is a voiceless individual in a country in which s/he has no membership claim and yet wishes to claim protection. A comparative study enables some evaluation to be made as to whether a certain outcome can be expected from a liberal and democratic polity, or whether in the end national variations are so great and variable as to render an outcome unpredictable between different states. In other words, if the same asylum seekers, with precisely the same claim, were to test their claims in different nation-states, could we expect the outcomes to be the same or similar? It is with this question that I now turn, in the following chapter, to the role of non-state actors in representing the needs and rights of others.

## Chapter 3

# Non-government organisations and the state – partners and adversaries

As NGOs have become significant players transnationally in recent decades, we are faced with the question of what such proliferation of their role means at the macro level for the inter-state system and at the micro level for the autonomous expressions of individual citizens. This is the context in which this chapter will discuss how NGOs fit into the landscape of state and non-state players, and moreover, in considering the ways in which NGOs engage in political action.

The previous chapter has already discussed the significance of the category of citizenship, circulating debates over immigration, and integral to the way in which we conceptualise, formulate and carry out our obligations to others. This chapter continues this theme, with a focus on the question of political action, and what triggers such involvement; whether it be NGOs, social movements or other 'types' of non-state groupings. I will explore the concept of civil society, specifically the contemporary efficacy of a 'global civil society', before turning in more detail to the distinctions between non-state actors.

Three developments from the 1960s onward form part of the historical framework which assists in deciphering and contextualising non-government or non-state action today in relation to human rights advocacy. First, the 1960s and 1970s unfolded as decades of vital activity in 'movement' politics. This period witnessed the advent of the so-called 'new social movements' (Johnston and Klandermans 1995, Cohen and Arato 1992, Tarrow 1998), heralding renewed mechanisms and strategies of defensive and reactive action to policy and legislative processes of governments, as well as to issues which traversed national borders and were in the domain of inter-governmental organisations, or of transnational corporations. The majority of issues articulated by the new social movements remain transnational issues: relevant globally, yet with regional and local distinctions. They include; the rights of women and children, concern for the maintenance of the natural environment, peace and anti-nuclear movements, as well as numerous movements focused on the rights of minorities such as indigenous people. Such new social movements transcend the national focus associated with the traditional notion of 'interest politics'. Second, during the same period, the term non-government organisations (NGOs) came to be popularly used to describe organisations operating as non-profit, 'issue oriented' organisations. Initially the term was used to describe organisations in economically developing countries (or least developed countries – LDCs) organisations were in many cases an important part of democratisation processes. And third, new waves of refugees, unrelated to the post-World War II resettlement programmes, began to impact on Western countries in their search for protection from oppressive regimes. Though these developments may seem quite unrelated, I argue that they became inter-related in the political arena in local and international settings of 'issue politics' in the 1990s. What these movements have in common is advocacy on behalf of some of the most marginalised people in the world: people who are largely voiceless and un-represented, or under-represented, in their own countries and communities.

These three developments converged during the 1980s and 1990s, into overlapping modes of action and of reaction by particular nation-states to external pressure: pressure of the inter-state system, of international human rights norms and of economic restructuring toward 'global economies'. At the same time, social movements transformed into more formalised organisations, becoming increasingly institutionalised in various ways. NGOs are today recognised and valued as legitimate forms of organisation in economically developed countries and moreover have some common characteristics with social movements, in terms of strategy, tactic and action repertoires (Tarrow 1998). Some of the similarities and differences between NGOs and social movements will be explored in more detail later, particularly in relation to the potential to influence the decisions of states. At this stage I would like to characterise NGOs as organisations of importance to refugees and asylum seekers who most often do not have the means or opportunity to represent themselves.

As we have witnessed an upsurge in the volume of work undertaken by NGOs, so the number of organisations present within particular states as well as in the international arena has multiplied. However, the presence of NGOs and the work they undertake should not, in and of itself, be taken as a positive development, but rather needs to be carefully assessed in relation to the activities and responsibilities of states. While NGOs legitimately seek to influence states and to urge them in various ways to conform to norms such as those that relate to human rights, they are not a replacement for states, nor a solution to attempts to reduce the role of the state. Rather, the presence of NGOs, at least in some interpretations which I find most convincing, are part of a broader support structure for the roles of the state (Halliday 2000; 438). The consequences of NGOs moving into various roles of state activity is discussed later in this chapter with the example of the 'third way'. By now it is sufficient to note that NGO activity has had a marked impact on governments and on international bodies, providing first-hand information on various social issues; information into which large institutions are rarely able to gain insights. Through direct lobbying and advocacy activities, as well as public information campaigns, NGOs are able to provide an alternative voice in the public sphere (Fisher 1997, Lipschutz 1992, Cohen and Deng 1998, Rosenau 1990s, Keck and Sikkink 1998, Sikkink 1993).

What do we need to ask ourselves which will lead individuals to being stimulated to be involved in political action? Should such phenomenon surprise us, or indeed, should we rather be surprised by the absence of such involvement?

## Human action: the social and political manifestations

Human action is an expression of our creativity and our individuality – action which is 'doing' and 'speaking', rather than 'making' – utilising speech and contemplation in distinction from the labouring work of 'making'. Following Arendt, action and speech are so closely related, as we need a way of engaging with the 'whoness' of every newcomer that enters our horizon. In this vein, speechless action cannot remain action if the actor does not disclose him/herself in word, as well as deed (Arendt 1958; 178-79).

In acting and speaking, men show who they are, reveal actively their unique personal identities and thus make their appearance in the human world, while their physical identities appear without any activity of their own in the unique shape of the body and the sound of the voice. This disclosure of 'who' in contradistinction to 'what' somebody is – his qualities, gifts, talents, and shortcomings, which he may display or hide – is implicit in everything somebody says and does. It can be hidden only in complete silence and perfect passivity (ibid.; 179).

To be sure then, human agency is related to the constitution of the self. Collective action, as the amalgam of a group coming together on an issue in a consensual way, is a conscious choice to engage in public (open) activities as part of a group. Just as the rights of the individual are secured collectively (in a family, a group, a community, a state), so it is the product of collective action which represents the will *to act* of individuals: the transformative potential of collective power. Under what circumstances will individuals come together and engage in collective action? Moreover, under what conditions will those individuals come together in collective action on behalf of others rather than in self interest? Can we expect or predict such action, or is it a case by case, situation by situation occurrence, premised on the vagaries of sympathy and charity?

Political activity is marked for Arendt by dignity, as one form of a relationship between two people or groups, in that politics is inherently confrontational. What emerges consistently in Arendt's accounts is the relationship between politics and action. As we have seen, action for Arendt is analogous to speech in public about matters which concern public affairs (Arendt, 1958; 180). From this view, all citizens are likely to be engaged in what is essentially political action at some point in their lives. If this is not the case, we may perhaps take it as an indicator of a society in a state of atrophy or decline.

From another vantage point, Max Weber situates political activity much more decisively in the arena of power relationships, with some exerting their will over others, in the form of making decisions on their behalf and influencing outcomes (1946). For Weber, politics, from the very public to the personal, is marked by leadership and the use of 'soft' or at times 'hard' coercion. Of particular note in Weber's theory of politics are the two paths he articulates for making politics one's vocation: 'Either one lives "for" politics or one lives "off" politics . . . . He who lives "for" politics makes politics his life, in an internal sense. Either he enjoys the naked possession of the power he exerts, or he nourishes his inner balance and self feeling by the consciousness that his life has *meaning* in the service of a "cause"' (1946; 84).

Arendt's account of politics - though perhaps less 'situated' than Weber's account, nevertheless has applicability for the pursuits of refugee NGOs, in that the political deliberations of NGOs at times call for extraordinary solutions and deliberations. Arendt tends toward an idealisation of politics and political action as a 'pure relationship', untainted by deals and compromises. Though she does admit that the distinction between political activity and economic demands are often rather blurred, nevertheless Arendt maintains that we see enough evidence of selfless action aimed toward democratic political participation rather than individual economic gain in political action (Arendt 1958; 215-216).

Even the undoubtedly problematic and much criticised distinction which Arendt makes between social and political action may prove to be useful in the case of the NGOs who engage in political action. As I will clarify later, many refugee NGOs begin their life span in a service delivery role, providing social services of many kinds. Often, it is through this day-to-day work with those at the margins of a society, that NGOs move to an engagement in advocacy, or political action.

The unintended consequences of action are of central importance to social theory in so far as they are systematically incorporated within the process of the reproduction of institutions (Giddens 1979; 59). The relationship between civil society and the state, is interesting specifically because of the question of agency, or human action, with, in, and upon institutions and structures of the state. In other words, the feeling, shape and appearance of action and interaction is not static, nor can it be taken for granted.

Alongside analysis of human action, there are numerous other ways of understanding inaction – or *anomie*, following Durkheim. The impetus for *social solidarity* declines in a social environment characterised by disassociation of individuals from each other and from various forms of collective engagement. That is, where individuals do not recognise reflections of themselves and their own lives in events around them. The tangible expression of an individual's connection with the social world around her is formalised in democratic societies in *rights*. However, keeping in mind the distinction between negative and positive rights discussed in chapter one, in a state of *anomie,* negative rights would prevail with no triggering mechanism to demand some level of fulfilment. Only by presenting oneself communicatively and by engaging in action, can any demands be 'put on the table'. This becomes then only the beginning of processes of debate, deliberation and contestation by competing claims. Only by communicating your claim, can your *will* be known.

**Civil society: local to global**

The heterogeneous character of contemporary democratic societies extend beyond the visible borders that define a country, or an ethnic group or indeed a religious group. People form allegiances, interests and loyalties to others as well as to issues or causes, which defy being bound, regulated or controlled in the way in which matters which are the domain of the state and its institutions can be. In similar vein, the action repertoires and the concerns of NGOs, social movements and issue networks more broadly, are increasingly recognised as having an international character. No doubt the revolution in communications technology which has resulted in a shrinking of geographic as well as social, economic and political distance, has also assisted the proliferation of NGOs (Rosenau 2000; 183). The ability of non-government actors to disseminate information, gather support and lobby political leaders, has been greatly enhanced by the world-wide-web. Networks of activists are linked globally along issues concerns in ways that were unthinkable even a decade ago.

During the 1980s and into the 1990s, the role as well as the influence of the nation-state system has altered under the pressures of globalisation and economic globalism as discussed in the previous chapter. While many authors regard the nation-state as continuing to play a central role in world politics, an increasing number acknowledge the presence of new forms of organising outside the state, including the role of national and international activist and advocacy networks (Lipschutz 1992, Rosenau 1990, Beetham 1999). From this second perspective flows the concept of a *global civil society* – a linking of political networks of collective actors in a transnational way - across issues and borders. On a single issue, such as the environment for instance, political networks of collective actors can organise and forms bonds of influence and power across borders, seeking to pressure states and corporations who are perceived as endangering the long-term viability of the natural environment. The activity of other networks, also operating between states on a different issue, for instance the rights of women - also offer some new opportunities to other issue networks. I suggest that non-government activity in general, on any issue, prepares a groundwork for other issue networks that follow. States, political parties, and the many different 'publics' that exist, become perceptive and receptive to the activities of collective action of the non-government sector, and may be 'harnessed' or engaged with as the role of the non-state sector is understood and appreciated. Even opposition to non-state activity is preferable to ignorance of it.[1]

However, before launching too deeply into the specifics of NGO activity, issue networks and the distinctions between 'types' of non-state activity, we need to consider the genesis of the concept of civil society. What framework does social theory offer with which to analyse the outcomes, but also the initial stimulus for involvement in political action and other forms of action in civil society?

While it is certainly true that the concept of civil society has a long historical trajectory, it is one which has received renewed attention in relation to understanding social phenomenon in late modernity. This is particularly so in relation to processes of de-legitimisation of the state, or the 'shrinking state' in many locations around the world. As the de-regulation of state services, the privatisation of government utilities and the 'crisis' of the welfare state have gathered pace in economically developed countries, so the role of the state has been increasingly called into question. If the state fails to deliver what citizens ask of it, what other avenues are open to debate issues of concern and gather to public support? One of the significant impulses for raising the profile of civil society as a conceptual tool is the claim that a vibrant civil society is necessary for democratic institutions.

Following the emphasis of Gramsci, it is the ' . . . public spheres of societal communication and voluntary association (which are) the central institutions of civil society' (in Cohen and Arato 1992; 411). In societies with democratic

---

[1] This particular insight resurfaces later in this research in relation to observations on the NGO activity in Germany and in Australia as well as in international networks on refugee issues. At times this awareness of the need for public attention is acknowledged and actively sought by NGOs. At other times though NGOs have taken the decision to work behind the scenes and see their invisibility as an attribute.

institutions, founded on principles of equal human worth and dignity, at least minimal expectations exist regarding the treatment of marginalised groups: both citizens and non-citizens. There is a rift among theorists about the meaning of civil society. A degree of consensus does exist on the voluntary character of civil society which differentiates it from the state and some other forms of organised activity. Social movements and other non-government organisations, and to some extent political parties, are the vehicles through which citizens can become active in the political processes which shape their lives and the societies in which they live (Bauböck 2000; 101). Individual interest and choice are expressed in the institutions of civil society rather than the state which tends toward coercive and compulsory forms of compliance for members. The state exercises political authority in making decisions and affirming institutions which can limit individual choice, while civil society mechanisms, premised on voluntary activity, expand the choice and the plurality of association. In order for civil society to exist, at least a generalised, shared political culture has to be evident, with the virtue of civility, for instance, expressed in a certain attentiveness to the arguments of others. This might be expressed in the adherence to, and acceptance of, a common set of rules for conduct in everyday exchanges and transactions in social life.

In practical terms, a particular *civil society* will bear a strong relationship to, and be shaped by, the state alongside which it exists, with which it negotiates, and whose institutional base it utilises. Moreover, civil society also impacts on the state. In the countries under discussion, the public/private split is a positioning device for categorising or 'bracketing off' some aspects of social life to the private, and therefore non-state sphere. Civil society has been defined as a public space 'between household and state, aside from the market, in which citizens may associate for the prosecution of particular interests within a framework of law guaranteed by the state' (Bryant 1997). Following this interpretation, civil society could be expected to foster pluralism and the accommodation of difference, rather than a common 'subscription to primary values'. Civil society relates in central ways to the politics of influence in shifting or displacing entrenched systems or practices, or indeed defending some of the same (Cohen and Arato 1992; 563). In this vein, the practice of civil disobedience is a strategy, particularly of social movements, with tactics of shock and disruption aimed at creating or expanding both rights and democratisation (ibid; 567). Civil disobedience is discussed later in this chapter in conjunction with social movements.

To reiterate, it is civil society, distinct from the state which represents the collective institutions and formalised practices (laws) of the people, as well as from the market, representing private and often transnational corporations working for the interests (profit) of shareholders, that ordinary people can express and organise themselves. In becoming 'organised', NGOs and social movements represent this non-material culture of civil society.

Civil society cannot be expected to display similar characteristics in every setting. The distinctiveness of a political system, cultural orientation and specific social pressures, will shape the civil society evident in a particular place and time. In the case of Western democracies, civil society operates alongside the state, and in many cases, goals are difficult to set and articulate as no large-scale struggles occur as is the case in democratising societies. Markus, for instance, argues that social integration, able to be achieved during periods of rapid social transformation in 'heroic periods', is not able to be sustained after liberation from an oppressive regime. Such unity, able to be achieved by social movement organisations during a struggle, quickly dissipates as new forms of social stratification occur after conflict has ceased (2001; 959-60). We could further extrapolate that in 'non-heroic times', organised political action in civil society is more difficult to trigger.

Just as the test of success of any political party in an election cycle is the voting public's verdict, so the efficacy of political action undertaken by non-state actors must be established by the trajectory through which the issue they advocate for is taken. Needless to say, generating public opinion is an uneven process, buffeted by often unpredictable events and alliances. Yet a commitment to the democratic ideal which sees matters of mutual interest vigorously debated in the 'communicative arena' of the public sphere, remains central. Mediation between various 'publics' takes place across organisations, movements, clubs and gatherings of local citizens (Cohen 1999; 215).

## Non-government organisations as an aspect of civil society

The end of the Cold War witnessed a shift in international relations away from a bi-polar system, marked by nuclear weapon proliferation, to regional conflicts and conflicts within nation-states, often based on ethnic and religious tensions which had remained dormant during the Cold War. Since 1989 armed and unarmed conflicts have tended to be located intrastate, rather than inter-state: localised ethnic conflicts and civil wars have proliferated in many locations, rather than large-scale inter-state conflicts. Relief and development NGOs, as well as international advocacy and human rights NGOs have played an increasing role in mitigating some of the most tragic impacts of these events upon the most vulnerable groups. Relief and development NGOs provide on the ground assistance in the form of emergency relief such as food and shelter and medical assistance, as well as long-term development, such as rebuilding infrastructure in the aftermath of war, and natural disasters. Advocacy NGOs also lobby in various forums to resolve conflicts, as well as involvement in development work such as the fostering of local capacities for institution building. A significant role of NGOs is the dissemination of information to other organisations and in particular to the mass media. The first hand information and accounts of developments and incidents, make the insight of NGOs a valuable component in communicating diverse opinions and interpretations in the discourses of international migration, particularly unauthorised migration.

The reasons behind the proliferation of non-state actors are complex, with some developments being generalisable across cases and others being specific to an issue or a geographic location. Broadly two observations are most relevant for this research in relation to NGOs: 1) NGOs have increased in number as well as in the reach of their work due to the geopolitical shifts in international relations at the end of the Cold War, and 2) states have increasingly sought to divest themselves of some of the roles, functions and responsibilities they carry out (most often social-welfare-oriented provisions), and have encouraged NGOs to engage in delivering such services. This development is apparent with the increased influx of refugees into Western countries, as well as in areas of social policy.

During the height of the Cold War, NGOs were primarily synonymous with activity in less developed countries as significant players in the processes of economic, social and to a lesser extent political development (democratisation), in situations where the state was not able or willing to provide the institutional support or leadership roles required for solving local problems. However, in the changing international system, NGOs have also become increasingly involved in 'post industrial', developed nations. The promotion of human rights, of social justice and the various manifestations of protest-oriented activity is associated with issues affecting both developed and less developed societies. The impact of immigration is one such issue which has repeatedly tested the reactions of economically developed and less developed societies. This is particularly the case in relation to asylum seekers who arrive unannounced and with little or no immediate resources to draw on - unlike other categories of migrants.

The largest body of literature on NGOs refers directly to less developed countries (LDCs), and to the activities of associations either local or international, involved in development work, as well as relief work in emergency and post conflict situations (Cohen and Deng 1998, Keck and Sikkink 1998, Huddock 1999). There is, however, an increase in research related to the activities of NGOs in developed countries. While I concentrate only on the latter, some general trends and patterns identified in both bodies of literature are relevant here. NGOs in less developed societies have long been associated with the process of democratisation – part of which is the facilitation of development - particularly economic and social development in order that basic needs are met and people can lead fully productive lives. However democratisation can also be seen as an ongoing process, relevant to economically developed countries.

The growing ease of making and keeping international contacts, facilitated by more sophisticated communication networks and by an increasingly globalised media, has fostered an environment conducive to the increasing networks of human rights NGOs who operate across borders (Keck and Sikkink, 1998, 12). As Risse and Ropp (1999; 255) claim with the phrase 'talk is not cheap', governments only enter argumentative discourses on ethics and human rights norms when pressed by internal (domestic) or external (international) forces which they can no longer ignore. They reiterate this point in their assessment of the lessons for human rights practitioners (NGOs), with an additional emphasis: that 'words matter' (ibid.; 276). The point is, that rhetorical engagement remains vital, even with human-rights-violating governments, though not in the naive hope that governments can be persuaded to change their action by talk alone. Nevertheless, the importance of communicating ideas and values cannot be underestimated. Just as corporations in the full-profit sector, NGOs must search for avenues and modes of communicating their ideas and the interests they represent if they are to engage the various 'publics' identified as significant to their goals. The issues that stem from concerns over human rights often defy geographical borders, and have the potential to unite as well as to divide people and nations. The way in which such issues, and their impact on local communities are communicated about, can be the decisive factor in eventual outcomes. Keck and Sikkink indicate how local leverage can be applied through links with external governments, or other NGOs perhaps in other countries, a process which the authors label 'boomerang pressure' (Risse and Sikkink 1999; 119). That is, when NGOs who operate within a state, rather than across states do not have the power or capacity to directly pressure that state, international networks can exert pressure through external forces - either NGOs outside the nation, international NGOs, or inter-governmental organisations, as well as other states.[2] In addition the use of a 'spiral model' (ibid. ; 20), indicates the accumulation of pressure exerted at various points and over time to make certain parties or 'rogue' states comply with standards, such as human rights norms. By a unified effort of international non-government organisations, local NGOs and states who comply with human rights standards a prolonged campaigning of pressure 'from below' and 'from above'.

In terms of the role of NGOs in the international arena, a number of key international initiatives have pointed to the significance of NGO action and the

---

[2] The international campaign to ban land mines is an example of a network of NGOs within, and between nations which operated successfully utilising boomerang pressure on states which sell as well as those which use land mines.

growing recognition governments have given to the role of NGOs in social and economic development, in advocacy, and the fostering of human rights and democracy. Let me point to two of the most significant: the World Conference on Human Rights (Vienna 1993) which recognised the role of NGOs in promoting human rights at national, regional and international levels (point 38 of the Vienna Declaration). While recognising the key role of states in 'standard setting' on human rights, the declaration emphasises dialogue and co-operation between government and NGO sectors. And second, the Beijing Declaration (1995) following the Fourth World Conference of Women declares the contribution of civil society actors – especially women's groups, networks and NGOs in facilitating the human rights of women (at point 20). Moreover, a follow-up action strategy involved NGOs as key players in ensuring more than one-off or tokenistic attention to the issues at hand. Non-government actors must find ways of engaging in the decision-making process if they are to have any effect on policy development. At a local and grass roots level, NGO actions are small manifestations of what are often bigger social and political problems in a society or indeed internationally. This is certainly the case in relation to the representation of refugees and asylum seekers, where common problems and constraints are faced by NGOs across different countries.

*(a) From local to international issue networks*

As I argued in the previous chapter, an identifiable tension has developed, particularly in the last decade, as a result of the gap between the national and international human rights standards and their application. It is a consequence of the spread of human rights standards that the degree to which such standards are implemented and adhered to is increasingly scrutinised by NGOs as well as by the international media. There are some 250 such organisations whose primary role is the advocacy of international human rights and humanitarian affairs (Forsythe 2000). Such organisations include; Amnesty International, the International Committee of the Red Cross, Médicins sans Frontiéres, Doctors Without Borders, Human Rights Watch, the International Commission of Jurists, the Human Rights Law Committee, Lawyers Without Borders. There is a vast critical literature which deals with international NGOs and their role in human rights advocacy. However within states, the role of NGOs is often researched in terms of voluntary, philanthropic and charitable organisations with little or no link to international organisations or to the issue of advocacy.

In light of the increased presence and impact of NGOs in many locations around the world, what conclusions can we draw from the degree and penetration of such activity? Are NGOs replacing the action repertoires of other groups or institutions, or does their work emanate from distinctly new areas of social and/or political concern? Once such questions have been addressed, secondary questions as to the accountability of NGOs also emerge. To whom do NGOs answer? How transparent and open to scrutiny is their work and action?

Before continuing with the general discussion of NGO activity and cycles of dialogue and contention with the state, I now turn briefly to an analysis of the phenomenon of social movements.

## Social movements and NGOs: similarities and differences

The literature on social movements is, at first glance discrete from literature on NGOs. Yet on closer inspection there are significant areas of overlap which I will be seeking to highlight. Both social movements and NGOs are forms of mobilising sentiment and concern on issues that are perceived as inadequately dealt with, or outside the jurisdiction of the state. As previously outlined, various theorists point to the decline of the state, or the 'shrinking' state; a phenomenon marked by a shifting of power relationships with greater interdependence among various 'stake holders' in world politics. This development includes the rise in the activity and prominence of NGOs (Fisher 1997).

The various groups that constitute the non-government and non-corporate (non-profit) sector, contribute to a *public sphere* between the state and private individuals, and differentiated from the state and from the economy, yet informed, influenced and to some extent shaped by the activities of the state and of the economy (Cohen and Arato 1992, Young 1999). Moreover, it is in this arena where unfettered, self-determining agency occurs and claims for the satisfaction of needs and wants can be articulated. Social movements are non-formalised, largely non-bureaucratic groupings of people seeking to influence a particular vision of *public will* on an issue. Broadly it can be asserted that social movements usually have a short-term trajectory or life span - either withering away, or being transformed into more formal entities or organisations. NGOs may mirror many of the characteristics of a social movement - particularly in the advocacy process – of articulating an alternative path: lobbying or protesting for social change. However, most NGOs have their origin in the delivery of specific services, or fulfilling specific roles, rather than in public will formation; adding this later activity to their work through experience.[3]

An important aspect of social movements is the dual potential which 'movement' has of system transformation, challenging existing institutionalised forms of conduct, and self-transformation; both of the individuals involved in movements and potentially those who come in contact with the movement. Alberto Melucci has developed a clear formulation of this dual function of social movements. Habermas has also outlined this duality as the potential of articulating new social problems and placing them on the 'public agenda', a goal able to be achieved in liberal public spheres by advocates and collections of concerned citizens, rather than by segments of the state apparatus or large corporations (Habermas 1996; 382). By focusing on collective, rather than purely individual action, it becomes plausible to contemplate the emergence, reproduction and transformation of social order. However, new social movements do not usually aim at taking power, as earlier types of movements such as the labour movement once did (Walzer 1991; 301). This means that transformation which social movements achieve is from 'below', rather than above.

Social movements consolidate and focus individual energies in a common pursuit. Such a pooling of resources and of energies is identifiable in other areas of social, political and economic life, but it is the particularly transformative effects of social movements that make this type of collective action distinct.

By focusing on collective action, rather than purely individual action, it becomes much easier to proceed to issues such as the emergence, reproduction and transformation of social order. This is true in the twofold sense that not only do collective forms of action and social movements contribute significantly to developing and changing social order, but they can also be understood in themselves as models of social order in the process of self generation (Joas 1996; 199).

Fundamental to any social movement, be it a global movement, or a local one, is the presence of conflict - symbolic or tangible. In this sense social movements are a specific form of the life of civil society. The very essence of a movement is the contesting of a set of social conditions or political arrangements. Conflict of some sort is thereby to be expected. Commonly, movements articulate interests

---

[3] This is particularly so in the area of forced migration, where the experience of NGOs in Western Europe as well as in Australia has been *accumulated resistance* or *radicalisation*. Organisations which at first may have focused solely on delivering health services or legal assistance to forced migrants, graft direct or indirect political work to their action repertoire in response to the retreat of state responsibility. These developments are detailed in later chapters.

which have a broader 'common good' for others outside the constituency of a social movement.

At not too irregular junctures, social movements become involved in civil disobedience, such as boycotts, mass demonstrations and other forms of 'contentious' politics. Civil disobedience can be engaged in purely to exert some influence on a government or indeed a coalition governments, in a policy area or in resource allocation. However, acts of civil disobedience also relate to 'justice-based' claims, where the rights of a minority may be violated even by a 'correct procedure' of law (Cohen and Arato 1992; 583). States that accept civil disobedience are less likely to fan the flames of dissent than authoritarian states. It is in the repression of citizens that a state leaves itself particularly exposed to the mobilisation of dissenters when an opportunity arises (Tarrow 1998; 85). Even though civil disobedience is extra-institutional in that it cannot be part of a legal framework as it is antithetical to it, nevertheless it remains a measure of the value of democracy and of liberalism:

> . . . of liberalism because it reveals the political dimensions of civil society and the normalcy of social movements; of democracy because it implies respect for rights and for a moral standpoint that is politically relevant outside the democratic consensus and procedures that have been institutionalized (Cohen and Arato 1992; 604).

Civil disobedience is, then, a 'litmus test' of democracy in a constitutional state, where the disobedient act has the role of a plebiscite role for the wider citizenry; in sounding an appeal to the majority to support certain claims (Habermas 1985; 103). Acts of civil disobedience have become familiar forms of dissent and resistance, from mass movements to relatively small-scale protests, following the lead of such figures as Mahatma Gandhi and the American civil rights leaders. However, as the use of non-violent protests grew during the 1960s throughout the United States, Europe, Australia and elsewhere, the response of authorities, from police to the courts, changed from utilising incarceration as punishment, to increasingly accepting protest as a form of speech (Tarrow 1998; 84). As a corollary, state toleration of such non-violent protest activity may deprive protesting groups of the 'potent weapon of outrage', as protesters are handled with care by police and; 'reasonable-sounding public authorities . . . organize seminars for protesters and protect their right to free speech against opponents' (della Porta and Reiter in Tarrow 1998; 84). According to Tarrow, a movement or organisation must then turn to the formal representative systems or political parties and elections in order to achieve any of their claims. However, we could also assume that under democratic conditions, a movement or organisation may first have exhausted legal and political channels prior to engaging in acts of civil disobedience (Rawls 1972, Dworkin 1978). It is in this sense, that we may think of civil disobedience arising at those times when a significant group of citizens become frustrated with the normal avenues of change, or where those avenues no longer function, and grievances are either not heard, or not acted upon, or, on the contrary, where a government embarks upon, or persists in modes of action whose legality or constitutionality are open to grave doubts.

In distinction to civil disobedience, obedience to norms, and a conformity to conventions, along with a concern for the opinion of others, would reveal a social world of self-imposed inertia. It can be argued that in some situations nothing needs to be done. However, patterns of inaction or of repeated conformity by citizens are problematic for democratic societies. Arendt claims for instance that obedience should be challenged where it fails to engage in any meaningful resistance due to 'self-imposed' obstacles – when the social becomes like a parvenu writ large: 'an entire human collectivity's failure to acknowledge its powers and responsibility' (in Pitkin 1998; 182). I pick up this theme again in chapters five and six, with an exploration of the role of bystanders or onlookers in contrast to participants in social and political action.

Far from being subsumed in a large movement, the individual is revealed in action and behaviour, which, when joined with that of others, becomes impossible to ignore. In order, though, for an individual to leave the private sphere and engage in public forms of communication;

> . . . 'disclosing and exposing' oneself to strangers, [the character trait of courage is required]: 'Courage 'is the political virtue par excellence,' but it is a courage contrasting less to cowardice than to anxiety. Citizenship requires that kind of boldness 'not because of the particular dangers that lurk' in the public world but because to enter politics one must leave behind one's personal 'worries and anxieties – about being accepted or valuable, or making a living – because in politics the 'primary concern is . . . always for the world, not oneself.' (Arendt in Pitkin 1998; 263).

Returning to the practical features of social movements, as I have pointed out, social movements do not have the longevity and continued influence of a formalised and institutionalised system such as, for example, NGOs. Nevertheless, movements can embody cycles of action and recurrence even when seemingly dormant.[4]

---

[4] The women's movement in Western countries has not been as visible, and vocal during the last decade as was the case during the 1960s and 70s. Nevertheless, we do see irregular activity from this movement on issues such as child sexual abuse and domestic violence, as these issues have come to light in recent times. Rather than a full re-awakening of the

Particularly in circumstances of perceived crisis, social movements are able to harness political will to propose alternative visions; visions which Tarrow labels 'opportunity structures' (1998). Tarrow has categorised movement action as 'contentious politics', alluding to the rebellious, dissenting stance of much social movement activity. NGOs rely in a much more obvious way then social movements, on the institutional framework, constructed and maintained by the state. This means that while both NGOs and social movements rely on some form of dialogue with the state and access to state knowledge (the accumulated expertise of the administrative mechanisms of the state), NGOs, as organisations, have to temper their goals more obviously than do social movements, as they often have close partnerships with the state.

Though social movements and NGOs may represent the same issues and adopt similar strategies and activities, they remain as distinct forms of organising non-state action. Social movements tend to display greater spontaneity of action, are less hierarchical and bureaucratic in structure and rely far less frequently on state funding than do NGOs.[5] Though both social movements and NGOs rely on the recruitment of volunteers to carry out some of their work, NGOs often have an important core group of paid, professional staff.

In this research I focus primarily the commonalities rather than the distinctions between movements and NGOs, and more specifically on the public will formation that emanates from the advocacy/representation processes. What sort of impact are movements and NGOs able have on public opinion? Are the resources of movements and NGOs best directed toward advocacy activities, or would the issue domain of NGOs and movements be better served through less overtly political activity?

Before considering the impact of the politics of the 'third way' on the work of NGOs, I want to briefly mention the way in which NGOs and social movements are staffed. We may ask ourselves, are activists the same as volunteers? Are these terms interchangeable, or do they denote something quite different? It does matter whether the staff of NGOs are paid, professional workers, or volunteers. Most directly, this relates to how an organisation is viewed in the public sphere. When the work of NGOs is viewed in a philanthropic light, as is prevalent in the United

---

movement, some feminist activists draw on past experience and utilise new issue networks to advocate for the rights of children and abused women.

[5] It should be noted that governments do fund NGOs whose activities are largely or in some cases solely advocacy-focused. However, advocacy NGOs have found it increasingly difficult to rely solely on state funding. In the Australian case, NGOs whose primary role is advocacy, are increasingly having to turn to non-state forms of funding to continue their work.

States, for instance, the original premise of NGO activity can become skewed. This relates to 'good samaritanism' or a charitable approach to representing others, or delivering certain services, which is distinct from doing such things from the perspective of rights and obligations in the pursuit of universal rather than a particular vision of justice. While NGOs do rely to some extent on volunteers, the need for training and supervision is an ongoing problem within organisations.[6]

It is particularly at the point at which NGOs as formal organisations and social movements, as loose networks, cross over, at which the character and potential of voluntarism is most evident and able to be utilised positively. At particular moments in history when collective action and protest activity becomes focused in response to particular events or policies, the gathering of loose coalitions of activists is regularly observed to be most pronounced.

## The Third Way: a new deal with the state?

By now we have a clear picture that NGOs and social movements are potential conduits of political power and influence as they mobilise sentiment and action through various forms of *public opinion* and *public will*. It is *resources* that to some extent define as well as delimit the potential power of movements and of NGOs.

Formal *representation* in a parliamentary democracy is at arm's length from individual citizens. Moreover, this representation, in the capital cities and in the grand monuments and palaces of formalised political power, is not only physically removed from the people, but communicatively filtered by intermediaries parties: the media, political parties, interest groups, and so on. It is the spheres of state and economy which continue to wield the most direct power, certainly in terms of resource allocation. Moreover, as neither NGOs nor social movements have legislative power, they must gain the support of parliament in order for any proposed change to be legislated. Engagement with these spheres is crucial for NGOs, if their endeavors are to be fruitful and have some impact. I develop this argument particularly in relation to NGOs and their association with the state, in

---

6 Particularly in an area such as representing asylum seekers, the work undertaken by volunteers rather than professional paid staff needs to be carefully gauged. Laws and administrative rulings and entitlements that pertain to asylum seekers during the processing of protection claims are highly complex and constantly changing areas of government policy and administration. Volunteers need to be given sufficient training and supervision to deal with such complex and sensitive matters.

that the state is a critical partner to NGOs. A retreating, minimalist state does not result in a larger, enriched NGO sector, but quite the reverse. A short-term growth in the non-government sector may result in the withdrawal of state services. However, in the medium to long-term such a shift is not sustainable, first, in an economic sense and eventually in terms of the institutionalised forms of knowledge accumulation and generation. In other words, the specific knowledge and expertise within government bureaucracies, often accumulated over many years, is not easily replaced or replicated within non-government organisations.

The notion of political culture articulated by Almond and Verba (1963) in their cross-national study of differences in political participation related to culture, offers one useful perspective on the development of conditions conducive to collective action. Their three-part assessment of political culture divides such action into - *parochial* – *subject* – and *participation* or *civic* culture. Parochial associations or culture are those (pre-modern forms) where life circulates around the private sphere and political life is limited. Subject culture is denoted by modern political systems, but ones in which individuals see little of themselves or their own abilities reflected in politics, as the practices and institutionalised manifestations of governments. Individuals instrumentalise their action with, and towards political institutions, where most often assessments of success are premised on 'output'. A civic culture reflects high levels of participation and influence in politics by groups and individuals, and an activist role in public and in political life. This last form of political culture has been interpreted by Putnam (1993) as emblematic of high levels of *social capital* - which other theorists, such as Giddens (1998) have developed into an interpretation of social life between market-driven and state-driven system logic, called the 'third way'. Much literature on civil society, and the proliferation of the so-called 'new social movements' has celebrated the growing phenomenon of these groupings within society as the champions of plurality, difference and justice. Critics, however, have typified new social movements as often constituting well-educated, middle-class memberships, for example the women's movement, and the environment movement: the contention being that social inequalities often remain masked, or blatantly present for people in marginal positions in society. Moreover, transnational issue networks may extend such marginalisation, as those with resources and knowledge leap beyond territorial borders in ways which less privileged groups are not able to.

In contrast to the growth in numbers and influence of NGOs over the last decade, states have increasingly been pressured by their voting constituents regarding diminishing sovereignty. Sovereignty is relevant for the control of the economy and regulation of flows of finance in and out of a country; and for membership in tangible and intangible forms: citizenship and identity, including various displays of patriotism and nationalism. As I argued in chapter one, economic regulation and the control of capital has in the last decade seen power and influence shift from states to transnational corporations, with individual states unable to resist global economic forces. Economic deregulation has triggered a sequence of reactions in societies around the globe. The two most relevant reactions for my discussion are the crisis of the welfare state and increasing xenophobia. Rising fear and insecurity within economically developed countries has led in many instances to an increase in support for ultra-nationalist political parties.[7] Populist political parties tend to simplify the economic effects of globalisation through stigmatising visible minority groups such as foreigners.

The other point of crisis or rupture; the 'crisis of the welfare state', is manifest in as much as the satisfaction of needs and demands on the state for satisfaction exceeds what is able to be granted. The question becomes who or what should satisfy, or indeed re-articulate these needs, and by what mechanism? However, this so-called crisis did not arise in isolation, but rather is a response to a wider neo-liberal agenda which favors the market as primary regulator with a minimalist model of the state. The logic of a social welfare state model in contrast, has been premised on a vital distinction between the 'liberal constitutional state' and the 'social welfare state' (Habermas 1998: 224). Social welfare interventions by a state draw on notions of 'justice' which indicate a move from negative to positive rights: where an acknowledgement of structural inequalities is addressed through the redistribution of the 'goods' of a society.[8] With the reality of the state retreating in Western democracies from social services and economic redistribution, the fulfilment of such needs are *devolved* to private (business) interests or to the loose coalitions of actors in civil society. That is, the state either contracts certain services and provisions to third parties through tendering processes and the privatisation of public utilities or operates on a presumption that 'charitable' groups will fulfil particularly the welfare and social needs previously part of state services.

---

[7] We can think here of both Germany and Australia as well as Austria, Italy, France Switzerland and Denmark.

[8] Both Germany and Australia, through the 1990s, experienced a winding back of social welfare provisions by the state and an emphasis on a less interventionist state: both symptoms of the much wider phenomenon of the 'crisis of the welfare state', characterised by a dismantling of redistributive social welfare provisions premised on a neo-conservative philosophy evident in Northern Europe and the United States from the late 1970s (Cockett 1994). These developments are relevant for this research in relation to the social rights (to legal assistance and language education) and economic rights (to minimal food, shelter and medical assistance) of refugees and asylum seekers during the determination period of a protection claim in a host country.

The theoretical underpinning of a change in the balance between the service and welfare provisions of democratic states, has been drawn from strands of communitarian thinking (Driver & Martell 1997). The particularist opposition to liberalism which communitarians such as Michael Walzer, Michael Sandel and Alistair MacIntyre have articulated have been reinterpreted by theorists such as Anthony Giddens (1998) and eventually integrated into the framework utilised by political parties in legitimising a move away from universalist welfare schemes to targeted and 'tied' schemes which identify and obligate an individual recipient of benefits.

Anthony Giddens has grappled with the dilemmas outlined above through what he terms a 'renewal of social democracy' (1998), conceptualising a 'third way'. For Giddens, the state becomes the 'social investment state', with a tripartite balance of arrangements between the state, the corporate sector and economy,and 'third sector' organisations. The formula is premised on responsibility of all sectors for the 'common good'. Consumer sentiment and behaviour may sway corporate strategy, but only if the perception is that it will benefit the corporation. Giddens outlines the principle 'no rights without responsibilities' as an ethical principle which must not apply only to welfare recipients, but also to the behaviour of business (ibid.; 65-6).

At first glance this appears relatively unproblematic in a system premised on liberal democratic principles - that the extension of rights to members (citizens) is linked to certain responsibilities - outlined, for instance, in a constitution, in legal frameworks which are communicated and deciphered through institutions, such as education and understood socially in the public sphere. Sanctions can then be applied to members who fail to carry out the responsibility side of the bargain - who harm other members, for instance: in which case rights can be deferred or suspended.

One of the consequences of a devolution of roles and responsibilities of the state to the third sector is also that the tenure of duties is shortened, inasmuch as organisations are squeezed into a metaphysical revolving door; having to keep moving to search for funding, put in tenders as well as continue the delivery of services; while simultaneously competing with other organisations vying for the same pot of funding. This development has the consequence of deferring the impetus for long-term planning, as well as diverting attention and energy and *will* from engaging in political action. For instance, if non-government agencies are involved in providing assistance to job-seekers, and do so in a market-driven environment, energy and focus is on the delivery of services within fiscal constraints. Those agencies can be expected to be less engaged in lobbying and advocating for solutions to the root causes of unemployment. Client-based work which is tendered on a regular basis in the same way that the building of a bridge is tendered has a number of consequences.

Perhaps the most serious consequence of devolution of state responsibilities is that it puts state responsibility at arm's length from those seeking assistance from the state. The linguistic turn of transforming *citizens* into *clients* indicates the insertion and prioritisation of market-driven calculus into social contract relations where reciprocity should not always mean all things undertaken have to be returned with an equivalence value (Godbout 1998; 180): that the user (client) must pay (show cause) before leaving the premises - in other words, that there should be some mechanism for deferring payment.

I move now to consider what roles NGOs undertake and to distinguish the major features of such work. Both advocacy and service delivery functions are components of NGO activity:

1. Advocacy is the process of representing and communicating ideas on an issue. A presence of advocacy activities is not necessarily possible within every organisation, though both advocacy and service delivery roles should ideally be present within *networks of organisations* who can draw on each other's expertise and knowledge, and engage in the processes of will formation on similar *social issues.*
2. Service delivery amounts to various practical services or tasks delivered to a targeted group. Successful networking between movements and organisations can foster an environment where both aspects are valued, fostered and nurtured.

In line with the dual roles of NGOs, the above distinctions are important, as the processes of advocacy and of long-term change are informed by the attention to detail at a day-to-day level played out in the 'situated' lives of marginal groups, for instance. This 'case-work' information is part of a feedback loop to advocacy groups who can utilise this information to advocate for a change in policy or in the administrative practices which affect refugees. Similarly, research by advocacy organisations regularly draws on the information and insights gained by 'front-line' fieldworkers who are engaged in day-to-day activities such as the delivery of social, legal, welfare and emergency services.

The implementation of third way policies and strategies by governments in Australia and Germany, as well as in the U.S.A. and Great Britain, has been accompanied by rhetoric of 'self-help' and 'community responsibility'. The over-simplification of the use of a term such as civil society and of *social capital,* have been powerfully employed by politicians to reify the third sector as part of a 'self-help' strategy. Such a strategy of 'self-help' should be applied by those in need themselves and those closest to them (charities), rather than looking to a third party (the state) for assistance or hand-outs. By placing the roles and responsibilities which were previously in the domain of the state into the domain of civil society or third-sector organisations, some consequential outcomes can be anticipated. It is, I would argue, much more than exchanging one service provider (the state) for another. The rhetoric of handing back responsibility to citizens coincidentally shifts not only the outer edges, but the very principles of representative democracy. Citizens do not have the veto power of a regular election over NGOs that they have over the state. The state, utilising third way thinking to devolve roles and responsibilities, also loosens the ties that bind citizens to the state, and thereby to each other.

In short, the problems that I would highlight resulting from the implementation of a third way and the associated devolution of state responsibilities onto various agencies of the non-government sector are as follows:

1. The problem of long-term quality and sustainability of what NGOs are being asked to do. This also raises questions of continuing funding, and of the impartiality or independence of NGOs.
2. The blurring of boundaries that occurs with state devolution to the third sector also has consequences for the other organisations/movements that do not participate in activities previously the domain of the state. Modes of resistance, opposition and alternatives are weakened, as the public perceives the general domain of third-sector, or civil society organisations as compromised in independence as they are in a sense an arm of the state.
3. In the medium to long-term, social trust is eroded as the concepts of at least minimal access to basic social 'goods' which the state allocates under a model of the welfare state is replaced by market-driven contractual arrangements.
4. The accumulation of expertise and knowledge gathered over time in government departments and institutions is weakened or lost.
5. NGOs increasingly are viewed as service providers, rather than as advocates. That is, as they are providing services (participating in economic activities) the potential for political action and advocacy decreases and is compromised. The advocacy work of NGOs is difficult to quantify, therefore funding can be difficult to secure, and will, I think, be sidelined in favor of pure service delivery with little room for reflection, critique and change. Moreover, advocacy processes are more open to the charge of politicisation than service delivery functions.

This last point listed in the critique of the consequences of third way principles, is particularly relevant for the focus of this research. The diminishing possibilities and the undervaluing of advocacy activities have consequences for the long-term viability of NGOs themselves, but more significantly for the prospects of the most marginalised people in society.

The emphasis on local voluntarism and on self-help, which is at the heart of third-way philosophy, rather than universal reciprocity, re-emphasises the social over the political - feeling, affinity and preference over impartial principles and justice applicable universally. Voluntarism is indeed antithetical to the formulation of rights based on justice principles. It is, at most, part of the plethora of social 'goods' that citizens may, or may not choose to be involved in; either for their own needs fulfilment or in providing for the needs of others. In changing the system of entitlements therefore, justice is at best reordered; perhaps substantially diminished. The previous recipients of entitlements as a 'right' find themselves in a more precarious position, where needs fulfilment is negotiated as a 'right' only so long as selected variations of the 'good' are met (Cohen 1999; 239).

This chapter has indicated some of the ways in which NGOs and movements are involved to varying degrees with administrative and bureaucratic power structures, in attempts to influence the development of policy at the nation-state level. A synthesis of the central thrust of NGOs, of social movements, third-sector organisations as well as transnational networks of actors and the discourses around civil society, is necessary for making sense of the challenges non-state actors face in attempting to enter the processes directed by the state or by the economy. The orthodoxies of managerialism tend to flatten the nuances and distinctions underlying administrative practice, and view only the systematic, predictable paths of the 'units' (people) to be managed through the established structures of the bureaucracy (Degeling and Colebatch 1997; 13). It is, in other words, primarily an instrumental view of policy application and administration. NGOs are also part of the feed-back loop to government and the bureaucracy on the effectiveness or otherwise of policy, as they encounter the front-line or grassroots implementation of policy via their constituents.

The idea of a 'movement' society, as outlined earlier, is not so far removed from the Athenian idea of engaged citizens, as more than recipients of state and market direction and impulses. Rather a movement society comprises of engaged individuals and collectivities, shaping political and social life and potentially extending democratic ideals.[9] However, to be fully active, certain minimum social rights of citizens must be fulfilled. Fraser and Gordon, for instance, argue that

---

[9] In contemporary societies *citizen* has largely been subsumed into *consumer*. The consequences of this development may well be the self-imposed parvenu status of modern citizens described by Hannah Arendt; the social as 'blob' which anchors us to political inaction as bystanders, with the stickiness of consumption shaping our desires and flattening our creativity.

social citizenship is distinct from civil citizenship, citing Marshall's 1949 essay *Citizenship and Social Class*, as the first consistent conceptualisation of social citizenship (1994). The stages of citizenship which Marshall outlines are three-fold. First, civil citizenship, emanating from the eighteenth century and establishing the rights for individual freedom, to property and above all to justice. The second stage is political citizenship, occurring initially in the nineteenth century, included the right to participate in the exercise of political power, to hold office, to vote. The final stage is social citizenship, which emerged in the twentieth century, and is marked by the idea of the right to at least minimal economic security and a share in 'social goods' prevailing in a particular society (in Fraser et al. 1994: 92). Marshall's concept of citizenship is also dynamic, resting on a crucial component of participation. The development of the secular state and the ideal of universal norms goes hand in glove with the idea of membership embodied in citizenship. It is with the insertion of nationalism that exclusionary components of membership come to the fore. For an individual to be an engaged member of a civil society, I would argue he/she must have the 'goods' of civil, political and social citizenship – particularly when seeking to represent the interests of others. That is, a *group* of citizens may become active in protest movements with the intent of gaining access to certain social citizenship rights for themselves and the *group* to which they belong, such as access to low-cost housing, to public transport and health services, even in more remote areas or isolated suburbs. Only when such rights are established is an individual sufficiently 'free' to engage in political action on behalf of others.

As citizens have also been transformed into 'clients', 'users' and 'customers' (Eriksen and Weigárd 2000;21), the ties which bound them to a place, to institutional mechanisms which support various aspects of life's needs, and even to fellow citizens, have been loosened.

Many scholars have interpreted increasing privatisation and political ambivalence in modern states as a result of consumer- and utility-oriented morals. In other words, citizens seem to show a somewhat passive orientation towards rights rather than actively participating in society' (ibid.; 31).

Such developments impinge on the willingness for collective problem solving or indeed collective action. It is my hypothesis, though not a central problem for this research, that the measure of a 'good society' can be gauged, among other indicators, by the level of 'engagement' or movement activity of citizens. Citizens are only likely to have the will for autonomous action where their needs, or 'social citizenship' are met. We could further hypothesise that such activity, engaged in for others, confirms or enriches a 'good society', perhaps making its edges less brittle, in contrast to more instrumental action, focused purely on self-interest.

Some of the key factors emerging from this discussion which will appear in the subsequent chapters in relation to assessing the relationships between NGOs, states and the inter-state system are: 1) the careful assessment and evaluation of NGOs and social movements indicating that the presence of NGOs and movements is not of itself positive and valuable, but rather must be carefully and regularly evaluated; 2) this assessment and appraisal has to be ongoing, particularly since the mechanisms of critique and assessment that are in place to guide and limit state action do not exist in the same fashion for the non-state sector; 3) how effective are the links between local to transnational networks?

As this chapter has indicated, NGOs, social movements and the myriad of formal and informal groupings in civil society indicate a potential force for issues and developments that concern people, not only in Germany and Australia, but globally. In the area demarcated for this study, this means in particular the issues of human rights. Having argued the case for a vibrant NGO and movement sector, it follows that the international human rights movement must continue to find ways to assist ordinary people in constructing and working for strong civil societies and viable states. This is particularly so in the face of international terrorism, which has the potential to hijack the ability to use strong moral arguments of international human rights.

I now turn to the case studies of Germany and Australia, bearing in mind the theoretical framework I have articulated in the last two chapters. I begin the case studies with a discussion of the historical and cultural significance of immigration in both countries in order to be able to analyse the particular problems which claims for protection have yielded in both societies.

# PART II
# HISTORICAL AND CULTURAL DEVELOPMENTS IN IMMIGRATION AND PROTECTION: THE CASE STUDIES

## Chapter 4

# The search for protection in Germany

To be an asylum seeker in Germany today is to join the significant ranks of people categorised as 'foreigners' or 'aliens' who find themselves as economic, social and cultural outcasts; fringe dwellers in a society undergoing its own identity crisis. The consequences of the historical marginalisation of immigrants and the more recent efforts at integrating these newcomers in ways which are palatable enough to the majority of Germans, is a substantial task for the unified Federal Republic of Germany. Asylum seekers are taken into account in the official immigration debates in Germany, though until their status is determined, they remain in a sense 'in-between' people, figures in the shadows, leading a suspended half life while they seek the official status that will grant them protection, residence and the right to work, to education and other aspects of human development.

At a German film festival screened during 1995 in Sydney, a short film titled *Schwarz fahren* ('to ride black'), provided a powerful commentary on contemporary German society. *Schwarz fahren* is a colloquial German phrase which means 'fare dodger'. A mini drama is played out on a tram in some large German city. People board the tram. The focus is on a young black man. We see him seated beside an elderly white woman, who stares at him with suspicion and scorn. Is she frightened of him? Does she think he will rob her? There must be something unsavory about this man. Perhaps he is one of the large, indeterminable mass of irregular, undocumented people who walk the city streets like ghosts. Tension builds. An inspector boards. Surely now the black man will be ejected from the tram. The inspector challenges him; he shows a ticket and the inspector moves his attention to the old woman. She is the fare evader - the 'black rider'. Like this short moral tale of the fare dodger, the political and social landscape of the Federal Republic is often ambiguous in dealing with strangers. Apparently straightforward and transparent procedures and rules may obscure layers of culturally specific complexities and rigidity which newcomers cannot penetrate. Added to procedural complexities is the question of identities and belonging. What does it mean to be

German in the new millennium? How are the boundaries of belonging and of entitlements demarcated and realised in the lives of citizens, denizens and aliens?[1]

The trajectory of 'asylum politics' (*Asylpolitik*) in Germany in the 1990s cannot be understood in isolation from earlier developments. As I have outlined in chapter one, I argue that the way in which immigration policy is formalised and administered by state institutions and communicated publicly, has repercussions in all areas of the immigration 'system'. The right to citizenship, as well as measures of social integration of newcomers and the adjudication over protection claims made by asylum seekers, all accumulate to constitute the public understanding of immigration and a generalised terrain of foreigners encountered in everyday exchanges. In addition, information flows in the public sphere, interpret and reinterpret the 'foreigner' and 'alien' for public consumption.

This chapter begins by outlining contemporary asylum politics in the context of Germany as a 'de facto' country of immigration. In the first instance, a brief history of the major emigration and immigration waves will assist in understanding the contemporary response to non-Germans generally and to 'alien', uninvited arrivals specifically. I address the consequences of official descriptions of Germany as a non-immigration country. What is the status of foreigners in German society? What formal and informal processes demarcate the lives of non-Germans from those of Germans? These are complex and open-ended questions. To be sure we can identify asylum seekers as synonymous with the lowest rung of an imaginary ladder or hierarchy of foreigners in Germany. Both legal and social understandings of citizenship – of 'belonging', will be discussed in this chapter. In this respect Germany, in contrast to Australia, is an ethnic nation, with an exclusionary form of citizenship based on descent, though modifications by the Schroeder SPD/Green coalition, which came to power in 1998, have begun the process of easing some German citizenship restrictions and re-engaging the immigration debate.

In order to be able to contextualise non-government activity in Germany, the role of the major churches also will be discussed. An overview of some aspects of unification after 1989 will allow us to consider the role of NGOs and social movements in the new Germany, aspects which make certain German responses unique.

---

[1] 'Riding black' or fare evasion, which is practiced commonly in cities such as Berlin, is also an example of the impact of the restrictive citizenship laws, which make it relatively difficult for immigrants to gain naturalisation compared with other Western countries. The laws relating to foreigners codifies among other things, the expulsion of non-citizens if they are found to have practiced fare evasion five times.

## The basis of nationhood and identity

Hand in hand with any discussion of immigration, or an analysis of the merits of immigration systems and models of integration, is the issue of nation and identity: how they are constituted, maintained and reinforced. A variety of interpretations of nation and nationalism circulate sociological and political views of human action and of the organisation of societies in search of solidarity and consent among members. Ernest Renan expressed an account of common national will as gathering consent through a 'daily plebiscite' (1994). In contrast, we see other interpretations of the national will as engaging with the relationship between *will* and *culture* in nation formation, as dual processes which express and reinforce ways of life generationally, as much more nuanced and layered social processes; with cultural life informing a general will (Poole 1999; 35). Hans Kohn's distinction between 'civic' and 'ethnic' nation is aligned with the idea of political development: those nations which developed with the enlightenment ideals of liberty and of reason hold to a 'civic' nationalism; while those nations, including Germany, which form shared identity on the basis of cultural or ethnic preference and codes, look to natural, organic modes of belonging, rather than political modes, and are in contrast 'ethnic' nations (Kohn 1967; 329-32). While civic nationalism looks to law to bind a society together, ethnic nationalism situates attachments as inherited, not as chosen (Ignatieff 1993; 4-5). To be sure though, while these distinctions are significant and inform government policy and the political action of citizens along potentially quite distinct trajectories, these different nationalisms regularly overlap in the same country. Ignatieff cites the examples of Northern Ireland, India and Canada as cases where; 'ethnic nationalism flourishes within states formally committed to civic democracy' (ibid.; 5). While the memories and traditions of different historical developments remain unique to certain groups of people, and are tied to geography and to monuments, it is in the end a question of politics and of moral values which drives both 'ethnic' and 'civic' versions of nation (Poole 1999; 43) and the extent to which they continue to flourish in particular countries.

In relation to Germany, the idea of nation and the realm of identity have undergone a remarkable transformation in a comparatively short period, while some traces of distinctly German historical roots remain (Münch 1996; 33). At a time when countries such as France, Britain and the Netherlands emerged as nation-states in the seventeenth and eighteenth centuries, Germany remained divided into a number of individual states, until the relatively late unification into one nation-state under Bismarck in 1871.

Until 1871, strong regional distinctions from north to south, were exemplified through linguistic and religious differences. More than three hundred German principalities existed under the Holy Roman Empire. Germany was essentially a 'state of mind' until the late nineteenth century with strong roots in Romanticism reflecting the physical environment of soil and forests. Johann Gottfried Herder was one of the most influential and eloquent exponents and custodians of folk memory in Germany culture, rooted to the idea of native soil. Romanticism continued through the eighteenth and nineteenth century with such literary figures as Schlegel, Fichte and Goethe influencing the development of nationalism. Romanticism inspired both a political and a cultural variant of nationalism, the former expressing the sovereign political will embodied in the nation-state, while the later was evident in national culture, especially language (Margalit 1997; 77). However, it should also be borne in mind that the typification of Germany as a nation grounded solely on ethno-volkish principles may omit other inclusive forms to be found in German nationalism, such as religious, humanist and even welfare-oriented forms of inclusion (Räthzel 1995; 264), which also continue through to contemporary periods.

In contrast to inclusive republican ideals, ethnic nationalism was a fertile environment for the growth of exclusionary politics in preserving unity against external threats and internal regional, religious and social forces. One consequence was the suppression of diversity for the 'higher good' of ethnocultural homogenisation and national advancement. Ascriptive and particularistic definitions were used to construct a homogeneous national identity. In other words, the ethnic nation-state created and enforced its own instruments and symbols of belonging. In a 'community of descent', the territorial boundaries are not at first as significant as the 'bloodline' of descent. Formal political citizenship is embodied in the principles of *jus soli* or *jus sanguinis*: the first, defines the citizenry as: 'a territorial community, jus sanguinis as a community of descent' (Brubaker 1992,123). In other words, the *jus soli* principle holds that a person, having lived in a particular place for a reasonable time, should be granted citizenship (as happens in Australia and the United States), whilst *jus sanguinis* holds that citizenship shall be granted when the person can prove a family link of descent by birth to a particular nation, thereby excluding immigrants of other ethnicities from formal membership.

The Basic Law (*Grundgesetz*), or 'temporary' constitution of the Federal Republic of Germany at its foundation in 1949 retained the ethnic concept of citizenship, based on the Reich Citizenship Law of 1913. The concept of 'ethnic' nation continued in Germany after 1945, with belonging continuing on a genealogical basis – of 'blood' ties. Although tempered by procedural democracy, post-war Germany remained committed to exclusive citizenship. Despite the fact that post-war West Germany was able to develop a stable political culture with liberal foundations enshrined in a constitution, 'ghosts of the past' remained.

The economic miracle (*Wirtschaftswunder)*, emerging constitutional patriotism (after Habermas), and the new cosmopolitan outlook of Germany were hiding the continuing existence of *völkisch* definitions of nationhood embodied by restrictive citizenship and naturalisation regulations alongside liberal republican and universalistic principles, represented most notably by the post-war constitution and its stipulation of an individual right of asylum (Kurthen 1997; 72).

The prevailing model of nation and belonging in a society are significant inasmuch as they delineate native from alien and become part of the public discourse, shaping opinion. Moreover, the formal aspects of belonging - citizenship and the extension of civil and political rights for long-term residents such as guest workers – have 'knock-on', or accumulative effects on other groups of 'strangers', or 'aliens'. If guest workers are largely excluded from gaining formal citizenship and the rights that accompany it, it follows that the number of foreigners officially deemed as living in Germany remains large. Those individuals living in Germany who are claiming protection from political persecution add to the perception of an increasing burden of 'foreigners living among us'. Later in this chapter I will discuss the changes to the German Constitution which occurred in 1992/93 on the question of asylum seekers specifically.

## Emigrations and immigrations from the 19th century: a brief overview

In the aftermath of World War II, Germany has witnessed three major waves of newcomers: ethnic Germans (*Aussiedler*), guest workers (*Gastarbeiter*) and refugees and asylum seekers (*Flüchtlinge* and *Asylanten*). Since unification, following the fall of the Berlin Wall in late 1989, East Germans have been considered by some analysts of German integration to be a new and special group of pseudo foreigners. It is predominantly socio-cultural and political factors which make sense of this categorisation of some Germans as newcomers. Such analysis would point to the different orientations toward free speech, individual rights, a free press and other indicators of democracy which distinguish East Germans from West.

In any town or city of Germany the evidence of large-scale immigration is evident in visible ethnic and cultural diversity. Yet Germany has for decades maintained the official line of being a non-immigration country.[2] This somewhat

[2] From late 1998, moves toward the reform of rules governing citizenship and the official approach to immigration began to take place.

schizophrenic approach has had long-term institutional as well as psychological consequences in German politics and society (Peck et al. 1997, Bade 1994a, Joppke 1999, Castles and Miller 1993). In short, this characterisation of 'non-immigration country' came to define the way immigration issues were approached in the German political system. There is for instance, still no federal bureaucracy which can address in a uniform fashion issues of immigration and integration. Germany has not equivalent of the Australian Department of Immigration, Multicultural and Indigenous Affairs (DIMIA) – no single responsible minister. Instead, the responsibilities of such a portfolio are shared between the Foreign Minister, the Minister for the Interior and a Federal Commissioner for Foreigners' Affairs (*Ausländerbeauftragte[r]*). The processing of asylum seekers' claims is undertaken federally, while the day-to-day responsibility and cost of the housing and welfare needs of asylum seekers is the responsibility of the States (*Länder*) within which the asylum seeker resides. All German *Länder*, including the 'new' eastern *Länder,* are allocated a 'quota' of asylum seekers.

After the cessation of the guest worker programme in 1973, which had brought a much-needed labour force to Germany from 1955 on, the asylum route become the primary mode of entry to the Federal Republic for prospective immigrants as well as asylum seekers. In the following years the category of bogus asylum seekers (*Scheinasylanten*) came to prominence, resulting in the first large-scale debate within Germany over asylum in 1980.[3] From this period on a cycle of legislative changes, speedier processing, and various challenges to the legitimacy of asylum claims oscillated in German politics, with the asylum issue rising to an all-time high in public awareness by 1992.[4] These changes will be discussed later in this chapter.

One of the most immediate consequences of the fall of the Berlin Wall was the movement of large numbers of people across Europe – primarily from East to West. For thousands of people from former Communist countries, the movement across borders into Western European countries with market economies and democratic political systems represented an environment safe from arbitrary violence and persecution, as well as potential economic opportunities. Germany became the destination of a large proportion of such East to West migration, mainly due to its geographic location in the centre of Europe, as well as historical and

---

[3] In the early 1980s Turkish newspapers reprinted the German form required to make an asylum application and the beginning of people-smuggling rackets began with so-called 'package tours' which included one-way air fares and instructions on the legal aspects of making asylum applications upon arrival in Germany (Teitelbaum in Joppke 1997; 277).

[4] From 1991 acts of right-wing violence toward foreigners escalated as a response to the increased numbers of new arrivals. In 1992, 2,285 acts of violence against foreigners and their homes occurred throughout Germany (Plaut 1995; 111).

cultural connections which many of these migrants had with Germany. From the early 1990s Germany experienced a large influx of people seeking refuge from Eastern Europe as well other refugee influxes from North Africa, the Middle East, Turkey and Yugoslavia in particular. In 1990 the number of people claiming asylum in Germany was just over 193,000, in 1991 256,000 and in 1993 over 438,000. At the same time recognition rates of asylum applications declined from a peak of 29 percent in 1985 to about 3 per cent in 1992 (OECD 1995).

We must bear in mind that Germany has by far the largest foreign population in Western Europe - at some 9 per cent of a population of 82 million: this equates to over 7.3 million non-Germans living in Germany. Unlike the 'classic countries of immigration' such as Australia, Canada or the United States, which developed through large-scale, yet controlled waves of quota immigration, Germany and many other European countries have not considered themselves as countries of immigration, with the consequence that there is a reluctance and indeed at times violent resistance to dealing with the social consequences of the influx of migrants. Public opinion polls indicate that over 60 per cent of Germans want immigration stopped or reduced, and confirm a wide-held belief that at least some of the foreigners living in Germany will return to their country of origin (Martin 1994; 188). Some of this sentiment is reflected in the small but significant growth of support for far-right political parties in Germany, particularly since unification in 1990.

However, the large-scale migration movements are not a new phenomenon in Germany. The history of immigration and emigration remains an informative undercurrent to present-day policies as well as public attitudes to newcomers, including the arrival of refugees and asylum seekers. Refugees and asylum seekers enter a 'general terrain' of 'aliens', of non-nationals, and therefore by inference must negotiate the same or similar tensions and exclusions experienced by other newcomers. When we look at history it becomes clear that Germany has experienced a myriad of cross-border migrations:

> . . . emigration, immigration, and transit movements; the labour migration of Germans across German borders and the influx of foreign labour into Germany; flight and forced migration of Germans into foreign countries, of foreigners into Germany, and of Germans as victims and offenders within and outside German national borders. In addition to the movement of people across borders, German history has also seen the movement of borders across people (Bade 1997; 2).

Through the collective memory of successive generations, Germans are familiar with both the experience of settling in new countries, as well as with others settling in German territory. From 1816 to 1914, for instance, it is estimated that some 5.5

million Germans emigrated to the United States and since 1914 that number was supplemented by another 1.5 million (Bade 1997; 5). Moreover, it is significant in light of contemporary perceptions of an 'asylum problem' in Germany, to consider that the motivation for this transatlantic mass emigration throughout the nineteenth century was social and economic – instigated most significantly by a lack of work opportunities, related to the transition from an agrarian to an industrial society. In today's understanding of forced migration, these early German emigrants were 'economic refugees' (*Wirtschaftsflüchtlinge*).

The Second Reich under the leadership of Otto von Bismarck saw some of the most dramatic and lasting changes to the German political and social systems. The period from the 1860s witnessed a late, yet rapid industrialisation, compared to other European nations. Concurrently during this Wilhemine period Germany underwent great social change. The population increased from 41 million in 1871 to 67.7 million in 1914 (Fulbrook 1990; 138). Towns and cities grew with a young population moving from the rural areas to industrial centres, in patterns not unlike that experienced in other European countries.

Complex factors lie behind emigration and immigration movements from and to Germany. Moreover, minorities have long been outsiders in Germany; economically, socially and legally – their exclusion being fostered by racism:

> . . . from the Kaiserreich to the Federal Republic, racism has existed throughout German history, usually led by the state. The migration situation in Germany in the course of a century reversed from mass emigration to significant immigration. In the nineteenth century some 5 million Germans emigrated with 90% going to the United States. By the start of the 1980s the foreign population in Germany, having migrated over three generations, was almost as large (Panyani 1996; 192).

During the National Socialist regime from 1933-1945, large numbers of people sought to flee Germany as a result of the anti-Semitic race laws and the discrimination against minority groups. In the aftermath of World War II, Germany struggled to integrate refugees from territories in Poland, Czechoslovakia and areas which had been annexed to Germany under Nazism. Between 1945 and 1950 some 12 million such refugees entered Germany (Peck et. al. 1997).[5]

I turn now to a chronology of developments in immigration policy and 'types' of immigration which is applicable across Western Europe. Post-war immigration

---

[5] There had, however, been earlier precedents of flight from Germany in the nineteenth century for political reasons. For instance, revolutionaries from the 1848/9 uprisings fled to the USA and to Australia, as did socialists at the time of Bismarck's anti-socialists law of 1878-90.

policy has broad similarities across Western European states. Policies which aimed to regulate and control immigration evolved in response to particular pressures, which though experienced differently by the countries of Western Europe, can be usefully broken down into five periods from the post World War II period until the fall of the Berlin Wall:

1. (1948-1964) – Post-war reconstruction and economic development with a free exchange of labour between countries.
2. (1965-1972) – The height of the guest worker period with about 1.1 million Southern Europeans moved to Western Europe under these agreements.
3. (1973-1982) – The beginning of entry restrictions with annual immigration decreasing.
4. (1983-1988) – The beginning of mass asylum movements with total annual inflows to 1.2 million.
5. (1989-) – The ongoing search for new international solutions of 'harmonisation' with regard to 'irregular' arrivals.

## 'Foreigners', 'strangers' and 'aliens': on classifications and their social consequences

Since 1945 one of the most significant movements of people to Germany has been the influx of 'ethnic Germans' (*Aussiedler*), who arrived in two significant 'waves'. This group of newcomers constituted expelees from the former German territories and refugees who fled Germany during and in the aftermath of World War II. *Aussiedler* who are able to prove their association with Germany have been returning to Germany sporadically throughout the post-war period until the East was sealed in 1961 with the erection of the Berlin Wall. In the late twentieth century Germany become a *de-facto* country of immigration, with a greater influx of newcomers both in real terms and in relation to the size of the German population, than the majority of classic immigration countries, with the exception of the United States.

### *(a) Expelees and Ethnic Germans*

Before World War II it is estimated over 17.5 million Germans lived in Eastern, Mid-Eastern and South-Eastern parts of Europe. For instance, east of the Oder and the Neisse Rivers about 9 million Germans lived in Silesia, in East-Brandenburg, in

Pomerania and East-Prussia. The remaining 8.5 million Germans lived in Czechoslovakia, in other parts of Poland, Romania Hungary, Yugoslavia and in the Soviet Union (Bade 1994c; 4-5). Following the end of World War II, the majority of Germans living in territories which were lost as a consequence of the war were expelled. Those who remained largely assimilated linguistically and culturally to the host society, and constitute parts of the groups which have recently returned to Germany.

The most recent influx of *Aussiedler* has occurred since the late 1980s. Bade contends that in a both socio-cultural and psychological sense the integration of these ethnic Germans has taken on all the usual dimensions of the integration process of foreigners, despite the fact that *Aussiedler* receive full civil rights upon arrival (Bade 1994b; 3). This new groups of *Aussiedler*, as opposed to earlier groups, often speak little or no German, as the use of the German language was regularly suppressed in Eastern Europe under assimilation pressures in the post-war period. The latest wave of ethnic Germans were predominantly born and raised as members of other societies with little or no memory of a German past. It is significant in considering the reception of 'foreigners' or 'strangers' in Germany, that this group are not part of the official count of 'foreigners' living in Germany, though they are part of the social reality and mental picture of foreigners formulated in everyday interactions with neighbours and fellow workers, adding to the societal anxiety with the unfortunate name of 'over-foreignisation' (*Überfremdung*).

Germans are aware of what it is to be a refugee, often as personal memory, but certainly as 'collective memory'. As a result of World War II millions of Germans became refugees or displaced persons. It has been estimated that between 1945 and 1950 some 11-13 million Germans were affected by forced migration (Rystad 1990; 290). By the time of German reunification in 1990, the figure of newcomers represented more than 25% of the total population of the Federal Republic. When non-German newcomers are added to this figure the total number of newcomers settling in West Germany since 1945 is almost one third the total population of the Federal Republic as at 1990.[6]

Ethnic Germans, or *Aussiedler,* must be able to trace German descent through their family heritage, and thereby have a claim under German law for entry and the acquisition of citizenship. As I have stated, this group is not officially considered foreigners or even immigrants. They are re-settlers, according to the Federal

---

[6] With the recent arrival of *Aussiedler*, a piece of forgotten and perhaps repressed German history returns to the present. And with it come forgotten people with traditional norms of orientation and moral concepts long ago given up in a modern Germany. Ethnic Germans seem to come straight out of history, as a reminder of aspects of German history which are at times repressed (Bade 1994a; 8).

Constitution (Article 116 paragraph 1): German citizens in the territory of the German Reich as it was in 1937 are the basis for this Article of the Constitution.[7]

The relatively favorable acceptance of *Aussiedler* is summed up by Klaus Pritzkuleit of the Ecclesiastical Office of the Protestant Church in Berlin in relation to attitudes toward other 'strangers' or newcomers. *Aussiedler*, he contends are:

> . . . our quasi immigrants. First they automatically get citizenship, plus the infrastructure is developed to make social integration possible in the form of education and gaining work. Secondly the psychological impression in the broader community is fostered by the federal government, who present a positive picture. they keep the discussion of ethnic Germans out of the media for instance – thus naturalising the process. But the will is not there to do that for refugees. Germany however, is a country that is historically responsible, economically able and logistically capable, to create and keep a situation where refugees who are really in need, persecuted, can be given protection (Interview No. 12).

Pritzkuleit's comments reflect an non-government sector which works across the spectrum of 'aliens' living in Germany. Chapter five analyses the impact of NGOs in detail.

*(b) Guest workers*

Following World War II, additional labour was required for the task of rebuilding cities and towns, as well as industrial compounds destroyed during the war. The enormous economic expansion Germany underwent from the 1950s and through the 1960s further reinforced the need for foreign labour. This led to formal recruitment programmes with a sequence of Mediterranean countries. It was generally assumed that these guest workers would eventually return to their country of origin, and indeed many also did.

The first official labour recruitment agreement was signed with the Italian government in 1955. Subsequent recruitment agreements were signed with Spain and Greece in 1960, Turkey in 1961, and Portugal in 1964. Later agreements were signed with Tunisia, Morocco in 1965 and Yugoslavia in 1968. At the end of 1973, with an economic downturn apparent, the German government called a halt to labour recruitment without prior consultation with the sending countries.

[7] The *Aussiedler* are the largest state-assisted quota immigrant group in the world. Assistance for resettlement is also given to Jews from these countries without quota restrictions (Thränhardt 1996b; 19).

Nonetheless, the continued migration to Germany of the families of guest workers meant that guest worker-related migration flows continued to be a major source of migration movement to Germany. Though the term '*guest worker'* has been used primarily in relation to the migrant labour contracted to West Germany, the German Democratic Republic (GDR) also had a migrant labour programme, where labour shortages were filled by workers recruited from other communist countries - notably Vietnam. After unification, return programmes of some of these workers began. The term *guest worker* refers to the objective which underscored the government policy of recruiting these workers - namely that as 'guests' they would return to their country of origin after a period of labour. However, significant numbers settled in Germany permanently and are now in the third and even fourth generation. The German government has had to face the claims for proper integration and citizenship rights for these long-term residents. A book published in 1988 by a German journalist, Günter Wallraff, proved a powerful thorn to common public perceptions that *guest workers* had a good life in Germany, reaping the benefits of an overly generous country. Wallraff spent two years disguised as a Turkish guest worker, taking any job offered him. His book details the response of small and large business enterprises; of farmers, as well as everyday encounters with Germans in pubs, shops and at festivals, revealing discrimination, racism and everyday incidents confirming the second-class status of non-Germans. A similar situation to the one which Wallraff encountered is summed up by Dr Sepp Graessner, Director of the Berlin Centre for treating victims of torture:

> . . . we needed people to do work, the dirty work, as we were dying out - not reproducing ourselves. Only the migrants could guarantee our pensions for instance. Migrants were only ever seen in response to German wealth - contributing in some way to things we could not or did not want to do ourselves, but there was never an emotional connection with these people. After unification though we no longer need the Turks, we have the East Germans, as a reserve work force, we no longer need foreigners, they have no more function for us – this is the climate that facilitated violence against foreigners. Such violence has been exploited by the government to say, 'well look we just have too many (foreigners)' (Interview No. 6).

Apart from the people who come to Germany within the official labour recruitment programmes, there are various seasonal and unregistered workers in Germany. Most of these workers are evident in the construction, hotel, restaurant and entertainment industries, as well as domestic employment (Thränhardt 1996a; 241). They are part of an economy of 'illegals', which also includes a growing number of rejected asylum seekers, who are tolerated by the state and utilised by business as a cheap labour force. Germany's Ministry of Labour has instituted various methods for cutting down on black-market labour through such methods as a social welfare card required by employers and databases, which are increasingly utilised across the countries of the European Union.

In 1982, the Christian Democrat government of Helmut Kohl declared migration policy as one of its priorities along with economic and foreign policy. In 1983 a Commission was appointed to investigate solutions to problems associated with foreigners living in the Federal Republic. The Commission comprising national, regional and local representatives agreed on a number of basic elements of future migration policy:

1. The integration of foreigners living in Germany
2. A limit on the entry of other foreigners
3. The promotion of the repatriation of foreigners

The first decision taken by the new federal government of Helmut Kohl with regard to migration policy was to offer foreigners a financial incentive to repatriate.[8]

Let us now consider the most controversial influx of newcomers to Germany; those seeking protection.

### *(c) Refugees and Asylum Seekers*

In the period from 1951 to the mid-1970s, West Germany experienced a steady influx of refugees and asylum seekers predominantly from Eastern Europe. Until 1976 the number of asylum applications did not however, exceed 10,000 in any one year. After this period arrival rates increased and asylum seekers from countries in the developing world began to outnumber those from European countries. The general trend through the 1980s saw an increase in numbers of asylum seekers from about 108,000 applicants in 1980, to 193,063 in 1990. The year 1992 saw a record number of asylum applications at 438,191, a 70% increase from the previous year (UNHCR, Country reports).

Particularly since the mid-1980s refugees and asylum seekers have been the central preoccupation in the politics of immigration. From the early 1990s the entry of asylum seekers to Germany replaced other categories of immigrants to Germany as the most urgent 'problem' facing social cohesion within Germany and the limits of tolerance. This development was at least partly connected to the political

---

[8] This repatriation assistance amounted to 10,500 marks, plus 1,500 marks for each child (Körner in Räthzel 1995; 191).

transformations in Eastern Europe as well as rising refugee numbers in other parts of the world. To be sure, the increase in those seeking protection and the quite dramatic rise in overt actions of xenophobia and far-right violence against all foreigners in the early 1990s appear to be closely associated. I explore the issue of violence against foreigners in detail in chapter five, beginning with the assertion that a simplistic cause and effect analysis of the triggers of violence and intolerance fails to address the more substantial problems Germany must face with regard to the long-term integration of immigrants who are resident in Germany for a variety of reasons. Meier-Braun, for instance, claims that in political debates and media typification the word asylum seeker could merely be substituted for Turk in similar debates a few years earlier (Meier-Braun 1995; 19). Sensationalist rhetoric typified by such labels as 'the boat is full', have been utilised repeatedly in relation to the arrival of those seeking protection, but also more broadly to throw a blanket over foreigners, ignoring the complex reasons for the presence of foreigners and aliens, as well as the differential moral and legal obligations due to different categories of immigrants. Later in this chapter I analyse the development of asylum policy through the 1990s, as well as the social status of those seeking protection in Germany and the entitlements they can draw on during the determination period.

Though those involved in policy formation, as well as the non-government organisations that advocate for the rights of immigrants, guest workers and more recently, refugees and asylum seekers, stress the need to differentiate between various categories of migrants, there can be no doubt that the conditions of one group affect the others: the category of 'alien' or 'stranger' applies to them equally. The reception and integration of guest workers, or of ethnic Germans, for example, does have a bearing on the possibilities of asylum seekers. If there is a negative perception and representation of guest workers and of ethnic Germans as being an economic drain or a social threat, it follows that the social and economic 'space' left to negotiate for asylum seekers is decreased. Though in strict legal terms the different categories of migrants do not overlap – and they do have varied needs and capabilities – in the consciousness of a citizen who encounters them in the street, the general category of 'stranger' still applies.

Despite the internationally accepted definition of refugee, attitudes to asylum seekers are primarily formed within a nation. It is also primarily an individual nation which can assure what is a three-step process of protection of those claiming asylum;

1. Grant an individual the right to have his/her claim for asylum heard; first by ensuring 'reasonable' access to a determination process and subsequently through access to judicial review.
2. Support them financially, legally and socially during this process.

3. Grant protection where an individual meets the definition of a refugee.

As I have already argued earlier, the integration measures afforded other categories of immigrants have an often substantial bearing on the reception of asylum seekers in receiver societies. Integration measures encompass both formal legal entitlements to citizenship and less tangible entitlements to respect and tolerance which also require some institutional support to become embedded as societal values.

## Citizenship: an exclusive entitlement

Naturalisation for non-Germans has historically been a long and painstaking process in Germany. The Aliens Act of 1990 gives first-generation immigrants the right to German citizenship once they have lived in the country for 15 years, can support themselves, have no criminal record, and are willing to give up their previous citizenship (Bryant 1997; 161). Those with permanent resident status may vote in local elections but not in federal elections. Joppke categorises Germany's citizenship regime as assimilationist, at least until some minor changes were made after unification (1999; 202). Germany has one of the lowest naturalisation rates of European countries (Thränhardt 1992; 176). The number of persons living in Germany who are counted as foreigners is much higher than would be the case in Australia, for instance, precisely because of the length and difficulty of the process of gaining citizenship. An easier path to citizenship became a prominent topic of political discussion in Germany from the early 1980s (Lohmann 1994). The ethos and rhetoric of nation-building has to account for newcomers in some way, even in countries which do not consider themselves immigration countries (Kurthen 1995).

As one of the first major reform measures of the Schroeder government, a new citizenship and nationality law passed both houses of the German parliament in May 1999. The new regulations mean that immigrants can gain citizenship after eight years of residence in the Federal Republic, and children born in Germany to non-German parents can gain citizenship automatically (*Bundesregierung* Press Release, 16th May, 2000). Following the introduction of the new citizenship laws the naturalisation rate rose 30 per cent in 2000 compared to the previous year (Bundesregierung Press Release, 5th July, 2001).

It is important in developing an understanding of the contemporary asylum situation in Germany, to reiterate that the symbolic inter-relationship between the different categories of foreigners and the level of institutionalisation of rights granted to those foreigners has a bearing not only on the reception asylum seekers face, but also on the national 'self-image' of Germans in relation to 'outsiders'.

There is a huge relationship between the general fear of strangers, foreigners . . . and this discussion of immigration to Germany (of asylum seekers) . . . it is anything but new in Germany. I say that there is not just a relationship, but a causal and intentional link between the political use of '*kein einwanderungsland*' (not a country of immigration), and the thoughts of the general population against foreigners, or more specifically between unemployment and foreigners (Interview No. 18).

The question of German citizenship (formal admission) and integration (informal admission) in relation to foreigners emerged as a central theme in the interviews conducted for this research in Germany during 1996-97. The first aspect, formal citizenship, has been a topic of political debate in Germany for some years, with the SPD and Greens, as well as the minor coalition partner, the FDP, advocating a speedier process of *Einbürgerung*, in the form of social integration measures, as well as granting citizenship to permanent residents in a shorter period. Social integration measures, unlike formal citizenship, are measures which under Germany's strong federal system have marked regional variations. In some areas, permanent residents without citizenship are permitted to vote in local elections, so the informal integration measures in local communities and neighbourhoods regularly precede any formal integration measures by local authorities or government. Often such social integration relies at least to some extent on the voluntary activity of citizens. Valuable as such voluntary activity often is, it must be borne in mind that it is also ambiguous in outcome: at least in longevity and sustainability. The aquisition of formal citizenship does not necessarily coincide with 'social membership' of the group of 'insiders' as is the case with the aquisition of Australian citizenship where ethnic and cultural difference is by no means as deep a barrier to acceptance as an 'authentic' citizen, as seems to be the case in Germany. A selection of interview extracts follow which illustrate a diversity of views on foreigner integration.

In an interview I conducted, with Hanns Thomä-Venske, the spokesperson on foreigner issues of the Protestant church, Berlin/Brandenburg, he stated:

> What we are experiencing is an isolation of ethnic groups, not much exchange. That does not in itself have to be such a problem. But what I fear is the German nationalist line which has an influence when conflicts escalate. And it is important whether you are a foreigner or not. It has been drummed into Germans for years that you are the real Germans, and all the others are only guests who will have to go back eventually. Society is not prepared to work through this peacefully if there were to be conflicts. They (the people) do not understand such concepts, and the government does not have an integration politics, such as, that when foreigners become citizens, they are actively fostered to work and become part of the community; not just 'foreigner work'. It would be important for federal politicians to stand for such things. To prepare the society for

> harder times, so we can peacefully deal with conflict. I don't see that happening in the present climate (Interview No. 5).

The Federal Commissioner for Foreigners Affairs, Cornelia Schmalz-Jacobsen, comments on the easing of citizenship restrictions as being significant to the prospects of foreigners living in Germany:

> I have worked on this for the last three years, and we are at present negotiating about this within the coalition. One must see clearly that we must also learn as Germans to be happy when someone wants to belong to us, and not just grudgingly give it to them. I find it a positive development and decision. I would rather live in a country that is one which protects human rights and those who have suffered persecution, rather than one from whom one runs away (Interview No. 16).

On the question of integration, the UNHCR spokesperson in Germany, Judith Kumin, stated that integration was:

> . . . [it is] a very difficult question because the level of foreign population varies so much regionally in Germany and therefore reactions are very hard to quantify. But there is something you can't really put your finger on in Germany: a pervasive belief that it is not a good thing to have different people in your society works to the detriment of people who need protection. An uncomfortable feeling that there is something not right when there are too many people who are different. An exception has been the surprising sympathy for some refugee groups, for example Bosnians, despite attempts by politicians to drum up negative sentiment. But the German population was bombarded by information about Bosnia and the conflict and victims. A real, direct connection with the victims was made; perhaps if that happened for others, the reaction would be different. . . But also the Bosnians are Europeans - they look and act like everybody else, you can't tell them apart on the street. That was an enormous factor. Race is a big factor in Germany, you can't avoid it (Interview No. 19).

The majority of interviewees identified the lack of clarity and leadership at the federal political level regarding the symbolic communication on the integration of foreigners as a highly significant ingredient in the negative outcomes such as acts of violence against foreigners, and the ghettoisation of various ethnic groups. Interviewees were largely united in the view that the political pursuit of Germany as 'not a country of immigration' was resulting in a negative social impact, exemplified in hostility toward foreigners. That is, as political leaders continued to communicate about migrants in a way which was antithetical to the lived reality of the majority of Germans, xenophobia and violence against foreigners rose. The reality that 8.5% of the population are foreigners must be digested in some way; this figure is a national average, with some urban centres such as Frankfurt having a population of 25% non-Germans. The rhetoric of political leaders has regularly been out of step with the lived reality in local neighbourhoods.[9] No doubt social attitudes are shaped 'from below', as well as 'from above', with negative sentiment toward foreigners being mutually reinforced. In such a situation a 'third force' – such as NGOs – may be able to break such mutual reinforcement from below and from above.

At the same time, though, some differentiation in interview responses is apparent, depending on whether the focus the interviewee's work is at the federal level, engaging with normative, ethical arguments, or work which is located primarily at local levels; focusing on service delivery, and in more direct contact with people outside the decision making arenas. The 'foreigner worker' of the Berlin Missionwerk, Edit Czimer, is engaged in grass-roots community work, as part of the Protestant church in Berlin. This work means not only an engagement with church members, but a strong focus on outreach to the groups that perceive themselves as affected directly by the presence of foreigners in their neighbourhoods; she says:

> Germans still have a bad conscience regarding their past. They will, for instance, not say anything about foreigners even if they have strong feelings because they do not want to be seen as racist. This attitude makes foreigner work difficult. They (Germans) have good intentions, but are not free of their history - have anxiety and shame about their past. And they want to see things put right. So when it comes to foreigner politics, there is a sense of political correctness. For instance, in a neighbourhood situation they will not say anything about the little things that disturb them . . . like loud music . . . and this is a problem, because you cannot move forward (Interview No. 2).

In some ways, both the advocacy work and service-delivery or outreach activities force the tensions about immigrant integration into the open, to be debated and deliberated over. The fact that NGOs, social movements, as well as neighbourhood groups are involved in such negotiations and deliberations is a positive signal to the broader host population that measures for inclusion and integration of newcomers can be negotiated and deliberated over at many levels, rather than being imposed from above.

Many analysts have documented and analysed the way in which the official lack of clarity and leadership on Germany's status in relation to immigrants through the

---

[9] Though foreigner integration has been addressed by various of the German *Länder* and by local authorities, the approach and the allocation of resource varies greatly between the *Länder* as well as between the local authorities of *Länder*.

1980s until the late 90s has resulted in a preparedness to scapegoat immigration as the direct cause of many economic and social problems in 'unified Germany (Thränhardt 1992;179, Bade 1994, Kurthen 1997). As I have already indicated, the official doctrine of 'not a country of immigration'; a denial of reality, reflects a deep social anxiety not just about the impact newcomers will have on German society, but also a national self-doubt about the ability to cope with change.[10]

Notwithstanding this, numerous studies have shown immigration has been a net economic benefit to Germany (Hof 1992, Aktion Gemeinsinn 1992, Spencer 1994, Mehrländer 1974, 1984). Demographic studies point to an ageing population in Germany, which is well below replacement level. Without immigration, the current birth rates would result in the German population decreasing by 20 million by the year 2030 (Mehrländer 1994; 12).

## Unification: one nation, many identities

The initial euphoria after the fall of the Berlin Wall, which had divided East and West Germany physically and spiritually since 1961, has been largely replaced by anxiety about the future and insecurity in relation to national identity. The West is distrustful of the East, and the East grows in resentment.[11] At first glance this anxiety seems to be rooted in uncertainty about the economy. It is of course an enormous task to integrate two social and economic systems which were diametrically opposed in core values. The most immediate task has centred around addressing the problem of high unemployment in the Eastern states of Germany resulting from reforms to the economy. However, though the concrete problems of work, of training and retraining for jobs in a post-industrial, technologically driven marketplace are the tangible outcomes which politicians and the public look to, the abstract issues of meaning and identity are no less significant, nor are the battle lines less deeply drawn.

---

[10] On an everyday level, the official response has also resulted in what many German commentators call a 'schizophrenia' of Germans, which continued through to the late 1990s. That is, citizens are aware they are sharing their country with many foreigners, who have come with varied claims for making a home, yet representatives of the government hold to the official untruth. Such rhetoric implies that perhaps somehow the immigrants would dematerialise and Germany would be left to 'Germans'.

[11] Wagner (1996) describes the process of unification from a cultural perspective - the shock being of the ex-DDR citizens attempting an integration into a 'new West', including the social construction of the Easten German 'other' as 'Ossis'.

Unification after the 1989 *people's revolution* led to renewed focus on the period which led to the division of Germany – the aftermath of World War II. The legacy of National Socialism and the particular consequences of Hitler's totalitarian regime have continued to gouge a track across the collective memory of Germans. Habermas, for instance, explains German unification in 1990 as causing social tensions through an overemphasis on German identity, perhaps a kind of glorification of a lost past, which reflects in a negative way on the status of asylum seekers in the public eye (Pensky 1995; 87). After unification East German states were allocated a proportional 'quota' of asylum seekers.[12] A renewed focus on asylum seekers in turn has led to a spiral of right-wing attacks and violence against various groups of newcomers, as well as the electoral successes of right-wing political parties throughout the 1990s. Ireland assesses the policies associated with unification as an unmitigated disaster, with the East German states unprepared for the new social problems that were to befall them (1997; 555). In addition to a quota of asylum seekers, East German states received one fifth of the intake of *Aussiedler*.

In an exchange of letters between the West German academic Jürgen Habermas and the East German writer Christa Wolf, some of the tensions and schisms between East and West Germans after the unification of Germany in 1990 are crystallised. From 1945 East and West Germany took very different paths. The events of 1989, however, have meant that it is primarily the East Germans who have had to walk away from their past understandings of society and culture and unite *to* the West, rather than *with* the West. Habermas and Wolf are at odds about the continuity of any single Germany identity prior to the Nationalist Socialist era; the demise of which saw the division of Germany into East and West. Habermas typifies the Western orientation of the Federal Republic of Germany in the post-1945 era as liberating;

> This westward orientation did not imply a warping of the German psyche but rather the practice of independence. Our unreserved assimilation of the whole range of liberal traditions did not merely include . . . American pragmatism . . . rational law of the seventeenth and eighteenth century down to Rawls and Dworkin, analytical philosophy, French positivism, and French and American social science . . . but it also extended to elements of the German tradition which up to then had been suppressed or marginalized; to Kant as an exponent of the Enlightenment and not as its so-called conqueror, to Hegel as a radical interpreter of the French Revolution and not its opponent, to Marx and

[12] The Germany asylum process is outlined later in this chapter, but in brief, an asylum seeker must reside in the state to which he/she is allocated, often in hostel-style accommodation, and regularly check in with the local authorities in which he/she resides. This means that in principle, freedom of movement is not restricted, though in practical terms, travel tends to be restricted to the close vicinity of residence.

Western Marxism, to Freud and the Freudian left, to the Vienna Circle, Wittgenstein, and so on. The German émigrés returning from the West were more important to us in this process than the wasted remnants of our own tradition that had survived National Socialism (Habermas in Wolf 1997; 116).

What Habermas is referring to in particular is the critical theory approach, fostered through the Frankfurt School under the leadership of such intellectuals as Horkheimer and Adorno. Habermas continues in the same letter to address Christa Wolf and East German intellectuals directly: 'the current upheaval of your lives creates special kinds of vulnerability. This makes it more complicated to understand each other, and demands more than the usual amount of sensitivity in the way we deal with each other . . . agreeing prematurely that symmetries exist between us (East and West Germans), would be a false courtesy that can only lead to new illusions . . . If we try to turn Germany into a one-pot stew, the result could be something that neither of us wants: the history of the GDR may get swept under the rug as West Germany writes its own victor's history' (Habermas in Wolf 1997; 118). Such sentiments were even more strongly expressed by Christa Wolf, who in reply to Habermas comments that those in the East knew more about the people in the West and their lives than the reverse: '. . . simply because we were more interested' (ibid.; 122).

Though the themes of a distinct German citizenship, nationalism and identity which I have so far explored are not the central concern of this book, they do form the context within which NGOs and social movements must operate. These factors moreover also impact on the possibilities of German NGOs and movements. The key activists and advocates, as Germans, are part of this national culture and identity even if they disagree with various aspects of it. That is, if it can be argued that there is a specifically 'German' way of operating and of 'being', then in the sense that Bourdieu uses *habitus* to denote an environment in which you negotiate day-to-day events and practices, asylum seekers and other groups of foreigners will be deeply and fundamentally affected by that German culture and identity. Moreover, NGO workers, activists and members of social movements will have an imprint of German culture and identity on their conduct, values and decision-making; even if it is expresses as a resistance to any dominant cultural norms.[13]

Let me return now to the question of the contemporary response to asylum seekers in Germany. To reiterate, as I have argued through an investigation of the different categories of immigrants, as well as the role of citizenship and the rights

---

[13] The majority of interviewees were only too aware of the specifics of operating within German culture and a 'German way of doing things', and often related anecdotes exemplifying the exclusivity of local cultural practices in dealing with foreigners.

that accompany it, I go some way to contextualise developments in asylum policy. The social unrest which the arrival of asylum seekers appears to have triggered in the early 1990s cannot be seen in isolation from the social pressures which other categories of newcomers exerted on the Federal Republic by their presence. Indeed the years 1989-1992 were a crucible, testing the priorities and resolve of the German state and of the people. Given the influx of some three million newcomers during this period made up of asylum seekers, *Aussiedler* and *Uebersiedler,* the logistic problems were enormous (Joppke 1997; 279). The representative of the UNHCR in Germany during the mid-1990s, Judith Kumin, acknowledges the 'burden' that Germany has been under in the 1980s and early 1990s, taking from around 62% (1984-93) of all asylum applicants in the EU, with a peak of 78.7% in 1992 (Kumin 1995; 28).

In the early 1990s, public debate became polarised between those who supported the intake of *Aussiedler*, as a 'coming home of Germans', over the right of asylum premised on Article 116 of the Basic Law which granted automatic citizenship to *Aussiedler*, and a contrary position, articulated by the SPD and the Greens favoring the introduction of an immigration quota which would also apply to *Aussiedler,* meaning an effective repeal of Article 116 (ibid.; 279). In short, the political debate held little common ground between these two positions, while the public lived with the daily consequences of this substantial influx of immigrants, with inadequate institutional support for dealing with new pressures. Rhetoric from both sides of the debate dominated the proffering of any practical solutions.

## Changing the Constitution in a quest to reduce asylum flows

During the 1980s a raft of federal legislative changes were implemented to shorten the legal procedures of assessing protection claims, and perhaps more significantly at the time, curtailing the social support which those claiming asylum could draw on. Thus, already in the early 1980s, a lack of social support and entitlements for asylum seekers amounted to a form of *deterrence*. In 1981 a new Asylum Procedure (*Asylverfahrensgesetz*) took the place of the regulations of the 1965 Aliens Act. The new procedures restricted avenues for appeal, activated expulsion provisions and reduced welfare allowances (Bosswick 2000; 46). After the recruitment stop of the foreign workforce in 1973, asylum became the only route of migration entry to Germany. While certainly some people entering Germany did have substantive protection claims, the public discourse shifted in the mid 1980s to a focus on the abuse of asylum (*Asylmissbrauch*). Both those with genuine claims for protection and others who were said to have economic motives came to be part of a negative stereotype associated with a drain on state resources and became associated in popular discourse with criminal activity. This discourse of 'system abuse' has also come to dominate asylum politics in Australia in recent years, as a correlation is drawn between falling recognition rates and undeserving or fraudulent claims.

In Germany the years leading up to the 'asylum crisis' saw the following recognition rates for asylum applicants; 1955: 29.15%, 1986: 15.95%, 1987: 9.4%, 1988: 8.61%, 1989: 4.97%, 1990: 4.38%, 1991: 6.9%, (Münch 1993; 179). The decline in the recognition rates in Germany was accompanied by a public discourse that predominantly cast failed applicants as abusers and defrauders of the German legal system (ibid.; 178). While about 95 percent of asylum seekers arriving since 1989 have been judged to be economic rather than political refugees, about 20 percent were subsequently allowed to stay in Germany legally with some form of humanitarian status, and many more remain illegally.

Over the ensuing years, and particularly in light of the pressures associated with German unification in October 1990, asylum came to be cast in public discourse as an unfair burden on a country already facing numerous social and political problems. By 1991, a rigorous national debate ensued over Germany's uniquely open constitutional provisions on granting asylum – found in Article 16 of the Basic Law (hereafter Art. 16a GG). This debate received widespread coverage in the German media, covering not only the issue of asylum seekers coming to Germany, but the place of foreigners in Germany more broadly. By late 1991, the issue of asylum seekers and the presence of foreigners amounted to the most significant issue of concern in public opinion polls (Marshall 1996; 6). Public debate came to be split into two camps: first, conservative critics of Art. 16a GG, who felt compelled to defend their local constituents who felt burdened by outsiders,[14] and second, those who viewed Art. 16a GG as fundamental to the continuing obligation to human rights. This second grouping included the SPD, the Greens and the many of the NGOs who worked on immigrant issues.[15]

It was the creation of the German Basic Law (the *Grundgesetz*) of 1949, which allowed the nation to move forward because of a sense of security in just laws, and a constitution which defined the new Germany, breaking totally with the past (Bade 1994; 94). The experiences of Germans in exile as opponents of the Nazi regime, was a strong motivational force, leading to the incorporation of the right to political

[14] Chancellor Kohl had advocated change to Art. 16a GG as early as 1986 (Marshall 1996; 8).

[15] During this period of intense debate over asylum seekers in 1991 and 1992, the related issues of Germany's approach to its status as an immigration country and towards the integration of foreigners were also debated vigorously (see for instance *Frankfurter Rundschau*, 29th September, 1991).

asylum into the new German Constitution (Bosswick 1997; 54). The Basic Law sought to make a break with the past by protecting the rights of individuals, associations and of political parties: 'In a conscious departure from Germany's 'strong' state tradition, the German Basic Law puts the individual first, the state second; it is conceived in the spirit of limiting state sovereignty by individual rights' (Joppke 1998; 284). Art. 16a GG refers to the fundamental right of any individual who has suffered persecution in her country of origin, to seek asylum in Germany. Many of those who drafted the 1949 Basic Law had personal experience of seeking refuge outside Germany during the 1930s and 1940s in exile from Nazi Germany (Martin 19994; 192). The difficulties they encountered in finding countries willing to accept them formed the impetus for Article 16 which states: 'Persons persecuted for political reasons shall enjoy the right of asylum.'

The amendment to the *Grundgesetz* on the 28th June 1993, resulted in the constitutional right to asylum being restricted in practice, while the fundamental principle of the right to asylum remained intact.[16] However the five sub-clauses which were added to the original article have resulted in what many analysts see as a restricting of the original character of the asylum right from a constitutional rule into an administrative regulation (Bosswick 2000; 30). Paragraph one of the amended article sustains the right to asylum for every persecuted individual. Paragraph two goes on to say this right does not apply to anyone entering the Federal Republic from a 'safe third country' (every country bordering Germany is deemed to be 'safe'), nor from a 'safe country of origin' (Paragraph three).[17] Paragraph four outlines measures for the judicious removal of those found to have 'manifestly unfounded' applications. Last, Paragraph five facilitates the ratification of international agreement in asylum policies by the Federal Republic (Ausländerrecht 1998; 135). The amendments to Art. 16aGG were part of a comprehensive legislative package, the overall objective of which was to limit access to German asylum procedures through a combination of speedier processing,

[16] The bitter battle which led to the asylum compromise is reflected in the fact that the Constitutional Court was called upon to endorse the change to the Art. 16a GG. This decision was ratified in May 1996.

[17] Asylum seekers who enter Germany from a so-called 'safe third country' are returned to that country on the premise that they could ask for asylum there. Further, a 'safe country of origin' list compiled under the Dublin Convention means that asylum seekers coming from countries on this list must substantiate their claim to asylum upon arrival or face immediate deportation. Countries on the 'safe' list include Bulgaria, Gambia, Ghana, Poland, Rumania, Senegal, the Slovak Republic. Germany has also signed agreements with its neighbouring countries securing the right to send back asylum seekers who have entered Germany through those countries.

as well as cutting social benefits to asylum seekers.[18] Nonetheless, the amendments stopped short of removing the possibility of seeking protection as a constitutional right altogether (Marshall 1996; 5).

An early prediction of the change to the asylum article in the German Constitution was that it would '. . . most likely have the effect of eliminating constitutional asylum protection for refugees who have passed through any of the neighbouring states' (Neuman 1993; 509). This raises the important question of whether those with genuine claims of political persecution were still able to gain access to the asylum process in Germany. Since 1993 some 98 per cent of cases are able to gain access to an asylum determination process only through illegal entry by concealing the route of entry (Bosswick 2000; 51). This conundrum is further exacerbated by the fact that a great majority of people seeking protection can only manage to gain entry to countries such as Germany through the use of people-smugglers. The use of such illegal and even 'criminal' elements in gaining entry to a country can in fairness be said to prejudice a claim for protection, even before the substantive causes of persecution can be detailed. The credibility (*Glaubwürdigkeit*) of an individual is tested and called into question by travel and arrival details even before any grounds of asylum can be tested.

In the lead up to the Basic Law changes in 1993, NGOs invested considerable energy in attempting to avert these changes. Disillusion and recrimination resulted after the amendments were finally passed. Grass-roots workers and advocates alike had to come to terms not only with personal and collective disappointments of a long and often bitter campaign to convince politicians and the public against the asylum amendments, they also had to familiarise themselves quickly with the practical implications of the new restrictions. An air of resignation dominated the NGO sector for some time after 1993, fuelled by a combination of factors including: a general public climate which saw the new restrictions in a positive light; a rapid decline in the interest the mass media took in issues related to asylum seekers; and a widespread assessment that the 'problem' had been solved. In other words, after the 'asylum compromise' NGOs were to a large extent silenced, with the avenues of entering a public discourse previously open to them, no longer attuned to the issue(s) which NGOs represented.

For many of the NGOs working in the area of advocacy of refugees and asylum seekers, the developments of 1992/93 marked a loss of trust and a certain *caesura* marked by modes of conduct, common understanding and negotiation which had taken long years to establish between state and non-state actors seemingly swept

[18] For a comprehensive commentary on the developments leading to the 'asylum compromise' see Bade (1994).

aside. The Jesuit priest, Jörg Alt, who was involved in the lengthy negotiations at both federal and state level in the so-called 'asylum compromise' which brought about the constitutional change to the asylum paragraph, notes:

> The big asylum discussion began already in the mid-80s, with asylum being linked to abuse and being seen as somehow fraudulent. For instance, in the heads of Germans 90% of asylum seekers are believed to be fraudulent, because the figure of those who get accepted is so low. And this situation is not clarified, certainly not at the political level as to why certain groups don't show up in the recognition rates, such as civil war victims. This is very much a need, because so many categories do not fit into the tight German reading of who qualifies as a refugee, and so people who have genuine claims are believed to be fraudulent (Interview No. 26).

Aside from the legal and administrative implications of the Constitutional changes to the asylum provisions, the events of 1992/93 also marked a symbolic turn for Germany. How this 'turn' is digested in the Federal Republic in the medium to long-term is, I would argue, largely dependent on the success of integration measures for foreigners already living in Germany. As I have argued in earlier chapters, the approaches taken to all categories of 'other'; of 'stranger', accumulate over time, and are expressed in the often unwieldy form of public opinion. The German constitution, which enshrined the commitment to grant asylum to anyone who suffered political persecution, did so mindful of the nationalist past, and the excesses that had resulted from it. As such, post-war, liberal Germany behaved in a manner contrary to the 'national interest' in relation to Germany's needs in the international migration system:

> Thus for Germans . . . the asylum crisis is the first moment in the post-war period where they feel forced to renounce the utopia of a post-nationalist state and think more soberly of Germany's national interest. Even for liberals, in other words, some nationalist discourse is unavoidable. They have to talk about quotas, limits, repatriations, putting the German unemployed first. All of this would be natural enough, were such a language not disgraced by its association with the Right (Ignatieff 1993; 75-6).

The compromise on political asylum, finalised in May 1993 is, according to Habermas, characterised as emblematic of a European wide phenomenon of seeking to prevent immigration from third world countries (in Gutman 1994; 136). In Germany the conditions for changing the Basic Law were also consolidated over a longer period through the public and political representations of foreigners in an overwhelmingly negative way. This is not to deny that the rise in asylum applications through 1992 was a startling development, with over 430,000 asylum seekers arriving in that year. However, the numbers of asylum applicants alone is insufficient to explain the constitutional change. The government of the day had tapped a much deeper, historical well-spring of apprehension, fear and social distance toward foreigners in the German psyche. Chapter five will explore in detail the rise in xenophobia and violence before the 'asylum compromise'; violence which also continued in unpredictable waves and outbursts well after this period.

### *(a) 'Out of Country' through the airport procedure*

Accompanying the constitutional changes of the 'asylum compromise' was the introduction of a special airport procedure (*Flughafenverfahren*, Fhv as §18a Asylum Procedure Code). This procedure was modelled after similar regulations already in force in France, the Netherlands and in Denmark, resulted in those travelling without valid documents and wishing to apply for asylum being detained in the 'international zones' at an airport. In this way the asylum applicant was deemed not to have entered German territory (Bosswick 2000: 51, Hailbronner 1998; 161). The airport procedure faced criticism for legal experts and in its ruling on the Constitutional amendments of 14 March 1996, the Federal Constitutional Court required major modifications to the practice of the airport procedure, and in part found it to be unconstitutional (Schelter in Bosswick 2000; 51). Along with the new procedures came new time limits for appeal: to avoid expulsion in the airport procedure a lawyer has to file an appeal within three days. It is noteworthy that the sum total of the regulations of the new asylum law came to be characterised as an 'expression of the executive's deep distrust of the courts' (Pfaff 1994; 11). A similar level of distrust became evident in Australia by the late 1990s; a development which will be discussed in chapter six.

German NGOs and human rights activists hold the view that the practice of holding asylum seekers in 'non-state' territory, was a circumvention of protection obligations. The airport procedure appears to be a revolving door to deportation, and legal access across land borders is effectively closed down through the safe third country regulations.[19] Moreover, as the airport procedure keep asylum seekers largely invisible from the receiver society and segregated from the bulk of the NGOs who could offer legal advice and other assistance, frustration both inside and outside airport holding facilitates accelerates. Hunger strikes, other forms of self harm and suicide attempts by asylum seekers, are regular occurrences in the

[19] From July 1993 when the amendment to the Basic Law, including the airport procedure was made, to July 1999, only 17,058 applications for asylum were made at German airports. Of these 14,307 went through the asylum procedure. Just 14 asylum seekers were recognised in the airport procedure (BAFI in Bosswick 2000; 51).

detention facilities at airports. NGOs expressed particular concern at the detention of unaccompanied women and of children.[20] Aside from the airport procedure, Germany does not practice detention of asylum seekers in the comprehensive and mandatory way in which Australia does, usually detaining only those who have a 'manifestly unfounded' claim and are awaiting deportation.[21] After 1993, the airport procedure did, however, become a mandatory form of detention for those entering at German airports. In particular Frankfurt airport, which has the highest volume of air travellers, has become the focus of much scrutiny by human rights groups and NGOs, the focus of sustained protest activity, particularly on occasions such as International refugee day (AI Press Release, October 1, 1997). Since 1998 Pro Asyl, the quasi federal refugee council, has staffed a legal advice centre at Frankfurt airport with over 50 lawyers being available at different times to advise asylum seekers of their rights and of the German asylum process.

## The asylum process

Only once a potential refugee has entered the territory of the Federal Republic can an asylum process be invoked. A person can enter the asylum process (*Asylverfahren*) in Germany in a number of ways depending on how s/he has entered the country. As is the case in Australia, the way in which an individual seeking protection enters Germany may ultimately have a strong bearing on the validity and ultimate success of the application. In the first instance at a border (land or airport), authorities follow regulations (§18 Abs. 2 of the AsylVfG, the *Asylverfahrensgesetz*), which directs them to 'turn around' those who have entered through a 'safe third country', or those who otherwise are judged as not being in fear of persecution, or those who pose a security risk to the nation. An obligation to deport individuals is enshrined in the same paragraph where the relevant travel documentation is not in the possession of an individual and that individual cannot adequately articulate the need for protection. Otherwise the border authorities have

---

[20] Flughafen-Sozialdienst, a church-based NGO who delivers social services to detainees at Frankfurt Airport regularly documents the situation of detainees (see 'Erfahrungen des Flughafen-Sozialdienstes Frankfurt am Main mit dem 'Fughafenverfahren' nach§18 a AsylVerfG', 31st October, 1996, see also 'Positionen und Mindestanforderungen zur Abschiebungshaft', Diakonie Korrespondenz, Mai 1996).

[21] However, legislative changes in November 1998 have broadened the scope for detention to new arrivals. Of particular concern to NGOs has been the detention of children, as, under German law, asylum seekers from the age of 16 are considered adults and therefore not subject to the strict time limitations which apply to children in detention.

a duty to allow an asylum process to begin. Second, those individuals who are not detained or apprehended at a border may enter the asylum process through a local foreigners' authority (*Ausländerbehörde*). Local officials are also obliged to deport individuals who have entered through a 'safe third country' (for instance, across a land border) under § 19 Abs. 3 AsylVfG, which also obliges them in other cases, to direct individuals to make an application for protection. In other cases individuals may approach either police authorities or the staff of asylum hostels, who have an obligation to direct individuals to the appropriate authorities able to guide them in lodging an application or determining that no such right to make an application exists.

Once an asylum application has been lodged an individual has the right to remain in Germany until such time as a determination is made. During this period an individual has a provisional visa (*Aufenthaltsgenehmigung*). Not every case is decided with a personal hearing or interview, though the law states that everyone is entitled to an individual hearing (§24 Abs.1 Satz 2 AsylVfG). An asylum seeker does not have the right to decide in which of the *Länder* s/he will reside during the determination process. After the 'asylum comprise', new regulations over social assistance came into force on the 1st November 1993, known as the *Asylbewerberleistungsgeset* (AsylbLG). This legislation regulates the extent to which the local authorities are obliged to assist an asylum seeker. Noteworthy is that cash payments are now rare, with most assistance being in kind, utilising coupons and other pre-selected goods, although practices vary considerably between the *Länder*. In April of 1997 assistance to asylum seekers, to 'civil war refugees' and to those on temporary visas were again reduced. Largely, asylum seekers are required to work for their upkeep in a refugee hostel or other group accommodation where local authorities cater for them for the first three months. Freedom of movement is restricted to the area of the local police authority. Asylum seekers are not permitted to work in outside employment while they are in asylum reception centres, nor are they permitted to study in German educational institutions. Even once some form of visa is granted, access to work is very limited, and work permits are granted only is cases where a job has first been offered to German nationals or other 'privileged' foreigners, such as EU passport holders. Asylum seekers are not entitled to any German language tuition, though NGOs regularly organise classes. The consequences of the living circumstances of asylum seekers are discussed in more detail in chapter five, in tandem with an analysis of the role of NGOs in identifying and highlighting problem areas in how receiving states manage asylum seekers.

There is a central office which hears asylum cases, located in Nürnberg. This office has grown in staff numbers and in the number of regional offices which hear asylum cases through the 1990s. During the 1980s one of the frequent criticisms made of the bureau was the length of time the processing of applicants took – often years rather than months. Every asylum applicant is entitled to a personal hearing. All offices of the central asylum office are connected to a central computer system which utilises several streamlined computer systems of information exchange across all countries of the European Union. An automated fingerprint identification system - AFIS, and a double identity system for identifying people who have claimed asylum elsewhere – DIAS have been introduced in recent years to assist in processing protection claims. In the early 1990s, when the influx of asylum seekers was at its peak, and the backlog of cases to be determined had reached over 500,000, the waiting period on an application averaged eighteen months. During this period, the processing staff in the central office was doubled and processing times decreased.

An application for asylum must be put promptly upon arrival and must be lodged personally. Once a decision is made it is forwarded by mail to the last known address of the asylum seeker. Where the notification of such a decision is not promptly answered, the authorities put in place a deportation order to be carried out within one month, even where a decision was in favour of an applicant. In such cases the local foreigner's authority in the district where an asylum seeker is known or thought to have lived, is authorised to order a deportation with the assistance of the police. An appeal to an initial decision can be lodged with the courts within a two week period.

One of the most serious protection gaps in the German interpretation of international refugee law has been the status of those fleeing from civil war.[22] Two main groups have highlighted this gap; the first the Bosnians fleeing civil war in the early 1990s, and second the Kosovars fleeing ethnic cleansing in 1999. Germany received by far the highest number of Bosnian refugees – almost 60 per cent of all those seeking refuge in the EU (Koser 2000; 29). As part of the 'asylum compromise' of 1992/93 the SPD succeeded in having a new status, known as 'paragraph 32a status' added to the German Law for Foreigners (*Deutsches Ausländerrecht*). The intention of this new regulation was to bypass the asylum procedure and provide 'temporary protection' for a period of three months; a period

[22] It is noteworthy that Germany's first Immigration Bill which passed through the through the Lower House of Germany's parliament, the *Bundestag*, on March 1, 2002 and was ratified by the upper house, the *Bundesrat* on the 22nd March 2002 after a heated debate, has among other things, address the issue of persecution by non-government agents and on gender specific grounds in line with the *Refugee Convention*. Previously Germany had used a tight interpretation of the *Refugee Convention* where protection was granted only in cases of persecution by a state.

able to be continued if the war in the country of origin continued. However paragraph 32a, despite having been intended for the Bosnian civil war refugees, was not invoked until April 1999 in relation to the Kosovars. In the early 1990s, the Bosnians received various more restrictive forms of temporary status, and were required to return to their homeland from October 1996 on, after the signing of the Dayton Peace Accord. The return to Bosnia from late 1996 was the highest from Germany of all EU states. Returns from Germany accounted for some 95 per cent of returns for all of the EU by late 1997. Chapter five will analyse the NGO response to what was perceived by many as a hasty repatriation process by the German government, given the lack of infrastructure in Bosnia after the war.

A national policy of burden sharing between the states of the Federal Republic means that asylum seekers are allocated to all the German states by the federal Minster for the Interior, who gives a monthly briefing on new numbers and responsibilities to the states. In general approximately 80% of asylum seekers are sent to the old Federal *Länder* (of the West) with about 20% going to the new *Länder* (of the former East). The *Länder* are then responsible for the day-to-day living circumstances of asylum seekers. The concept of burden sharing between member states of the EU has also been a high priority for Germany, which will be discussed in chapter five. In the allocation of asylum seekers between *Länder*, only married couples and those with children are considered for dispersal in groups. Otherwise quotas are directed according to country of origin.

The sixteen *Länder* of the Federal Republic vary greatly in terms of local capacity as well as societal openness and tolerance toward asylum seekers. The strength and historical connections and capacities of NGOs also vary greatly. The former Eastern *Länder* have less well developed non-government networks that deal with immigrants and issues of integration, as there was largely no call for such organisations until after 1989. Nevertheless, the practical implementation of the integration measures, and the subsequent institutionalisation of such processes are in their infancy throughout Germany. Though it can be argued that in one sense integration measures are never complete, having to adapt and be modified in response to immigrant groups as well as to societal change within the receiver group, I would maintain that until integration is 'normalised' in the public mind, substantive progress cannot be made. There is ample evidence that a variety of regional and local integration initiatives in a particular city or a community (*Gemeinde*) have been highly successful, yet only a co-ordinated federal approach with political leaders communicating positively about such initiatives over a period of time, as well as allocating sufficient and ongoing resources to such initiatives will ensure the long-term success of such projects and initiatives.

The Director of the Berlin Refugee Council, Frauke Hoyer, who has been working with immigrant communities in Berlin over a long period, put it this way:

> We need a form of integration where people do not sit on suitcases for years, and go crazy in light of their uncertain status. The question is one of who uses who in the relationship between politics and public opinion. Politicians use the community as an alibi, to say 'well the people don't want more money spent on integration'. The cost of the civil war refugees in Germany is constantly highlighted, for instance. And then, when there are a few isolated cases of fraud in relation to an asylum claim, it is splashed all over the media. Out of proportion with the incident. But the Olympic advertising campaign for the Berlin bid, cost DM 50 million of public money. That is not seen as a problem (Interview No. 9).

I turn now to a brief overview of the groups and organisations that advocate for asylum seekers in Germany as well as those that act internationally, across borders. In chapter five I analyse the work of these organisations in more detail. I begin with an overview of the organised churches in Germany which generate both large welfare organisations and small initiatives emerging from individual parishes, and constitute such a significant part of the NGO sector in Germany.

## Church and state: welfare of body and soul

The Reformation and the Counter-Reformation set in place Protestant and Catholic networks which extended to schools, seminaries, universities and the court. The outbreak of the Thirty Year War in 1618 marked unresolved tensions between the German nobility as well as the Austrian Habsburgs, largely played out along religious lines. The Austrian emperor Ferdinand led a strong Catholic coalition, including Maximillian of Bavaria, as well as support from Spain and Poland, against the Calvinist Frederick V and the Bohemian Protestant nobility (Fulbrook 1990; 55-6). With the Peace of Westphalia in 1648, a certain secularisation became evident in the formal separation of religion and politics. Some commentators assert that the Protestant church in particular developed a position of conformism and even deference to the state, associated with a Lutheran distrust of the masses (Balfour 1992; 3). Even so, church networks, both Protestant and Catholic, operating primarily through the institutions of education and of welfare, continued to have a considerable influence from this period on.

It was, however, the experience under the *Third Reich* that led the churches to rethink their ties with the state, moving away from the traditional stance of passive subordination to the state and its authority. The Protestant Church in particular gradually developed a critical and independent judgement of the state. The Catholic Church similarly developed a new approach, becoming an active lobbyist in the political process (Dalton 1993; 254). The two major churches thus became an important part of the recreation of social and political life in the Federal Republic after World War II. An example is the Christian Democratic party, (the CDU), which was an effort to overcome the differences between Catholics and Protestants:

> . . . the Christian Democratic party directed post war reconstruction. In addition, the churches were one of the few functioning institutions that could be relied on to assist in this development. Moreover, in contrast to the U.S. tradition of the separation of church and state, the two institutions were closely intertwined in the West. The state legitimised the political role of the churches, granting them a special legal status as public law corporations (Dalton ibid.).

The right to levy a church tax evolved from the nineteenth century, with arrangements negotiated by individual states. The Catholic and Protestant Churches both have large and well-established welfare associations which attract substantial state financial support. In 1957 the two Protestant welfare associations which had been founded in 1848 and 1945 were merged into the Diakonisches Hilfswerk. Caritas, the Catholic counterpart, united in 1897 as an umbrella organisation to what had been largely decentralised work by various Church and lay organisations to effect a counterpoint to the social costs of industrial capitalism in the late nineteenth century (Katzenstein 1987; 7). The two-pronged financial support of the state and the institutionalisation of church tax collected by the state, results in a unique strength and role for the major churches in the provision of social welfare. As de-facto immigration movements to Germany grew in the post-war period, these church welfare organisations developed specific services for immigrants. Over time this has resulted in a significant level of expertise residing in church organisations which is only thinly developed in state institutions. The Church is granted a certain legitimacy and significance in German society, quite distinct from the more secular orientation of Australia.

Non-religious welfare organisations like the German Red Cross, founded in 1864, and the *Arbeiterwohlfahrt* (Workers' Welfare League) are also important in the welfare lobby in Germany. The diversity of other organisations involved in work with immigrants, refugees and asylum seekers is discussed later.

The role of the mainstream churches in Germany has been a vital part of citizen mobilisation and involvement in political action at various moments in history. The most apparent difference in citizen engagement in overt political action as well as neighbourhood initiatives has been between East and West Germany. Padgett outlines the development of an emerging civil society in East Germany through the process of democratisation leading up to the events of late 1989. Germany is a special case of post-communist transformation because of the existence of the Federal Republic as an alternative 'German identity' (Padgett 2000; 37). Leading up to the events of 1989, the Protestant churches in East Germany provided an umbrella for a 'constellation of opposition groups similar to that in other communist states' (ibid.; 38), which were ultimately instrumental in bringing down the communist regime. However, in similar fashion to other countries in Central and Eastern Europe, these opposition movements disintegrated and were marginalised or absorbed into the party system which had its roots in the West. The associational activity of civil society relies on a relationship *with* the state as outlined in chapter two. That is, though state and civil society may, according to democratic theory be cast as oppositional forces, it is not only the state that depends on legitimation through the various mechanisms of civil society but civil society which relies on the state to encourage and facilitate associational activity among citizens. This is evident through the provision of infrastructure from the state, which can be drawn on by civil society, as well as giving the demands of civil society some legal institutional mechanisms to invoke. This element of state support for civil society and 'movement' activity was largely absent in the GDR, as in other East European societies. In the West associational activity has continued and been encouraged by the state as complementary to state activities and roles.

Associational activity was retarded by a syndrome that is endemic to post-communist society. Poised between state socialism and the market, economy relations were insufficiently developed to generate the complex patterns of social differentiation in interdependence that lie at the heart of civil society in sociological discourse (Padgett 2000: 51).

Post-communist societies display social atomisation, in that communism has laid waste to the institutions of autonomous collective action (Offe 1996: 70). With the exception of the Catholic Church in Poland and the Protestant Church in the former GDR, social trust and co-operation for group interests are low in such societies, displaying a deficit for the collective action of NGOs and social movements. This is borne out by the fact that NGOs which do operate on migrant and refugee issues in the former GDR are primarily church-based organisations.

A significant development in Germany is the place and relevance of the social movements, which have at times been highly active in the German political landscape - mostly in the West before 1989, but of course most potently in the East in the demonstrations and civil disobedience which culminated in the fall of the Berlin Wall. Before the period of high 'new social movements' activity from the 1970s, the majority of citizen initiatives and autonomous activity were largely institutionalised, thereby lacking an autonomous and spontaneous character.

Historians often draw attention to German 'traditions' or pre-dispositions such as authoritarianism, legalism and nationalism (Martin 1994; 193). However, particularly since the 1960s and 1970s a distinct counter tradition informed by social movement principles has been evident at least in West Germany. The combination through the 1970s and into the early 1980s of a thriving economy and an increase in social and political pluralism in West Germany, resulted in discussions of new social issues; the issue of foreigners living in Germany including ethnic Germans, guest workers, as well as asylum seekers.

As indicated at the beginning of this chapter, Germany has historically been a place both of large-scale emigrations and immigrations, with war and economic depression being the two primary 'push' factors for emigrants from Germany from the mid nineteenth century. In the late twentieth century Germany has become a *de-facto* country of immigration, with migration movement to Germany coming from guest workers, ethnic Germans and refugees and asylum seekers. Though the people represented in these three distinct immigration sources have distinct needs, differing legal status and integration opportunities such as access to citizenship, choice of residence, or the right to work, they overlap and indeed merge into the broader category of 'foreigner'; non-German. The overburdening of the category foreigner, due to historical factors and German law, does make a differencc in the day-to-day lives not only of those non-Germans, but also to the lives of Germans themselves. A perception of over-burdening of the public purse by foreigners, and of an over-foreignisation (*Überfremdung*) of Germany (disturbing what is a non-existent though nevertheless idealised cultural homogeneity), is not only encouraged, but indeed incited by legislation and a policies of exclusion with a long history. The impact of such measures over time on the symbolic representation of native and foreigner is ultimately expressed in the unpredictable and politically volatile force of public opinion. As has been discussed briefly earlier in this chapter, the groups who did become vocal as advocates for the rights of foreigners in the 1970s and early 1980s, became part of a more positive approach to societal change (Muller et. al. 1996; 46). Various organisations and initiatives, large and small, local and national, recognised that 'yelling from the sidelines' was not sufficient to achieving the changes they had in mind. Initiatives in Germany built on strong and long-standing cultural orientations among Germans toward involvement in clubs, associations and group-oriented activities and in turn strengthened the propensity for involvement in such activities. However, the growth of refugee initiatives through the 1980s and into the 1990s largely grew in distinction from other social developments pointing in a counter direction, namely toward a more introverted, increasingly individualistic orientation.

## NGOs in Germany: continuity and change

I shall turn now to a brief overview of the non-state sector which has responded to the issues triggered by the arrival of asylum seekers. First, let me outline the various organisations which constitute refugee or asylum advocacy and service delivery here, while analysing the major contribution of this non-state sector in chapter five.

The NGOs involved in the issue of asylum seekers fall into two broad categories: first, those whose primary work is advocacy and lobbying government and bureaucracy directly; and second, those organisations whose primary function is service delivery of one kind or another – health care, legal advice, or provision of a range of welfare services.[23]

The established interest representation groups in Germany include unions, churches and independent welfare organisations, some of which also have an international 'development' or aid focus. In representing the interests of immigrants, refugees and asylum seekers in particular, a variety of organisations exist in Germany at the federal, state and local levels. The German Trade Union Federation (Deutscher Gewerkschaftsbund, DGB) encompasses 16 unions, including memberships of industrial, white-collar and government workers. The DGB has a substantial social justice platform, and has undertaken significant work in the refugee area during the 1980s and 1990s. Both the Catholic Church and the Protestant Church in Germany (Evangelische Kirche in Deutschland, EKD) are involved at many levels in the lobbying for policy development at federal and at state levels, as well as grass-roots service delivery. The EKD has a chancellery office in Bonn, from where lobbying is undertaken The Catholic church maintains the secretariat of the Bishops' conference in Bonn, an office which monitors the decisions and debates of parliament and the ministries. Catholic leaders actively lobby government on legislation dealing with social issues. The extensive resources and network of the Catholic church allow Catholic leaders and representatives have a role in the development of policy.

The social welfare services of both the Protestant and Catholic churches in Germany have substantial programmes for immigrants, including refugees. The Protestant 'Diakonie' and the Catholic 'Caritas' carry out these programmes. Both organisations work across the Federal Republic and have specific refugee desks. However, as these organisations carry out welfare roles across the various needs within German society, there is also an anxiety among those working directly with refugees that this area can easily become secondary to other areas of social need concerning German citizens rather than non-nationals with an undetermined status. This sentiment was expressed to me during interviews by workers from both

[23] The size of this NGO sector is indicated by the directory of refugee assistance which the ZDWF published in association with the UNHCR (1996). The directory runs to over 200 pages, including social and legal advice centres, airport social services and asylum hostels and centres.

agencies. The business lobby forms another interest group which is significant to the immigration debate in that this lobby has been calling for increased immigration to Germany. Although business interests do not lobby from an explicitly human rights perspective, some of the NGOs find their positions sympathetic, and find alliances to strengthen lobbying useful.

The UNHCR has been a prominent presence in the Federal Republic of Germany since 1951, when it established a Branch office in Bonn, and in 1953 a sub office in Zirndorf. The office of the UNHCR in Germany has been pro-active over time in establishing relationships with both government and non-government bodies and individuals involved in the asylum area. The UNHCR's role is one of monitoring the situation of refugees and asylum seekers and advocacy with government in policy formulation. In addition the UNHCR has assisted in the negotiations over return and readmission agreements for persons found not to qualify for refugee status.

By 1985 it had become apparent to those involved in advocating for the rights of asylum seekers, primarily church organisations, welfare and human rights groups, that a coordinated response to the diminution of rights was needed. Pro Asyl was founded in response as a peak body of the regional refugee councils, in 1986 and registered as an association in 1988. At that time the German representative of the UNHCR, René van Rooyen, was also pivotal in assisting with the founding up Pro Asyl. One of the founders of Pro Asyl, Herbert Leuniger, took up responsibility of European representative through ECRE in 1994. Since its inception, Pro Asyl has identified the gathering and dissemination of information to German and European citizens as a vital part of its lobbying efforts. Because of its relatively high public profile and often critical approach to government policy, Pro Asyl had been typified as radical and extremist by numerous politicians of the major parties by the mid 1990s.

Local, and regional initiatives instigated by and for local communities, aimed at solving local problems, have a long history in Germany. So-called citizen initiatives, clubs and associations of various kinds are common as forms of involvement in the political life of local areas. After the arrival of significant numbers of foreigners in Germany in the early 1970s - at that time through the guest workers programme - local initiatives began which specifically addressed concerns with the integration of foreigners. These initiatives spread in number through the 1980s, searching for amicable and conciliatory solutions to local problems. Their aim was to achieve strategies for living together with foreigners in harmonious rather than confrontational ways. Such localised initiatives have on the whole been highly successful as they have tackled the fear of the unknown which generalised characterisations of foreigners have created. Rather than reproducing simplified stereotypes, local initiatives have been pivotal in raising debate and dialogue through personal contact in neighbourhoods.

Immigrant associations who represent the interests of particular ethnic or religious groups have historically not been particularly well organised in Germany, with the exception of the Council of Jewry, the *Zentralrat.* Turkish immigrant groups have also organised into numerous associations, though only relatively recently. Joppke indicates how this development among Turkish immigrants is evident in two trends: associations which are pragmatic and 'host-society oriented', and those which focus on 'renationlisation of the diaspora' and evoking a protest culture among Turkish people in the receiver society (1999; 218). It is noteworthy that such associational activity among Turkish immigrants began largely only after the xenophobic violence of the early 1990s, which was carried out against German-born Turks as well as asylum seekers. However, most of the ethnic groups living in Germany as foreigners tend not have established their own associations and organisations, relying to a large extent on NGOs. While to some extent the asylum NGOs are distinct from the much larger and broader grouping of NGOs involved in 'immigration work' per se, it is also the case that the relative institutional and resource weakness of asylum NGOs, draw them to coalitions with the wider NGO sector. While some NGOs criticise foreigner communities for their lack of self-organisation, the very conditions and culture within the German foreigner lobby has historically not been conducive to immigrant self-representation. Rather than facilitating the self-representation of immigrants, the foreigner lobby, including churches, the unions and other charity and welfare organisations led 'a discourse about the migrants and not a dialogue with them' (Radtke in Joppke 1999; 209). Though this development related in particular to guest workers, the instrumentalising of the foreigner, as the object of (voluntary) assistance, has continued with asylum seekers.

In summary, this chapter has indicated the way in which Germany's refugee policies reflect the politicisation of the asylum issue since the late 1980s (Schnabel 1994; 6), in the sense that the arrival and presence of people seeking protection, though indeed having a significant impact on German society, was regularly and repeatedly miscommunicated to the German people. Habermas assesses the public and political responses to asylum seekers from the early 1990s as a 'de-civilizing' of German society, mindful in particular of the increased hatred and violence toward all foreigners which escalated from 1991 (1994:127). This politicisation is on the one hand unique to social and political developments in the Federal Republic of Germany, but on the other hand such developments correspond to similar developments in neighbouring countries as well as in other Western countries in response to 'irregular' and illegal arrivals. What we see across Western countries is an increase in internal and external deterrence of such arrivals. Similar patterns of legislative and administrative response are also evident in Australia and other receiving states. I turn now to a short history of immigration in Australia and an assessment of the development of refugee policy and the role of NGOs as advocates for the rights of those seeking protection.

# Chapter 5

# Selection and control in Australia – from old habits to new techniques

> For travellers on the empty Stuart Highway that passes 1,600 kilometres through the vast, lost desert country from the sea at Port Augusta in the south, north to Alice, Woomera is a largely forgotten town.
>
> Spuds' Roadhouse, at the hamlet of Pimba on the highway, advertises the old rockets and broken-down aircraft that can still be seen in Woomera . . . out on the gibber plains where the British came in 1947 to test-fire rockets into the desert.
>
> Out there, pencil thin metal towers stretch in perfect lines to the horizons and mark out the now little-used firing ranges . . . Later, the Americans came and built one of the early joint facilities, the Nurrangar Missile Early Warning Station, about 15 kilometres south of the Woomera township. From there, Saddam Hussein's scud missiles – used against Kuwait and Israel in the 1991 Gulf War – were detected at blastoff by Nurrangar's huge white radar domes and warnings flashed to the Gulf.
>
> . . . But now new buildings are going up outside the town that once helped the Western powers combat the 'butcher of Baghdad'. Behind high wire fences are Iraqis who have fled Saddam's rule by illegally entering Australia. The wire also holds back Afghanis, who fled the murderous Taliban militiamen who control much of their country. Again, it is Woomera's isolation and emptiness that have proved an attraction for the Australian Government as a place to build its newest detention centre for illegal immigrants (SMH, September 9, 2000).

Newcomers are not a rarity in Australia – rather the norm. As a thoroughly modern nation, Australia has a highly refined set of administrative filtering and constraining measures, tuned to differentiate between categories of such newcomers. What this chapter will outline, is the way in which practices of *disciplining* such newcomers, especially non-European newcomers, is a continuing feature of the Australian social landscape since White settlement, rather than a distinctly new development.

As has become clear through the German case, a nation's historical relationship with immigration and emigration, the practices of granting citizenship and the policy responses to the needs of newcomers, have a bearing on the formulation of refugee policy, as well as demarcating the potential and the limitations of lobbying by third parties such as NGO advocates.

Though the planning and policy response to refugees and asylum seekers is different in the German and Australian cases, and historical trajectories have had different constraints and pressures, the cases nevertheless have many similarities. I have already discussed some specificities of the German case. In what follows, I will elaborate on the considerable layering of historical and cultural significance of immigration to Australia, including multiculturalism and the various ways in which tolerance is an ambiguous entity in Australian society. It will then be possible to focus on the way in which the reception of refugees and asylum seekers operates. However, it is not the aim of this book to detail the history of administrative, and legislative changes in relation to refugees. Rather, only the key moments with reference to the central problem of this book will be considered; namely how can a balance be struck between the protection obligations which those claiming asylum seek to engage, and the local needs and interests within societies which are asylum destinations?

Since the arrival of the First Fleet, bringing with it primarily convicts and their guards and administrators, Australia has experienced small and large influxes of European and non European settlement instigated by a myriad of 'push' and 'pull' factors. Included in this immigration intake have been those who have escaped dangerous and intolerable situations in their homes, and others who have come to reunite with family members. Unlike Germany, Australia has developed a pro-active approach to immigration – actively recruiting and selecting prospective newcomers. Immigration has been utilised as a mechanism of nation-building by successive governments.

In 1901, with the federation of the states of Australia, the new Australian Parliament passed the *Immigration Restriction Act*. This legislation confirmed what was to become know as the 'White Australia Policy', which was to preserve the social and political fabric of a settler society (Collins 1988, Hawkins 1989, Freeman & Jupp 1992, Jupp & Kabala 1993). The legislation remained the basis and justification for selective immigration for the next seven decades. The White Australia Policy effectively excluded all but British and some European migrants; its aim was particularly to exclude immigrants from Asian countries and by extension, all non-white immigrants (Hawkins 1989; 22).

The policy was premised on the racism and xenophobia of white European settlers toward non-whites and particularly Chinese immigrants who had been brought to Australia as indentured labourers in 1848. By 1858, Victoria was estimated to have a Chinese population of 40,000 and in New South Wales there was a Chinese population of 15,000 by 1861 (McMaster 2001; 129). Anti-Chinese sentiment rose as the settler population feared for job security, fuelled by populist notions that Australia could be 'swamped' by 'Asian hordes from the north'. However, the racism of the early settlers was directed most virulently against the Aboriginal population.

Australia's convict past, together with the forced removal of Aborigines from their lands coinciding with the development and growth of towns, agriculture and of mining, is not irrelevant to the experiences of refugees and asylum seekers in Australia in the late twentieth century. In chapter six, I explore the issue of the mandatory, and non-reviewable detention of asylum seekers who arrive without prior authorisation, arguing that this practice is at least in part acceptable to the

Australian public because of a history associated with the cordoning-off and segregation of strangers who were viewed as a threat. Such strangers included Aboriginal people.

While the White Australia Policy effectively excluded non-Europeans from entering Australia, the Aboriginal population in Australia was excluded by other means; by the denial of citizenship; and through containment in settlements and missions in remote regions and overt as well as hidden acts of violence, resulting in the death of large sections of the Aboriginal population. Certain government programmes were aimed at 'cultural genocide'[1] and the actions of early settlers and their descendants had in mind the 'extermination' or 'extinction' of Aboriginal people, though this was not achieved (Reynolds 2001;3).

Reconciliation between white and black Australians remains an issue of great contemporary significance. It is a fundamental strand of modern Australian identity which is yet to be fully explored and understood. School curriculum and texts, up to the early 1980s, regularly depicted Aborigines as savages in need of civilising. It was not until the 1992 Mabo judgement by the High Court of Australia that the legal fiction of *terra nullius* (a land without people), was finally struck from the Australian legislature. However, substantive discrimination of Aborigines continues through uneven access to health, education and other services, as well as excessive policing in residential areas with a high Aboriginal population. Legal battles over native title claims continue.[2]

Let us consider then, the place of the stranger in Australian society after white settlement and the issue of racism. As I have already argued, the stranger who could once be either excluded or assimilated, is a common figure in contemporary life. Understanding the historical particularities and dispositions associated with strangers requires some conceptual tools. Pierre Bourdieu's concept of *habitus* is one such tool which has a usefully broad application in relation to the complexities of a social system. A *habitus* is understood as a set of durable and transposable dispositions, akin to principles which; 'generate and organize practices and representations that can be objectively adapted to their outcomes without presupposing a conscious aiming at ends or an express mastery of the operations necessary in order to attain them' (Bourdieu 1990; 53). In other words, we may think of a *habitus* or several *habitus[es],* as informing our attenuations and

---

[1] The notion of cultural genocide has been exemplified most profoundly in Australia by the practice of taking Aboriginal children away from their natural families, and placing them with white families or orphanages and church run missions. This practice has been documented most comprehensively by the Human Rights And Equal Opportunity Commission (HREOC) in the 1997 report; *Bringing them home. Report of the National inquiry into the Separation of Aboriginal and Torres Strait Islander Children from Their Families.*

[2] The United Nations race discrimination committee has found the Australian Government's amendments to the Wik legislation breaches the international pledges against racial discrimination.

evaluations of the social world, even if unconsciously and outside the use of language. The concept of *habitus* is linked in Bourdieu's formulation to the *field* as the site of struggle and strategy, together forming an insightful explanation of the use and location of relationships more traditionally classified as power. We may go through life engaging in several overlapping *habitus[es]* without necessarily being conscious of any distinctions between them, nor of the shaping and constraining possibilities of various *habitus[es]*.

During the period of white settlement in Australia over the last two centuries, there are perhaps three factors which have come to predominate in the formation of *habitus* as a set of durable, transposable dispositions within which an Australian understanding of immigrants has been constructed. These factors are: the White Australia Policy, multicultural policy development from the mid 1970s, and the treatment of indigenous people in Australia. The latter have most often been completely separated in academic and mainstream writing and analysis from immigration, multiculturalism and 'ethnic affairs'.[3] This separation is an acknowledgement that indigenous people cannot be conflated with another group of ethnic 'others'. For many Aboriginal people the cultural divide in Australia is a *bi-cultural* one, between themselves as indigenous people, and all others who have come after 1788 (Vasta 1996; 50). While the scepticism Aboriginal people express toward multiculturalism is understandable in view of the extreme racism they have experienced during the colonial period and after, the dilemma of a 'partial' multiculturalism continues for white Australians and for black/white relations. This raises the question of what model of cultural diversity and difference is acceptable to the various groups and minorities which make up Australian society.

I will now consider now the various ways in which newcomers have been accommodated into Australian society. Though Australia has received refugees from various conflicts in Europe during the 19th century, it was not until 1945 that a specific refugee policy was adopted, and the first Minister of Immigration, Arthur Caldwell was nominated. Since then, the emphasis in Australia has been placed particularly on administrative control over the processes by which people are selected to come to the country, and upon the entitlements they receive upon arrival – such as settlement services. Previously, the focus of immigration policy had been on helping British immigrants and discouraging 'alien Europeans', resulting in at least a partial exclusion of non European immigrants (Freeman & Jupp 1992; 131). After 1945, economic expansion was accompanied by similarly rapid population growth. The often used slogan, 'populate or perish', was employed to win over a sceptical Australian citizenry to the view that selective immigration would benefit the country. This large-scale immigration programme was accompanied by a policy of assimilation, considered necessary to the

[3] After winning a third term in office in November, 2001, the Howard Government broadened the responsibility of the immigration portfolio to incorporate indigenous affairs. The Department (previously DIMA), is now know as the Department of Immigration, Multiculturalism and Indigenous Affairs (DIMIA).

maintenance of homogeneity, as well as responding to popular local fears (Castles 1996). Citizenship came to be viewed as a pivotal aspect of successful assimilation, putting the nation's arms around newcomers by joining them formally to the nation. The role of the state has been central to immigration in Australia, encompassing both the social, economic and political rationale for immigration as well as responding to the consequences of immigration with policies which have shifted in emphasis over time.

Before elaborating the various political modes of accommodating newcomers to Australia, it is important to consider some factors influencing the recruitment of immigrants, which largely are not dissimilar to Germany's. There is no doubt that immigration has been of economic and social benefit to Australia. Rather than being a drain on public funds; a characterisation which usually circulates around the debates over migrant intakes, migrants have generally been an economic boost to Australia (Collins 1988). It is no wonder therefore, that there is a historical link between labour shortages and increases in immigration intakes. Immigration at crucial points in Australia's development ensured the continued creation of local wealth. Migrants characteristically filled the difficult, dirty and low paid jobs, which Australians of earlier migration phases did not want to undertake; a pattern not unlike the recruitment of guest workers in Germany with the notable exception that in Australia there was no expectation of return of the migrants to their countries of origin.

Up to the 1960s, assimilation was the emphasis of government policy and of the popular discourses surrounding newcomers and how they ought to conduct themselves. Ethnic enclaves were discouraged and immigrants were to adapt to what was conceived as a culturally homogenous society based upon British values and institutions (Castles et. al. 1988; 46). However, by the 1960s several policy changes were implemented when it was found that many migrants were living in poverty, and often isolated from mainstream Australian society (Martin 1978). Assimilationist policies had been based on the assumption that adult immigrants would most quickly adapt to a new environment by working and living among Australians. It was assumed that no special educational measures were needed, past rudimentary English tuition. Similarly, children were to attend mainstream schools and more 'immersed' in classes taught in English (Castles 1999; 25). It was not until the late 1960s that education authorities began to change policies to target the particular needs of immigrants. In 1971, after the Immigration (Education) Act was passed by Federal Parliament, funding was provided for specialist English teachers of English as a Second Language (ESL).

The White Australia Policy was finally abolished in 1973 - 11 years after Canada which previously had a similar policy of exclusion based on race and ethnicity. However, moves away from the White Australia Policy had already begun during the 1960s, with a recognition among some groups that assimilation was not working for the benefit of Australia and certainly not for the immigrants who were subject to this policy. The demise of the policy has been typified as a slow erosion, rather than one uniform act (Lack & Templeton 1995; 152, Warhurst

1993; 196). Along with a shift away from assimilation came a recognition that ethnic communities could maintain distinctions such as a unique culture and language without any risk to the legitimacy or institutional strength of Australian citizenship. This approach came to be embodied by the Whitlam Government as *multiculturalism*. Alongside a gradual policy shift on the integration of immigrants from the post 1945 period, dramatic demographic changes had taken place. Between 1947 and 1992, Australia's population rose from 7.5 million to 17.5 million. By 2001, Australia's population reached over 19 million, with one in four Australians being born overseas.

## Modes of incorporation

The institutional structures of Australia's legal basis of migration and multicultural policy is provided through the Migration Act of 1958, the Migration Legislation Amendment Act of 1989, the Racial Discrimination Act of 1975, and the Sex Discrimination Act of 1984. These laws are monitored by the Human Rights and Equal Opportunity Commission (HREOC).

The particular form that a response to newcomers takes at both official (policy) and unofficial (community) levels has a considerable bearing on the early settlement period of immigrants in all categories, including refugees, as well as on the extension of rights (formal and informal) to which they are entitled. Castles (1995), has proposed three models which have informed policy on newcomers in countries of immigration: the 'differential exclusion' model, the 'assimilation model' and the 'pluralist' model. Germany is a country which has utilised differential exclusion – particularly applicable to guest workers, in that their entry is thought to be temporary for short-term labour demands, therefore permanent settlement needs would not apply. However, differential exclusion is being challenged as an ineffective, unjust and damaging policy in the first instance for immigrants, but in the long term also for the receiver country. Australia has moved from an assimilationist model to a pluralist one, though such adjustment is not seamless and a certain 'slippage' is evident in policy, in funding decisions, and most obviously in the political rhetoric and in public opinion which have accompanied the pursuit of multicultural policies.

Multiculturalism has, over more than two decades, been a significant part of the development of Australian society. Moves away from assimilation have been accompanied by a recognition of the contribution of immigrants and of the inequalities in work, in education and life chances more generally. Multicultural policy has been part of an institutionalised approach to such issues. The presence of diverse ethnic communities has generated new initiatives of co-operation between the government and the non-government sector due to the institutionalised support ethnic communities have been able to draw on. Specialist non-government agencies provide information, counseling and specific services to particular migrant groups such as youth and women and are often funded, or subsidised by public funds.[4]

The incorporation of the immigrant population was comprehensively re-articulated during the period of the Whitlam Labor Government from 1972-75. This period marked the beginning of what has become a comprehensive institutionalised response to ethnic diversity in the form of multicultural policies. The Immigration Minister at the time, Al Grassby, embraced the idea of multiculturalism, which came to be associated with the welfare state due to the link between immigration, a growing awareness of the particular needs of 'ethnic' Australians (Castles 1996; 262, Collins 1988) and the benefits of integration to the receiver society. In the previous assimilationist period, immigrants were expected to suppress any specific needs which did not reflect the majority (Anglo) culture. Under the Whitlam Labor Government, multiculturalism signified part of a general policy programme for social equity, focusing on 'cultural pluralism' as a marker of broad tolerance, while largely leaving historical and structural inequalities to the corrective forces of the market (Pusey 1991). The tenure of the Whitlam Government had witnessed an enfranchisement of 'ethnic' Australians which future governments had to consider and incorporate for longer term political viability, as the voting base of non Anglo Australians had broadened considerably (Jakubowicz, 1984; 38).

The underlying impetus for policies of multiculturalism do not remain static over time. Jakubowicz contends that the conservative Fraser government (December 1975 – March 1983), harnessed the idea of multiculturalism and further institutionalised it as a management *tool* to control and influence an increasingly disparate society. However, it must also be noted that the Fraser government was responsible for a number of reforms which seemed to strengthened Australian multiculturalism. Some of these initiatives came from recommendations of the Galbally report, commissioned by the Fraser government in 1977, concerning post arrival programmes and services. The changes resulting from the report included: the expansion of the Adult Migrant Education Programme, the Telephone Interpreter Service, radio and television stations broadcast in languages other than English, and the launch of Migrant Resource Centres, which remain a vital link between migrants and refugees, the local community in which they live, and government services. Ethnic specific services have fostered positive contributions toward inclusiveness of newcomers with benefits for the broader receiver society. Yet, at the same time such services were,

4 The state Ethnic Communities Councils and the federal body, the Federation of Ethnic Communities Councils of Australia (FECCA) focus on multicultural initiatives. The embeddedness of ethnic groups and associations in Australian life, distinct from the German case, has also led to widespread co-optation of various ethnic organisations into state structures as state agencies seek to utilise ethnic community structures and associations (Castles and Miller 1993; 121).

and still are, regularly attacked in various public discourses as unfairly favouring one segment of society.[5] Support for Australian multiculturalism and its impact on institutions varied over time and with changes of government.

Opinion polling in the late 1980s suggests that about half the population agreed (with multiculturalism) while half did not. Assimilationist attitudes were much stronger than overt racism. Strongest feelings were towards Muslims, Arabs and Vietnamese, while previously rejected groups such as Chinese, Jews or Aborigines were viewed more tolerantly than in the past. The inheritance of White Australia was undoubtedly still present. But it did not manifest itself in organised or political racism, despite the debates of the 1980s (Castles 1995; 106).

By the mid 1980s, during the Hawke Labor Government's first term in office, reservations about multicultural policies and funding allocations began to be expressed more broadly and vociferously. Some analysts have interpreted these actions as part of the promotion of a 'new' nationalism (Dorais, Foster and Stockley, 1994; 385). The derogatory use of the term; 'multicultural industry' was coined during this period, casting activities and funding allocated to immigrant communities with the pallor of corruption, while simultaneously de-legitimising the institutionalised processes of multiculturalism. Debate had moved away from the earlier consensus on the desirability of extensive immigration programmes toward a growing anxiety over Asian immigration (Inglis et. al. 1994; 15). In 1988, John Howard as Opposition Leader, attacked multiculturalism and in particular Asian immigration. This followed the lead of prominent historian Geoffrey Blainey who had earlier called for immigration restrictions and in particular warned of an 'Asianisation of Australia'; sentiments which received widespread support across the political spectrum. Blainey and other figures such as Frank Knopfelmacher criticised multiculturalism as a recipe for future social disunity and national fragmentation. Other critics of multiculturalism from the political left, on the other hand, pointed to the policy initiatives of both the Fraser Government and its successor, the Hawke Government, as a distraction from more serious social reforms needed for all Australians, no matter their ethnic background (Lack and Templeton 1995; 220).[6]

---

[5] Galbally had noted in his report which was confirmed in a 1982 review, that he found major problems present within public agencies other than those dealing directly with immigrants in recognizing the changing needs of the public they were providing with services. He made particular mention of employment programmes, as well as heath, welfare, education, womens' services and aged care (Jupp 1992, p.134). This situation has somewhat since changed, at least partly as a result of the lobbying as well as educative role of the NGOs who work with immigrants, refugees and asylum seekers. There have been numerous initiatives in the form of training for instance directed specifically at government service providers such as housing and health care, many of whom were largely unaware of the specific needs of refugees.

[6] At least in part, this debate over Asian immigration was grounded in Australia's geopolitical and economic location as a European nation.

Emphasising the economic and social benefits of multiculturalism, the Hawke Labor Government launched the *National Agenda for a Multicultural Australia* in 1989. The *National Agenda* outlines multiculturalism as a system of rights and freedoms, tempered by a commitment to the nation, an acceptance of the Constitution and the rule of law. Rather than defining multiculturalism as cultural pluralism, or minority rights, this new approach centres on the cultural, social and economic rights of all citizens in a democratic state, emphasising a citizenship model of multiculturalism rather than an ethnic group model. The successive Liberal Government of John Howard, has endorsed the principles of the *National Agenda*, including the three dimensions of multicultural policy: cultural identity, social justice and economic efficiency ('The Evolution of Australia's Multicultural Policies' DIMA, June, 1998).

Australian multiculturalism in the main, has been conceived as pertaining to 'ethnic' immigrants, excluding both white British immigrants and Aborigines from the discourses on cultural diversity. While the *National Agenda* admits, the place of indigenous Australians is crucial to a valuable discussion of multiculturalism – that debate has yet to fully flourish in Australia (Vasta and Castles 1996; 50).

Clearly, immigration and multicultural policies have never been without controversy, with vociferous public debates over levels of immigration, the cost of services, selection of immigrants and the social impact of cultural pluralism:

> The public debate frequently takes on racist overtones, evoking spectres of being 'swamped' by mass immigration from Asia. Although there are no riots (like in Britain) and little organised racist violence (as in Germany), there is considerable evidence of racism, taking the form of abuse, harassment and even physical violence, particularly against Asians. Multiculturalism still has a long way to go before it secures universal support (Castles 1996; 269).

In his first term in office as Prime Minister, John Howard rejected the view that Australia had a racist past, accusing educators of giving children a misguided view of Australian history:

> I sympathise fundamentally with Australians who are insulted when they are told that we have a racist, bigoted past . . . Australians are told that quite regularly. Our children are taught that . . . some of the school curricula go close to teaching children that we have a racist, bigoted past. Of course we treated Aboriginals very, very badly in the past - very, very badly - but to tell children whose parents were no part of that maltreatment, to tell children who themselves have been no part of it, that we're all part of a sort of racist, bigoted history is something that Australians reject (SMH October 25, 1996; 1).

The rise of the One Nation Party, after the election of Pauline Hanson in March 1996 as the federal member for the seat of Ipswich, gathered significant support for anti-immigration and particularly anti-Asian immigration policies. Pauline Hanson called for the abolition of multiculturalism and a halt to the 'special treatment' given to indigenous Australians.[7]

Whether or not the use of the term multiculturalism survives its many critics is ultimately of debatable significance. However, the tolerance for cultural, ethnic and religious difference and the due recognition of such difference in various institutions of the state is critical on a number of fronts. Australia is, alongside Canada and the U.S., a country with large numbers of immigrants who have been permitted, at times encouraged, to maintain their cultural particularities and distinctions. Having been well established, and comprehensively institutionalised over more than two decades, the policy outcomes of multiculturalism are facing a renewed attack from significant segments of Australian society. Germany on the other hand, remains resistant to the language of multiculturalism, while moving closer to mechanisms of positive integration.

Practices of inclusion or exclusion are institutionalised by the state in concrete policies aimed variously at either a positive and efficient settlement (inclusive); or at barriers for newcomers to ensure the existing social and economic order (exclusive); or more often, a differential mix of inclusive and exclusive policy. The impetus to include or exclude also emerges from a variety of reference points in social exchanges, and the embedding in culture of those exchanges over time. The White Australia Policy was able to be maintained for seventy-two years only through a legitimisation in several succeeding generations of support for overtly discriminatory practices. No doubt, the assimilationist attitudes and policies which stemmed from the White Australia Policy, established a prevailing attitude which views people from a non Anglo background as outsiders. While an institutional framework for positive multiculturalism has provided a comprehensive acceptance of these newcomers as Australians, the extent to which multiculturalism has touched the bedrock of white, Anglo Australian attitudes to newcomers from diverse cultural and ethnic backgrounds is open to debate. Hage suggests that some supporters of multiculturalism, particularly those from the dominant culture (Anglos), are practising a tolerance which operates only from a dominant position (1998; 86-87). A 'strategy of condescension', is the process whereby the dominant group symbolically deny the social distance (inequality) which exists between them and the newcomer. In this way support for multiculturalism is a covert protection of one's own relative power/position through a bracketing-off of the newcomer to a recognisable position:

> . . . it seems that the ones who are concerned by the call to tolerate can only be the *same people* who feel entitled to engage in intolerance: those we have analysed as belonging to the White dominant culture. When the request 'Tolerate!' is made, only those who

[7] Pauline Hanson's political career and the fate of her 'Pauline Hanson's One Nation Party' seemed to be in rapid decline after the November 2001 federal election with support in decline from near 10 percent to 4.2 per cent. Pauline Hanson failed to win a Senate seat and was, at least temporarily outside the political system (SMH November 12, 2001; 8E).

> recognise in themselves the capacity not to tolerate are likely to raise their heads (Hage 1998; 88)

Charles Taylor situates multiculturalism within a politics of 'recognition' (1994), with recognition marking the way in which social actors negotiate the politics of inclusion and exclusion through various mediations and filtering mechanisms, where only select others are offered recognition and thereby inclusion. Similarly, the connection between recognition and meaningful reflexivity is the ability to inspect oneself critically and be able to choose actions and recognise their consequences (Calhoun 1995; 198). It follows then, that to enhance inclusion, a model which encourages multiple entry points and possibilities for reflexivity is preferable. Such a model can be expected to enhance self knowledge as well as improve the receptiveness to develop knowledge about others. Importantly, it is not only minorities who are to be recognised, but in the process of broadening the 'base' of recognition, the original members may be challenged to re-recognise themselves. Perhaps an unintended consequence of inclusive recognition, is the need for a reappraisal of the original, or dominant community. Exactly this need for re-recognition of oneself seems to be a stumbling-block to a broad acceptance of multiculturalism in Germany, where a generous intake of foreigners on the one hand, is countered on the other by a reified and brittle representation of German identity, resistant to the malleability and openness which cultural diversity demands. The extent to which multiculturalism is an accepted part of Australian society is also being renegotiated in a world terrified by the spectre of terrorism in a new way since 2001.

A variety of conceptions of how 'identities' and 'difference' is understood constitute the various *habitus[es]* within which the dual process of recognition and re-recognition takes place. Newcomers and their advocates must articulate needs and requests for incorporation into the nation, while the receiver society filters their perceptions of and interactions with newcomers through institutionalised processes of recognition. Multiculturalism remains both an idea and a mechanism by which recognition of difference and a balance between the needs and aspirations of multiple cultures living within one nation-state, or indeed across borders, can be struck:

> Uncoupled from its associations with unbridgeable, absolute difference and reconfigured with a wider sense of the unevenly developed power of sub national (local) and supranational relations, multiculturalism can force nationalisms and biosocial explanations of race and ethnicity into more defensive postures (Gilroy 2000; 244).

Tolerance of the 'other' may be espoused, while essentially changing nothing – or very little – about the location of power: '. . . White Australians are cast in the role of governing subjects . . . where the non-White other is a passive object (Hage 1998; 96).

If the traditional ideological function of nationalism is to unite a country around some fundamental characteristics, or historical memories, which defines the nation and who.is *in* and *out* of an 'imagined community', then it can be argued that multiculturalism as idea and later policy, has been able to make incursions into the orthodoxy of Australian 'national values' which have tended to emphasise Anglo early settlers and their offspring as the builders and architects of the nation, by reference drawing exclusionary boundaries around others (Castles et. al. 1988).

Let us turn now to consider Australian identity and the integration of newcomers through citizenship.

## Identity and belonging

Most countries in the late twentieth century have populations representing a variety of ethnic, cultural and religious groups. This is particularly true of countries in which immigration has played a significant role in the development of the nation. A country with ethnic, cultural and religious diversity must find ways of 'managing' such difference and must make decisions regarding the formal and informal processes of inclusion, or exclusion of newcomers. The motivations for recruiting migrants are highlighted in the contradictions between residents (without full rights) and citizens (Jupp 1993). In Australia, in distinction from Germany, the acquisition of citizenship by new immigrants is encouraged as a social 'good'. The qualifying period for citizenship is two years permanent residency. Immigrants are encouraged to take out Australian citizenship in what has been a bipartisan approach to full formal inclusion. Immigration up to the late 1980s saw primarily permanent resettlement of newcomers. From this period, indications are that there has been a surge in temporary migration; primarily skilled migrants and students who enter temporarily to acquire new skills and experience without the intention of settling permanently (Davidson 1997; 153). Until the introduction of a Temporary Protection Visa (TPV) in 1999, Australia's refugee intake was also premised almost exclusively on permanent settlement of individuals entering Australia under protection obligations. The effects of the TPV will be discussed later. The focus of immigration policies and quotas set by both the Labor and Liberal/National coalition governments in recent years has been on economic development and the role that skilled foreign workers, and foreign students (who must pay full university fees) can play in strengthening the Australian economy.

Identity, displayed in the meanings attached to national belonging, embedded in culture and in the formal citizenship conferred to members of a polity, form part of the context within which refugees and those seeking protection must conduct themselves. Although formally the international protection mechanism takes no account of the particularities of different countries who comply with protection obligations, there can be no doubt that the variations in formal and informal mechanisms of belonging between nations have a considerable impact on a refugee's day to day experience during a determination process. That is, their everyday living circumstances as 'foreigners' can be expected to be 'softened' and mediated by a variety of established practices that reflect tolerance in a multicultural society.

Australia does not have a clear-cut foundational moment, such as the American Declaration of Independence, or a 'historical turn' such as the French Revolution, or the National Socialist rule in Germany. That is not to say that there were not moments and events of enormous significance in the period since 1788 – the arrival of the First Fleet – but rather that Australians have no sustained, collective memory defining the nation. Perhaps the federation of Australia in 1901 would be named as one such moment by historians; or perhaps the spirit of the Anzacs who fought under British command with valour in World War I. The extent to which these, or any other particular events or moments in Australian history denote common and shared memories is however debatable.

In the case of U.S.A, religion served as a hegemonic and unifying force, granting a certain homogeneity to a diverse population, as well as the significant affirmations of a strong republic which had been built 'from below'. Australia, in contrast, as an immigrant society established 'from above', lacks common, unifying memories which can be said to *bind* across the society. In popular usage the ideal of egalitarianism, expressed as 'mateship', is understood to cut across class, race and ethnicity in promoting shared experiences and attributes, rather than differences. Australian multiculturalism may be thought to run parallel to this egalitarian ethos. Largely, though, 'mateship' is a decidedly masculine national myth, built on unstable foundations. Mateship grew from the memories of the early settlers as pioneers in a harsh environment. It is an exclusive concept, excluding particularly Aborigines and women. Doubtless, Australian identity has expanded in the multiplicity of meanings encompassed in what it is to be Australian; particularly resulting from immigration. However the acceptance of multiple identities and of diversity *per se*, remains as 'unfixed' as the identities themselves.

Before discussing the situation of refugees and asylum seekers in detail, let me revisit once again, the issue of refugee discourse within the general immigration framework. Although I maintain that the overall immigration system, the public perception of it, and its impact on the host society are fundamental factors in the reception of refugees and asylum seekers, it must also be remembered in what ways migration and refugee issues diverge. The decision to accept migrants, whether for permanent resettlement, or as short-term workers, is an aspect of state activity, influenced by a range of domestic factors including the economy, the labour market, and the social impact of immigration. The active recruitment of immigrants can be administered and controlled in an ordered and predetermined way which does not challenge nation-state sovereignty, but rather, enhances it. The intake of refugees, particularly spontaneous arrivals who claim asylum, intersects with the state's international obligations – and in principle should not be subject to domestic considerations. However, in the case of refugee resettlement countries, such as Australia, this principle is to some extent compromised. The United Nations High Commissioner for Refugees (UNHCR) organises resettlement of refugees in co-operation with countries which volunteer places for individuals who have been found to meet the criteria of the *Refugee Convention.* Refugee resettlement has generally been subsumed in public discourse in Australia under the general rubric of the yearly immigration quota. This 'humanitarian programme' has thereby been quarantined from controversy and has been supported in a bi-partisan fashion.

Australia operates immigration policy under a yearly quota system, whereby the government sets a numerical target for the various categories of immigrants who are to be considered for entry in the following year. Apart from quotas for skilled workers, business migration, and a family reunion quota, yearly quotas have, over the past decade, consistently set aside around 12,000 places for the 'humanitarian' intake, which comprises various categories of refugees, or people in 'refugee-like' situations.[8] Over recent years, a community consultation process has preceded the setting of this yearly quota – giving community groups, and NGOs a platform to advocate their positions, as well as engaging with government on areas of concern. The Refugee Council of Australia (RCOA), puts forward a detailed case each year for refugee and humanitarian intakes based upon changes in international conflicts and detailed country information of changing refugee situations. Asylum seeker arrivals have been tied to the yearly immigration and humanitarian quota since 1996/7, setting an artificial cap for the number of asylum seekers able to be accommodated in the programme in any given year.[9] The number of such 'unauthorised arrivals' is thereby pegged to the humanitarian programme (people selected 'off-shore'), with the result that as the number of asylum seekers successful in their applications exceed the quota set aside, the corresponding numbers from humanitarian places offered that year are 'knocked off' the quota.[10]

---

[8] The Humanitarian Programme consists of three main categories: Refugee, Special Humanitarian and Special Assistance. In addition, in 1989, a new category; 'Women at Risk', was added to the refugee component for women who were deemed to be in particularly vulnerable situations. Between July 1989 and June 1997, 2,222 'Women at Risk' visas were issued (DIMA 1997; 14). The establishment of the 'Women at Risk' category was established after long-standing and determined advocacy by Australian NGOs.

[9] This numerical link - though officially not having an absolute ceiling, is nevertheless at least a potential psychological barrier to processing officers aware that a certain 'absorption level' has been preset.

[10] The Australian Government has not given any clear indications how it would proceed should the number of spontaneous arrivals exceed the total humanitarian quota.

## The treatment of refugees and asylum seekers

The arbitration on refugees and asylum seekers entering a nation, whether for short-term protection, or permanent resettlement, intersects with the fundamental concepts of membership of a nation and how boundaries of meaning for people are constituted through identity-formation processes and through formal citizenship, as already discussed in chapter one. The contemporary refugee 'crisis' or 'problem', is complex and many-faceted, both in the origins, as well as in possible solutions to various crises. The large and growing number of individuals who are outside their country of origin and in need of protection, heightens the question of how goods are allocated in a global context: not only the allocation of economic goods, but the allocation of a scarce good internationally; membership in a prosperous and democratic state (Adelman 1994: 65). This dilemma requires that a concept of justice be articulated which transcends and prefigures the particular social, political and economic circumstances of a nation-state. Refugee and asylum policy can be expected, from a justice perspective, to reflect much broader concerns than those of national interest. What does Australian refugee and asylum policy tell us about the nation? In addition, arbitration on the forms of inclusion or exclusion of newcomers is generally legitimate for a nation-state under the guiding principle of sovereignty, embodying national interest and integrity over influences outside the nation. However, an obligation which defies national borders exists for individuals who seek protection under the *Refugee Convention.* In other words, if an individual is a refugee, then there is an obligation to include that person at least until such time as the threat from which she sought refuge has disappeared. The dilemma increasingly to be faced by asylum seekers, is the burden of proof; being in a position to substantiate a claim for protection within the legal framework of a particular state which is a signatory to the *Refugee Convention.* While I have already discussed the situation asylum seekers face in Germany, I now turn to a brief overview of refugee arrivals in Australia after 1945, before exploring developments in asylum policy and the response of NGOs during the 1990s.

It was particularly in the post-war period after 1945, that the needs of refugee entrants as a specific group of immigrants emerged with the resettlement of refugees and displaced person from Europe.[11] Camps, later known as 'hostels', were used for refugees as well as other arrivals. Early refugee arrivals in the post-1945 period,[12] experienced at times harsh resettlement processes not least due to

---

[11] In 1938 shortly after the annexation of Austria, President Roosevelt convened a conference of 20 nations at Evian in France. The conference was convened to seek solutions to the refugee problem in Europe. Australia offered to accept 15,000 Jewish refugees from Germany and the Sudetenland. In the months before the outbreak of war, 7,500 arrived in Australia, the rest being unable to flee (Hawkins, 1989,165).

[12] Australia received displaced persons and refugees after World War Two, numbering some 170,000; the Hungarian refugee movements of 1956-7, where 14,000 were settled; the

the lack of recognition given to professional credentials, training and expertise (Martin 1965). Many of these early refugees had professions and were highly skilled, yet were regarded as manual labourers by the government. This development reflected a 'two tier' pattern of immigration, with British immigrants immune from the conditions and constraints which refugee arrivals faced. The British arrivals were able to compete with locals for jobs and houses, unlike other new arrivals, who were required to take particular types of work. Such distinctions created a tier of 'second class citizen', premised on ethnicity rather than on qualifications or ability (Collins, 1988,56). By the early 1970s, Australia was not involved to any significant extent in international efforts to settle refugees, nor was it affected by spontaneous arrivals, 'on-shore'. It was in mid 1975 that the first groups of Indochinese refugees began arriving in Australia, having been selected from refugee camps in Thailand. The 'first wave' of refugees to arrive in Australia by boat reached Australia's northern and north western shores in April 1976. By 1979, 2,011 boat people had arrived (Hawkins, 1989,173). Between 1975 and 1984 some 90,000 predominantly Vietnamese refugees were resettled in Australia (Collins 1988, 60). In March 1978, that the Fraser Government established the Determination of Refugee Status Committee (DORS) to consider applications for protection. Even though many of these 'first wave' of asylum seekers arrived on boats, they were not classified as 'unauthorised arrivals' and became the first significant group of Asians to arrive in Australia since the end of the White Australia Policy. This indicated the successful transition to more open, non-discriminatory approaches to newcomers (Viviani 1984; 114). During this period Australia was one of the leading countries of admission of Indochinese refugees in the period 1975-1985, as indicated in Figure 4.1.

**Table 4.1 Leading countries of Admission of Indochinese Refugees, 1975-1985**

| Country | Number admitted |
|---|---|
| USA | 583,049 |
| People's Republic of China | 262,853 |
| Canada | 98,424 |
| France | 97,827 |
| Australia | 96,262 |

*Source:* UNHCR (in Hawkins 1989; 182)

It has been the response to boat people and 'unauthorised' air arrivals arriving since 1989, which has raised concerns about Australia's standards of refugee

Czech refugee movement of 1968 with some 5,000 refugees (Hawkins, 1989,165) and the Polish Solidarity activists who arrived during the 1980s.

protection under international obligations. The 'second wave' of boat arrivals from November 1989, marks a departure in the Australian approach to boat arrivals and illegal arrivals more generally. This period was rapidly followed by a 'third' and then 'fourth' wave of boat arrivals. The 'third wave', from 1994 to 1997, constituted primarily Sino-Vietnamese and Chinese arrivals. The 'fourth wave' began in 1999, with the arrival of Iranian, Afghani and Iraqi 'boat people'. All but the first wave of boat arrivals have been subject to mandatory and non-reviewable detention. The bi-partisan support of mandatory detention continues to have a significant bearing on the public acceptance of this policy. The policy and practice of mandatory detention had been contested in a relatively narrow public debate until the lead-up to the so-called *Tampa* incident, of August 2001. The most recent developments surrounding the opening of new detention facilities, notably at Woomera in 1999, and the *Tampa* incident, have led to unprecedented scrutiny of Australia's treatment of asylum seekers and detention policy both domestically and internationally. These developments are detailed in chapter six with an analysis of detention policy.

I now consider in more detail the asylum procedures in Australia and the actions of NGOs who advocate for the rights of asylum seekers.

## The asylum process: legal procedure and social entitlements

The refugee component of the yearly immigration intake has been an important feature of Australia's immigration programme.[13] To a large degree the 'off-shore' refugee intake has remained out of public contention, as previously stated. NGOs have, over time, built strong links with government and bureaucracy in the area of refugee resettlement, evident in a relatively high level of co-operation. Refugee resettlement in Australia has been accompanied by a comprehensive system of refugee-specific services and initiatives, many of which have their origin in the efforts of NGOs. Asylum seekers are able to draw on some, but by no means all, of these services while they remain non-residents and non-citizens during a determination period. 'Off-shore' arrivals are provided with resettlement services under the Integrated Humanitarian Settlement Strategy, which identifies specific services.[14] Certainly with regard to the provision of resettlement services to

---

[13] The institutional recognition of the distinction in needs between refugees and migrants led to the creation of a Refugee and Humanitarian section within the Department of Immigration (DIMIA).

[14] The services offered to refugees under the 'off-shore' programme include: ***Information and Orientation Assistance***, helping refugees to make links to essential services such as income support; ***Medicare***, the Australian universal health cover scheme; education and training and employment services; accommodation support, which provides interim accommodation and assists with finding long-term accommodation; household formation, which helps in establishing a household with provision of basic items; early assessment and

refugees, the Australian case is markedly distinct from the German case, where specific services and programmes for refugees are not well developed by the state and where NGOs tend to focus on the needs of asylum seekers who are still awaiting a determination of their status.

As stated earlier, the 'on-shore' asylum seekers, arriving without authorisation, have become an issue of concern for the federal government since 1989. While in 1989, the number of claims for asylum was just over 500, in 1990 there were over 12,000 applicants. Most of these applicants were Chinese students already in Australia on student visas at the time of the suppression of the democracy movement in the People's Republic of China, in 1989. Even though statistically this dramatic rise in applicants in 1990/91 was due to specific political developments, nevertheless, it caused major upheaval to the planned and controlled approach of the immigration bureaucracy. However, rather than constituting an unpredictable 'crisis', as is true of the spontaneous arrivals in Europe, the issue of the Chinese students was a departure, though a momentary one, from established protocols of refugee determination. Rather than being assessed on a case-by-case basis, in June 1990 the Hawke Government granted permanent residence status to 27,359 Chinese students who had arrived before 21 June 1989, as a 'special group'. This decision has been robustly criticised as creating an asylum crisis where none existed (Nicholls 1998; 63). During this same period, several hundred Cambodian boat people who had arrived in 1989-91, were condemned by Prime Minister Hawke as 'queue jumpers and 'economic refugees'. As will be explored later, this development has had long-term repercussions for asylum applicants in Australia. Apart from such domestic political developments, the illegal trafficking and smuggling of people, which is a phenomenon that has gathered pace since the period around 1989, has accentuated the dilemma for those asylum seekers with a just claim, as well as for governments seeking to meet their obligations. People are smuggled across national borders for often large sums of money, and smugglers are known to sell 'refugee stories', likely to meet the *Refugee Convention* requirements. The twin problem created by this phenomenon is that on the one hand, it heightens the fear of incursions on sovereignty and on the other hand, once an asylum seekers' claim is labelled fraudulent, unbelievable, or inconsistent, the likelihood of success on a second hearing or appeal seem to be diminished.

As I have already noted, due to Australia's relative geographic isolation, travelling to Australia either by sea or by air is a lengthy and often costly undertaking. In addition, the lack of appropriate travel documentation, can result in

---

intervention, which provides services to refugees with physical or psychological health problems; community support, with a register of volunteers, who can provide support as well as raising community awareness of refugee experiences. Providers of these services, through DIMIA initiated and controlled tendering processes include; NSW Migrant Resource Centres, ANGLICARE, St Vincent de Paul Society, the Service for the Treatment of Rehabilitation of Torture and Trauma Survivors (STARTTS) and other torture and trauma counselling and community development services.

immediate removal, unless judicious claims for protection which are seen to engage Australia's obligations under the *Refugee Convention* are able to be articulated to airport or border officials.[15] NGOs have consistently expressed unease and dismay at the initial screening process which takes place both at detention centres and airports;

> Only people who tell a story that obviously fits within the Refugee Convention are allowed to apply for refugee status. For example, people who speak of fear, torture, or of being hunted will be screened in, while those who say simply that they want a future for their children could be screened out. This has caused concerns that immigration officials are failing to recognise refugees who have not spoken up about their claims. Many asylum seekers are also suspicious of authority figures because they have been ill-treated by the authorities in their own countries (Crock and Saul 2002; 54).

Border arrivals ('on-shore' asylum seekers) are not automatically given information about the determination process and in many cases have little or no idea of the significance of what they are saying. In detention centres, new arrivals are initially kept apart (*incommunicado*) from other detainees as part of this pre-screening process.

Kerry Murphy, a Sydney lawyer and previously researcher for the Jesuit Refugee Service (JRS) Australia, expressed concern about the lack of public scrutiny of the screening process of border claimants and particularly of the process of 'airport turn-arounds':

> I think there is a policy of deterrence and interdicting arrivals before they can even enter Australia. There are [Australian] immigration officers in overseas posts, checking people who board planes for Australia. 'Forward defence' is what we called it in the Vietnam War, and we're using the same policy in terms of people coming here now (Interview No. 39).

The law firm which Murphy works for, has handled several Federal Court injunctions to halt deportations. The problem remains how an individual claimant can receive independent advice or alert a third party to his/her predicament. In a submission to the Senate Legal and constitutional References Committee with regard to turning potential refugees away at the border, lawyer, Nicholas Poynder states:

> There is a strong suspicion amongst refugee advocates that genuine asylum seekers are routinely being 'turned around' at the border. This suspicion is supported by the example of a Sri Lankan man who arrived at Sydney Airport in July 1998 . . . [and]

[15] From 1 July, 2000, the fine to be paid by airlines who carry arrivals to Australia rises from $3000 to $5000 for each individual without a passport and relevant visa.

claimed to have been displaced due to the war in Sir Lanka, that he was forced to work by the Liberation Tigers of Tamil Eelam (LTTE) and that if he was returned to Sri Lanka he faced persecution by the Sir Lankan Army forces because of his Tamil ethnicity and his perceived involvement with the LTTE. The airport officer's notes . . make disturbing reading:

> (Senior DIMA [sic] official) consulted at approx 2000 hrs. Story put to him – he stated that prima facie, pax did not provide sufficient info to engage our protection obligations. Pax informed of decision thru Tamil interp at 2015 hrs. ACM (Australian Correctional Management) collected his at 2025 hrs. QF 125 flight at 1230 hrs.

It was only the fact the man's relatives were on the other side of the airport border control – and were able to alert lawyers to get an injunction to prevent his removal – that the man was able to enter Australia and apply for refugee status. He was granted asylum by a Departmental officer at first instance [primary stage] (Submission No 35. 18 June 1999).

Amnesty International (AI) has also expressed concern regarding the practice of 'turning around' persons at airports to whom Australia may have obligations (Amnesty International, AI Index: AUS/POL/REF 1998;19). The treatment of border claimants has been highlighted in a report by the Australian Auditor-General (1998). In assessing DIMIA's entry screening processes the report notes: 'there is a risk to DIMA [sic] that the screening process will be perceived as de facto refugee determination system which lacks important features of the actual refugee determination system such as the provision of assistance to the applicant and the availability of administrative and judicial review' (point 6.38). Although this report focuses on boat arrivals, pre-screening and removal processes are relevant to all unauthorised arrivals - whether by sea or air.[16]

All persons who want to avail themselves of Australia's protection obligations must apply for a Protection Visa. In the first instance, an application is processed by DIMIA in what is known as a *primary* decision. From the mid 1990s, the fast-tracking of *primary* decisions, has meant that the majority of claimants are not interviewed as part of this process. An independent tribunal for the review of refugee claims, the Refugee Review Tribunal (RRT), established in July 1993, grants protection visa applicants the right to appeal a primary decision with an oral

---

[16] In addition to the Auditor-General's report, the last ten years has seen a number of major government reviews of Australia's refugee and humanitarian systems by the Australian Senate and by HREOC. The reviews and inquiries have come about for variety of reasons, though all reflect a growing level of public anxiety, about the management and administration of Australia's refugee programme. Complaints procedures under the HREOC guidelines have instigated the HREOC inquiries. The overwhelming concern and focus of these reports related to the treatment of unauthorised arrivals subject to detention. I discuss the substance of these reports in chapter seven.

hearing of their claim in a non-adversarial setting.[17] The Minister for Immigration is also invested with the power of *ministerial discretion* in humanitarian cases, though the appeals to the Minister must first have been heard by the RRT. Until recent legislative changes following the *Tampa* incident which are discussed later, appeals to an RRT decision were able to be made to the Federal Court in relation only to misinterpretations by RRT members on points of law in relation to the *Refugee Convention*.

Let us consider briefly the social and economic circumstances of those pursuing protection claims in Australia. Asylum seekers who live in the community have access to only limited legal advice unless they have the means to pay for their own immigration advice, while those in detention are given access to a government funded lawyer once they have been 'screened in' to a protection process. The Immigration Advice and Application Assistance Scheme (IAAAS)[18] grants assistance to asylum seekers only if their case has 'merit', if they are in financial hardship or have suffered torture or trauma (DIMIA Fact Sheet 70).[19] One of the major hurdles faced by asylum seekers who live in the community, is meeting their everyday social, economic and health needs. The majority of those living in the community are granted little or no government assistance, relying on the major charities and church groups for their basic needs. Customarily, they have little or no access to Medicare (the universal health care scheme); and, after the imposition of the '45 day rule', have very limited access to work, as an application must be submitted within 45 days of arrival in Australia. In the main, it is the myriad of regulations and time limits that govern eligibility criteria for government assistance which have the effect of 'screening out' the majority of asylum seekers for government assistance. For instance, eligibility for the Asylum Seeker's Assistance Scheme (ASAS), administered by the Red Cross with federal government funding, is premised upon a waiting period of six months after arrival in Australia, and is available only while at the primary stage of a protection claim. Since the mid 1990s, the primary decision-making processes have been fast-tracked, with a decision usually taken within three months.

[17] An asylum seeker must lodge an application for review of a primary decision with the RRT within seven working days after notification of a primary decision has been given where the applicant is in detention and 28 days in all other cases. The RRT is given no discretion to hear cases outside this time limit which grossly disadvantages many asylum seekers facing not just language difficulties but also unfamiliarity with the legal system (Taylor 2000; 39-40).

[18] Under the IAAAS Scheme contracts for advice and assistance are granted by DIMA to private law firms, private migration agents, NGOs and legal aid commissions through a competitive tendering process in operation since late 1997.

[19] From the 1st July 1998, legal aid funding was no longer available in making protection visa applications at the primary or RRT stage.

## East Timorese asylum seekers: a special case

One group of asylum seekers who generated particular attention and support within the Australian community through the 1990s were East Timorese. Some 1,650 East Timorese fled to Australia where they sought protection; many after the Santa Cruz massacre in Dili on November 12, 1991, when the Indonesian military fired on a peaceful protest which had formed after a funeral. These asylum seekers had been waiting for a determination of their status for between five and ten years as the Australian government sought to have them apply for refugee status in Portugal as the former colonial power of East Timor. Most of this group remained stalled at the 'primary' stage of decision-making, with the constant threat of imminent deportation. Australia's foreign policy ties with Indonesia were an additional factor in the government's reluctance to grant refugee status to East Timorese. In the case of East Timorese asylum seekers as in so many other areas of refugee policy, a bi-partisan approach is evident:

> Back in 1995, the Shadow Minister for Foreign Affairs, Mr Alexander Downer, appeared sympathetic to the asylum seekers' case. 'Not one of the 1300 East Timorese asylum seekers . . . is by any stretch of Mr Keating's vivid imagination a Portuguese citizen.' Now in Government, however, the Liberals argue as Labor did. To Mr Ruddock the case turns on whether asylum seekers can find protection in any other country. 'It is not a matter of choosing where you want to be a refugee.' (*The Age*, May 3, 1997; 24).

A 'sanctuary' network, similar to the Germany case of church asylum, evolved by the end of 1995, from the Catholic organisations which worked most closely for the East Timorese in providing social services and other forms of support. A network of some 15,000 people around Australia evolved with a large number of 'safe houses' which could be activated in the case of an imminent deportation. Sister Kath O'Conner of *Christians in Solidarity with East Timor*, describes the evolution of the sanctuary movement:

> The first thing I did about the church sanctuary movement was to go to the Timorese community. They go through their network and leaders here of course, are in close contact with the leaders in East Timor and the underground movement. We never do anything here in Australia in isolation, without the leaders in Timor knowing about it and getting their approval. They were thrilled that there was going to be a stand made. The could not believe that the (Australian ) government was going to do that to them (the asylum seekers); send them to Portugal. That threw them. But really the movement evolved day by day. As people saw it in the news they rang and said they wanted to be in the movement; parishes, unions, members of the Green Party and Independents, teachers (Interview No. 32).

By September 1998 a Full Bench of the Federal Court of Australia had rejected the government's argument that the East Timorese should apply for protection in

Portugal (SMH September 24, 1998; 9). The violence that followed elections in East Timor in August of 1999, resulted in the application of temporary safe haven status to the East Timorese. Before the Australian Government intervened in East Timor in September of 1999, with the sending military troops, some of the largest mass demonstrations in support of East Timor independence from Indonesian rule took place in all the capital cities of Australia.

## Temporary safe-havens and the Kosovars

During 1999, as the humanitarian crisis of displaced ethnic Albanians in Kosovo led to an international evacuation plan. After initial reluctance, the Australian government agreed in April 1999, to give temporary asylum under new 'safe haven' legislation, to 4,000 Kosovars, bearing the cost of airlifting them to Australia, and providing for their needs during an initial three-month temporary stay which could be extended if necessary. The Howard Government agreed to the airlift of the Kosovars after initially declaring that such a move would be an inappropriate response, as Australia was not in the region of the conflict. Both Prime Minister Howard and Immigration Minister, Ruddock, argued that countries in the region were best placed to meet the needs of the Kosovars.[20] However, public opinion in Australia reflected a strong desire for Australia to respond in a more practical fashion. Commentators drew a connection between the eventual 'policy back flip' which saw 4,000 Kosovars given temporary asylum in Australia,and public opinion which had expressed concern over the 'mean spiritedness' of the government (SMH April 7, 1999). Estimates suggest that the total cost of bringing the 4,000 Kosovars to Australia to be $100 million (SMH May 9, 2000). In contrast, boat people who arrived during the same period, seeking to invoke Australia's protection obligations, met with a renewed focus on tightening legislation, accompanied by a renewed and vigourous campaign of public denouncements of illegal arrivals as 'queue jumpers', associating them with criminal activities. In fact at the same time as Kosovars were being welcomed, asylum seekers from other parts of the world aroused public hysteria, portrayed in headlines such as 'Blitz on boat people. Rush to tighten laws as 10,000 head this way'(SMH November 16, 1999; 1).

The 'safe haven' agreement stuck for Kosovar refugees was a 12-month agreement, which all Kosovars were required to sign, agreeing to the temporary nature of their stay in Australia. The Kosovars began to return voluntarily in September 1999 and the majority had returned by April 2000. Around 10 percent

---

[20] The RCOA's position in relation to the Kosovar refugees was also that a regional response would better serve these people, and that the cost of airlifting 4,000 Kosovars was disproportional to what measures could be undertaken within Europe with such funds.

felt unsafe to return and wanted to make their stay in Australia permanent.[21] Of this group, 82 were later allowed to return to Australia as permanent residents sponsored by community groups (Crock and Saul 2002; 111). Two issues are particularly noteworthy in relation to the case of the Kosovar refugees: first, the generous community support; and second, the disproportionality of response to this refugee crises compared to other cases. The 4,000 Kosovars were accommodated in public facilities, such as vacant army barracks, in numerous locations around Australia. Local communities in close proximity to these facilities volunteered their time, and gave toys, clothing and social support to the Kosovars throughout their stay in Australia. Many of these same communities sponsored Kosovars' return to Australia on a permanent basis. At the same time, the public response to other asylum seekers, particularly those arriving by boat, was markedly negative.[22]

## A new strategy of deterrence

One of the most significant changes in recent years to the status of individuals found to be genuine refugees, is the introduction in October, 1999, of a Temporary Protection Visa (TPV, Visa Subclass 785). This change focuses on the documentary validity of entry to Australia as the determinant of the visa an individual may be granted once s/he has been found to be a refugee. The TPV grants a three-year temporary status, during which time no family reunion or access to other significant resettlement programmes is available. A TPV means an individual has no automatic right of return upon leaving Australia and restricted access to resettlement services and medical care.[23] On the other hand, those persons who arrive in Australia with valid travel documents and subsequently apply for refugee status, face an often arduous task in proving the legitimacy of their claims. That is, the *bona fides* of asylum seekers living in the community as individuals who have escaped some form of persecution may be called into question even before the particulars of their situation can be investigated, as they were in a safe enough position to avail themselves of travel documents from their

[21] The UN representative in Kosovo during the period of the refugee return in late 1999, Dr Bernhard Kouchner, was critical of the speed of return of Kosovar refugees before appropriate conditions and infrastructure had been established. Australia was the first of the countries which had hosted Kosovars on a temporary basis to insist on their return (SBS Dateline, 3rd May, 2000). Australian refugee NGOs also argued vociferously that local infrastructure could not yet support the returnees. A number of follow up visits by NGOs as well by Australian media indicate that the returnees are barely able to sustain their lives. Many have expressed a desire to return to Australia.

[22] The airlift of the 4,000 Kosovars to Australia has been criticised by the UNHCR as 'special treatment' which is contrary to the universal standards of protection which apply to all those who fear persecution.

[23] More recent amendments to the TPV, which are discussed in chapter seven, do not grant any access to permanent residency status.

government authorities and be able to purchase an air ticket to Australia.[24] Recent research on the impact of the TPV on the lives of refugees, suggests that this 'two-tiered' approach to protection has resulted in TPV holders being subject to poverty, insecurity and little access to services at a far greater rate than is the case for holders of Permanent Protection Visas (PPVs) (Mansouri & Bagdas 2002, Pickering et.al. 2003).

Two new categories of TPV were introduced to Australian law as a result of a raft of legislative changes under the *Migration Amendment Bill 2001,* which followed closely after the *Tampa* incident of August 2001, and only weeks before the federal election of November, 2001. Before September of 2001, individuals on a TPV could apply after a period of 30 months for a Permanent Protection Visa (PPV) if they has a continued need for protection. However, after September 2001, TPV holders may be barred from being granted a PPV even if found to have a continuing need for protection. Instead, another TPV would be granted. I will discuss the *Tampa* incident and the ensuing *Migration Amendment Bill* shortly. But first, the earlier introduction of the TPV in 1999, met with stiff opposition from NGO advocates, many of whom interpreted this measure as an erosion of Australia's commitment to its protection obligations and another indication of the development of a 'two-class' refugee system, where asylum seekers arriving without documentation are stigmatised as 'queue jumpers', fraudulent and criminal by elements of the media and by prominent politicians. The RCOA, in a position paper on the TPV, argues that this new visa class is being used as a form of punishment for those who have circumvented Australian immigration control by their unauthorised entry and to act as a deterrent to future arrivals. It lists the omission of family reunion rights as perhaps the most harmful limitation on TPV holders. In addition, the RCOA argues that Australia is acting in a manner contrary to its obligations under the *Refugee Convention*, which provides that contracting states shall 'not impose penalties, on account of their illegal entry' (Article 31), (RCOA, *Position on Temporary Protection Visas*, November 1999).

During June and July 2001, the Federal Government came under increasing pressure from an avalanche of media reports over conditions in detention centres and the high incidence of self-harm among detainees. At the same time, calls for a judicial inquiry into the detention of children received much public attention (AAP, August 16, 2001). Such calls were redoubled after *ABC Four Corners*[25] aired a programme about a six-year-old Iranian boy, Shayan Badraie, who was suffering post-traumatic stress disorder as a result of experiences in detention. The boy had refused food and drink for some period. Eventually the Badraie family were found to be refugees by the Refugee Review Tribunal, and the family released from detention. In October 2003 the lawyers representing the family

---

[24] If successful in their claim, however, such entrants are granted permanent residency through a Visa Subclass 866, have access to full social security benefits, to work permission and to 510 hours of English language training.

[25] A weekly current affairs programme on the national broadcaster, ABC.

lodged an action with the NSW Supreme Court suing the Federal Government for harm done to Shayan as a result of detention.[26]

We have already considered the distinctions between 'off-shore' and 'on-shore' refugee and asylum seeker arrivals in Australia and discussed the differential treatment which whose who arrive as authorised, as opposed to unauthorised arrivals face in Australia. Events in late August 2001, have witnessed the most dramatic escalation of the 'politics of asylum', and the ensuing treatment which those who seek protection in Australia face. On August 18, the *Sydney Morning Herald* carried a headline; 'PM calls for tighter law on asylum seekers'. The article begins: 'The Prime Minister yesterday declared war on illegal immigrants, saying Australia must 'redouble our efforts' to make it less attractive for them to come here'. On the 26th August, a small boat, carrying 433 asylum seekers which had embarked from Indonesia, was in distress and appeared to be on the verge of sinking some 140 kilometres north of Christmas Island, which is part of Australian territory. A Norwegian commercial container ship, the MV *Tampa* rescued the asylum seekers, and after initially seeking to return them to Indonesia, sought to take them to Christmas Island.

The captain of the *Tampa*, Arne Rinnan, was refused access to Australian waters, was threatened with fines and the impounding of his ship. A stand-off ensued with the Indonesian, Norwegian and Australian Governments negotiating on the responsibility for the asylum seekers, while the asylum seekers themselves were falling ill as a result of their journey and the conditions on the deck of the *Tampa* where they were being temporarily housed. The Prime Minister was interviewed by the national broadcaster, the ABC, on the evening of 27th August 2001. In response to a series of questions on Australia's response to the *Tampa* issue he stated:

> We are a decent, compassionate, humanitarian country, but we also have an absolute right to decide who comes to this country . . . It is an appalling human tragedy that people wander the world in search of a home. I understand that, but no country can surrender the right to decide who comes here and how they come here. We have an open, non-discriminatory immigration policy and obviously there are people who seek to exploit the generosity of Australia and what we are trying to do as we have done at all points is strike a balance between our decency and our generosity, but also making certain that if people come here on the basis of being refugees they are compared with all other people who are seeking to come here on the basis of being refugees (ABC 7.30 Report, 27th August 2001)

Captain Rinnan broke the deadlock, insisting that the safety of his passengers should be prioritised. As the *Tampa* made for Christmas Island, Australian Special Air Services (SAS) troops were ordered to board the ship and take over control. Eventually more multilateral negotiations, resulted in what has become know as the 'Pacific solution'. Prime Minister Howard insisted that the *Tampa* asylum

[26] This case is still awaiting a decision at the time of writing.

seekers would not be allowed to lodge protection applications in Australia. After hasty negotiations with neighbouring Pacific Island nations, the *Tampa* asylum seekers and all subsequent boat arrivals who have been intercepted by the Australian Navy, have been sent-on to processing centres in the Pacific. The *Tampa* incident is estimated to have cost the Australian government $120 million, and the 'Pacific solution' is still proving to be a drain on Australia's financial resources, as Australia covers the cost of detention as well as 'friendship' payments to the nations which are hosting the asylum seekers who were 'pushed-off' Australian territory.

By mid-September, the Government had placed before the Australian Parliament a raft of legislative measures (which were passed with minor amendments before the federal election of November 10, 2001). The *Migration Amendment Bill 2001*, facilitates stricter border control and further restricts the rights of asylum seekers. The effect of the bill is to excise from the Australian Migration Zone; Christmas Island, Ashmore Reef, Cartier Reef and Cocos Island. This means that boat arrivals landing their craft on these islands will not be considered in Australian territory for the purpose of lodging a protection application. Further, the *Border Protection Bill 2001,* authorises the removal of any vessel from Australian territorial water if it is deemed that the intention of the people aboard seek to enter Australia unlawfully. Indeed, § 7A of the Act confirms the power of the government and its administration to act outside of any legislative authority (Crock and Saul 2002; 39). As part of this package of amendments, the Judicial Review Bill, which was first introduced to the Senate in December 1998 was passed. This mechanism restricts access to Federal and High Court judicial review of administrative decisions under the *Migration Act 1958*, such as RRT decisions.[27]

The diplomatic stand-off which ensued and the raft of legislative changes which were passed through the Australian Parliament as a direct result of the *Tampa* incident, are disproportionate to the dilemma which 433 asylum seekers wishing to seek protection in Australia could be expected to generate. However, the *Tampa* incident and the unprecedented reactions of the Australian Government to a boatload of asylum seekers, coming as it did just two weeks before the terrorist bombing of the World Trade Centre in New York, and the Pentagon in Washington, has consolidated public opinion in Australia, firmly supporting the Government actions. Public opinion polls reflected a ten-point surge in support for the government after *Tampa* and another ten points after the September 11 terrorist actions in the U.S.A. (Marr and Wilkinson 2003; 174, *The Australian* 11-12 May, 2002; 24-5,).[28]

---

[27] This mechanism is known as a 'privitive clause'.

[28] Captain Arne Rinnan has received 13 awards around the world for his actions in rescuing the asylum seekers, including an Australian human rights award, 'The Sailor's Prize' of

## NGOs in Australia: from pseudo bureaucrats to activists

The legal interpretation that particular countries take into domestic law of the *Refugee Convention* are decisions over which national NGOs can, and do attempt to have some influence by engaging in lobbying. However, this macro area is also engaged in by international NGOs who may have more power and leverage allowing a more critical approach to concrete policies than may be the case by local NGOs.

As we have seen from the earlier discussion of multiculturalism and the institutionalisation of immigrant organisations, collaborations between government and non-government actors in the area of immigrant integration and refugee settlement have long had a close association. The RCOA, based in Sydney, is the umbrella body for the advocacy of issues related to both 'on shore' and 'off shore' refugees and asylum seekers. The RCOA places submissions before the federal government annually on the humanitarian intake. In addition, it is one of the key NGO players in regular consultation meetings on a bi-monthly basis between DIMIA, the UNHCR and NGOs.

Concerted and co-ordinated advocacy by NGOs in the area of non-authorised, 'on-shore' arrivals was limited in Australia until the arrival of Cambodian 'boat people' who were subject to detention in the Port Hedland detention centre.[29] From this period on, the need for some common strategies, information-sharing and more consistent use of the media became evident in the actions and collaborations of NGOs. Previously, most of the NGO initiative was directed at settlement services for the 'on-shore' refugee arrivals. Margaret Piper, Executive Director of the RCOA, contends that the NGO response to the detention of the Cambodia boat arrivals is marked by a lack of timely and effective intervention by Australian NGOs. In addition, NGOs lacked co-ordination, the ability to mobilise quickly, and communicate to the media effectively (Piper 1994).

By the late 1990s NGOs and human rights groups responded to issues and to individual cases in a more unified way.[30] In reflecting on the relationship between

[29] The case of long-term detention of one of these Cambodians (Mr A) was taken to the United Nations Human Rights Committee by an Australian lawyer, Nicholas Poynder. In April of 1997 the UNHCR brought down a decision unfavourable to Australia. Nevertheless, the mandatory and non-reviewable policy of detention of unauthorised arrivals which saw Mr A detained for some four years continues.

[30] Documents from the Refugee Council to the Joint Standing Committee on Migration Regulations 1992, give some insight in the painstaking process of lobbying which established some uniform rights for detainees (correspondence of the RCOA to the Standing Committee, 16 April 1992).

NGOs and government, John Godfrey, Deputy Principal Member of the RRT, states:

> There are certain critical areas where the NGO community have close involvement with government in policy development. The major breakdown with NGOs and government and the area where there is a lot of advocacy, is on the question of detention of asylum seekers. The whole NGO community, and I guess you could include HREOC in this one, have a very strong view on detention, which is completely at odds with the government view . . . It's an issue that successive governments have been very sensitive about. This issue sets up a lot of the conflict and noise between NGOs and government and masks the fact that eighty to ninety percent of the policy is done in full consultation and agreement with NGOs (Interview No. 52).

Paris Aristotle, Director of the Victorian Foundation for Survivors of Torture (VFST), regards the relationship between government and NGOs as one of ongoing tension:

> The residual effect of the period, 1992-1993 is still with us. Even though we have made progress, it doesn't take much to lift the lid off because so many people were so hurt in that time. Some people invested ninety percent of their time in that struggle, there were no winners, the residual effect of that seeps through sometimes into outrage (Interview No. 43).

Many groups who work on behalf of asylum seekers, are also involved in work with refugee and humanitarian entrants, and in some cases with other categories of migrants. An example is the various Migrant Resource Centres, located in regions in which a high concentration of migrants reside. The centres began initially to support the settlement of immigrants. However, they became magnets for refugees and particularly for asylum seekers who lacked family or ethnic networks within Australia on whom they could draw for financial, or emotional support, or indeed for advice about local customs, practices and the machinations of the bureaucracy with which they came into contact. Increasingly, it is the micro issues of social rights which national NGOs are addressing, and turning their advocacy activities toward: the eligibility for various forms of social assistance, work permits and legal assistance for the duration of a protection claim. For over a decade, the recognition of the specific psycho-social needs of refugees has been met through specialised torture and trauma counselling services in the various Australian States. The largest and first established of such specialist services is the Service for the Treatment and Rehabilitation of Torture and Trauma Survivors (STARTTS) and later the Victorian Foundation for Survivors of Torture (VFST). By now the other States and Territories of Australia offer similar services.

Many of the community initiated services for refugees and asylum seekers are auspiced by the major churches. The National Council of Churches funds specialist positions engaged in education programmes and advocacy on immigration and on the refugee intake. Various of the Catholic Church religious orders are involved in refugee work, in particular the Good Shepherd and the Mercy Sisters support numerous projects including the Asylum Seekers Centre in Surry Hills, Sydney and the Mercy Refugee Service, which has a long-standing involvement in visiting asylum seekers in detention centres. Since 1993, the Asylum Seekers' Centre has been seeking to fill the needs gap which asylum seekers who live in the community face during a determination process. In Melbourne, the Asylum Seeker Resource Centre and the Asylum Seeker Project, Hotham Mission, fulfil similar roles. The Jesuit Refugee Service (JRS)[31] is involved in the running of the Asylum Seekers Centre, and has a vocal, though small presence in Australia, running a social justice advocacy and research centre, UNIYA. The JRS has been an important, independent voice on refugee issues and particularly on the detention of asylum seekers throughout the 1990s, through staff members and key Jesuit priests such as Frank Brennan SJ and Peter Hosking SJ.

A community consultation process, hosted by the Asylum Seekers' Centre in November 1996, had the outcome of establishing a new forum where advocates for the rights of asylum seekers could co-ordinate their actions, as well as meet with relevant state and federal government agencies and the UNHCR. This forum is known as the 'Asylum Seekers Interagency', and meets on a bi-monthly basis in Sydney.[32] Various positions in relation to advocacy can be well illustrated by the excerpts from some Australian interviews conducted in the course of my investigations. While meetings, collaboration and information-exchange between NGOs existed prior to the establishment of the Interagency, such a forum has assisted the work of NGOs on a number of fronts. Margaret Piper, Executive Director, RCOA states:

> What happened from March 1996 onwards, was that so many of the things we had built up over a number of years were stripped away one after the other. If we were going to try to hang onto things, we had to work together. Also the individual needs of asylum seekers had rapidly escalated as the support structures were taken away. So, in order to meet those needs, people had to work much more creatively and constructively. If you have a client who has nowhere to live, what are the resources you can call on? Things

---

[31] The Jesuit Refugee Service is an international Catholic organisation, providing education, health, and legal services to refugees and asylum seekers in many parts of the world. In addition, the JRS is engaged in advocacy activities for the rights of refugees and asylum seekers. It is a network organisation, consisting of a secretariat in Rome and various regional offices.

[32] The Interagency has over 100 members and invited DIMA, the RRT and the UNHCR to report and answer questions from members. The Interagency has three working groups on housing, law and detention. The aim of the Interagency is to focus on practical issues that relate to the experiences of 'on-shore' arrivals and to distribute information as widely as possible through its networks. Since November 2000, the Interagency has made available a newsletter on the world-wide-web and through its e-mail network which details policy development, administrative changes and international developments in refugee policy. The newsletter also list useful links on relevant publications.

> are changing very rapidly, and the interagency has given the opportunity for those involved to get a handle on what is going on. For me, I find it invaluable because I am hearing from the people working at the coal face the impact of the changes. So when I go to argue at a policy meeting, I can trot out case studies, so that philosophical objections can be backed up with the practical implications (Interview No. 38).

In terms of strategies and approaches to government in advocating for asylum seekers, NGOs reflect some significant differences in approach. One group follows the view that a united front and conciliatory approach must be taken in appealing to government, while others remain of the view that individual lobbying, strengthens the capacity for change to policy (Interview No. 51). Eve Lester, the Refugee Research and Policy Officer for JRS Australia, and previously a lawyer for the Refugee Advice and Casework Service, Victoria, while supportive of the Interagency initiative, remains adamant that effective advocacy depends on a variety of NGO actions and initiatives:

> Individual organisations must have their say. Though we may all be heading in the same direction, some voices are louder or stronger on a particular issue. So the strength or emphasis comes from different places . . . The refugee lobby is such a small lobby and if that lobby becomes one voice only, it is a pushover. You need united, but separate voices. Not one voice (Interview No. 41).

In commenting on the co-operation between NGOs and government, Nicholas Poynder, human rights lawyer states:

> There's a tension between the NGOs about funding and a fear that if you criticise the government too harshly you are going to compromise your funding, which in turn compromises the independence of NGOs. . .  It can be couched in terms of 'look, the only way we can get anywhere is to get on with the Department, to continually criticise is going to get us nowhere, we've got to have a working relationship with them, so let's hold back a little bit'. But I've had off-the-record meetings with representatives of the Department who have said to me, 'look the reason we're cutting your funding is because you've criticised the minster so harshly', it's as simple as that (Interview No. 37).

In terms of NGOs building broader networks outside of refugee-specific advocacy, Chris Sidoti HREOC commissioner states:

> I do know that their advocacy could be more effective if they started penetrating other organisations with the message, and started building a much broader constituency. Certainly they have an advocacy role to the community . . . and groups such as the Refugee Council and the JRS do that well, but some others are so overwhelmed by the workload in individual cases, that their capacity to undertake broader public and policy advocacy is very limited. And yet unless we start turning around public perceptions of refugee issues, it is not going to be possible to effect significant changes in public policy. There does need to be a more explicit and concerted effort to work with non refugee NGOs and the broader community to convince them of the need to change policy in these areas (Interview No. 46).

NGOs themselves recognise the usefulness and indeed the logic, of fairness arguments, when advocating for the rights of refugees in public forums and settings (Interview No. 37). That is, there is a perception among the refugee NGOs in Australia, that the public is open to reasoned argument that asylum seekers should be treated with fairness. In contrast, the same NGOs are mindful that when lobbying politicians, different forms of argument need to be utilised. This sentiment has been severely tested though, by the overwhelming support for the Howard Government stand on the '*Tampa* asylum seekers' and the 'Pacific solution' which followed the *Tampa* incident in August 2001. Newspaper opinion polls suggest up to 75 percent of Australians continue to support the Government's actions.

In the search for pragmatic solutions to the dilemma which 'unauthorised arrivals' have generated in the Australian political system, a number of prominent activists in the refugee area have signalled that a departure from the present bureaucratic and administrative approach taken to refugees and asylum seekers would significantly settle the inflammatory public discourse on refugees and asylum seekers. Chris Sidoti, while serving as Human Rights and Equal Opportunity Commissioner, advocated a separation of responsibilities between migrants and refugees, with DIMIA responsible for the former and the Attorney General's Department for the later. This approach has much support among the NGO sector, reflecting the view that refugee determination, as a legal process should be separated from the controlled immigration programme run by DIMIA, which increasingly focuses on skilled migrants, with a view to Australia's economic performance. This sentiment and the advocacy of such a development to the Federal Government resulted from the culmination of long-term information gathering and investigations into the human rights of those individuals asking for protection as 'on-shore' arrivals. The thrust of this sentiment is part of the recommendations of a report into the detention of asylum seekers, tabled by the Human Rights Commission (1998), which is discussed in chapter six. Margaret Piper, Executive Director of the RCOA, argues in relation to this matter:

> My view of such a separation, is that immigrants and refugees are in fact motivated by two entirely different motivations. Immigration is something that the country does to benefit itself, enhance the economy, the skills base, the sociological base, it is a process of people engineering for totally self-centred reasons, to make Australia better. The humanitarian programme is about helping the individuals, irrespective of whether they can make positive gains to the Australian society, motivated by benevolence, recognition of being part of a broader international community, and international responsibility. The two motivations do not always sit neatly. To have a separation would remove the humanitarian programme from the vagaries of economic ebbs and flows. It would remove it from the arguments about such things as jobs (Interview No. 38).

As has been the case in Germany, local community initiatives, aimed at assisting asylum seekers in the community, and visiting those in detention, have emerged in Australia as the living conditions of asylum seekers in the community and particularly the mental health of those in detention have deteriorated. It is not only local parish groups of the major churches and various ethnic communities that have developed local initiatives to support asylum seekers, but student groups and most recently networks in country areas of Australia, such as 'Rural Australians for Refugees', which began in October 2001. The issue of children in detention has been a particular focus of community support groups in recent years, organising visits to detention centres and various forms of direct action.[33]

No doubt demographic distinctions have an enormous bearing on the receptiveness of local communities to asylum seekers. Unlike Germany, Australia has no system of allocating asylum seekers on a per-capita basis to the various States and Territories. As a consequence, Sydney, followed by Melbourne host the majority of 'on-shore' arrivals who live in the community. Regular contact by Australian citizens with asylum seekers is rare, especially in regional cities and towns which have no asylum seeker residents. Rather, media images are often the only association regional populations have with refugees and asylum seekers. Even more invisible are those asylum seekers who are subject to detention, who are often housed in some of the most remote locations in Australia, such as Port Hedland, Woomera and Curtin air-base.

## Some connections between the two case studies

In order to meaningfully connect the discussion and analysis of this chapter to the case of Germany, we should consider the discussion articulated in chapter two, which offered a framework for considering the actions of NGOs. First, let us again consider the possibility for political action, which I argued is potentially extended through day-to-day engagement and service-delivery work, where the human consequences of policy, law and administration are encountered first hand by NGO workers. Does such experience and the 'competency' gained over time, further the capacity for political action? Second, and perhaps related to the first point, do we see the possibility of forms of civil disobedience extended through the experiences at the 'front-line' of working with asylum seekers? Finally, in making any assessment of the efficacy of national NGO work, what role do international connections and networks play in particular campaigns and to the overall efficacy or longevity of NGOs? The hypothesis I proposed in chapter two considered that to some extent we may look to action and *movement* of citizens as an indicator of a 'decent society'. In view of this, what does the advocacy for asylum seekers in this case indicate? Further, I proposed that activity engaged in *for others*, rather than self-interest, confirms and consolidates civil society organisations as enhancing a society.

---

[33] The group, Chilout (Children Out of Detention) is a recent example of such community initiatives.

In substantive terms, to be sure, the routes of entry to Germany and Australia are at variance, with the 'universal visa system' and 'controlled immigration' dominating the Australian approach, while in the German case, the 'asylum route' remains the dominant form of entry with the exception of recent skilled worker recruitment schemes. The major difference between the 'asylum route' in the German and Australian case, is the numerical difference. When comparing 'spontaneous' or 'unauthorised' arrivals, Australia has a markedly smaller 'problem' compared to Germany. Nevertheless, despite these differences, the overall approaches to the 'asylum problem' have, over time, converged to a degree. The relatively small number of spontaneous arrivals in the case of Australia, may have led to an expectation of generosity, but in fact Australia is leading its Western counterparts in areas of surveillance and various forms of deterrence, in particular detention and deportation.

Chapter six and seven, will develop the parallel responses to asylum claimants in Germany and Australia, utilising the resource in particular of the in-depth interviews with non government advocates for the rights of those claiming asylum. As I have argued throughout this book, the way in which immigrants are included or excluded potentially creates a space for increased or decreased public acceptance of refugee entrants. Further, NGOs carry the potential to create a favourable space for a more positive public perception of asylum seekers if their advocacy role is effective. We have so far seen evidence of a reasoned dialogue between state and non state actors in the formulation and implementation of refugee policy. Though friction and conflict exists in such relationships, some progress is nonetheless made. In addition, we have seen evidence of the governments of both Germany and Australia acknowledging the expertise and knowledge of NGOs and the consequent importance of a continued dialogue between the two parties. Similarly, NGOs in both case studies, indicate a degree of sympathy with the significant dilemmas which governments must address in the administration of refugees and asylum seekers, and in balancing the myriad of other interests within a country.

Another issue which deserves some further consideration in view of the Australian case, is the question of various modes of inclusion of immigrants, including refugees and asylum seekers, discussed already in chapter one. The way in which a multicultural attitude or awareness influences the tonalities of everyday life that a newcomer faces, relates to the political and broader public discourses on immigration. As I have argued at the outset, the German and Australian case studies are in this sense, 'most divergent' examples, because of the dissimilar experience of the two nations in relation to immigration and the incorporation of immigrants. However, the divergent policies of Germany compared to Australia, may or may not be reflected in the local communities in which asylum seekers and refugees live. Some of these particularities are explored in chapters six and seven in relation to the advocacy work of NGOs in Germany and in Australia.

The appearance of uninvited newcomers such as asylum seekers in a society, requires not just state responses, but also community responses of tolerance and inclusion. It often appears that a straightforward relationship exists between tolerance and inclusion: the more tolerant one is, the more likely are tendencies toward inclusiveness, to foster inclusive policies, and on the other hand, the more intolerant one is, the more likely are exclusive tendencies. However, such a straightforward relationship seems to me to be over simplistic. I would propose a circular, rather than linear connection between tolerance and inclusion, or intolerance and exclusion. A circular connection leaves open the possibility that 'tolerance' may mean a tolerance toward exclusion, or a tolerance of ethnic labelling or stereotyping. If we imagine a spinning sphere with tolerance and intolerance at different points on the circumference, and a second sphere, spinning on the same central axis – the points at which tolerance and inclusion (or their opposites) intersect are arbitrary. The rate at which the two separately spinning spheres are rotating will be influenced by the environment around the spheres. Moreover, as the spheres are independent, though in the same general environment, it is conceivable that they are spinning at different speeds, perhaps even in opposite directions, with the result that any cross-fertilisation or contact between them could be at arbitrary points of the spheres - adding to the unpredictability of the relationship between inclusion and tolerance.

As outlined in chapter two, at a practical level, justice in immigration will vary according to the type of immigrant wanting to enter. The liberal dictum *ought implies can*, can be applied to refugees and asylum seekers much more readily than any other group of prospective immigrants. We *ought* to allow refugees and those claiming asylum into our territory (even if only temporarily), therefore we must ensure that we *can*. The *ought* can be applied in a number of ways: we *ought* because of the International Conventions we have signed (as a nation); we *ought* because it is just to give refuge to those whose lives are in danger, we *ought* because it does not harm us to do so, but prevents harm to others. Whether we *can,* or not, has a practical as well as an emotional component. We *can* accept refugees and asylum seekers because we have the infrastructure to support them as well as the *will* to allow them to live amongst us. Justice in immigration is the thread which connects the reality of inclusion or exclusion that immigrants, including refugees experience. The perception (public opinion) of the general population can form a force field of *public will* which nurtures the *can* component of the equation. That is not to suggest that public opinion precedes political activity (of state and non state actors) which can be said to be more directly involved in the *ought* component of the equation, related to obligations. Rather, a diachronic relationship exists - which is continually contested and unstable.

A balance between the legitimate claims of the state to restrict immigration, against the transnational human rights logic reflected in the advocacy of NGOs must be struck. If NGOs, whether located within a particular nation-state or operating across borders are to succeed in representing transnational human rights interests such as those of refugees and asylum seekers, broad engagement in multi-level activities with and between states and other NGOs need to continue and be strengthened. In addition, the support of the society being asked for protection must continually be re-engaged through various processes of opinion formation, through media engagement, education and information-sharing at many levels. To reiterate, the purpose of this chapter has been two-fold. In the first instance, the major developments in Australian policies towards immigration in general were outlined; necessary for interpretation of the contemporary response to refugees and asylum seekers. Second, the Australian interpretations of the obligations under the *Refugee Convention* and some of the practical implications of legislation and administrative practices of the Australian migration system were explored. I turn now to the issues within the 'politics of asylum' which have been of most concern and consternation to the government and the NGO sector in Germany and Australia in the following two chapters.

# PART III
# THE POLITICS OF EXCLUSION

Chapter 6

# Paths of resistance and NGO experience in Germany

**The Neighbor**

Strange violin, do you follow me?
In how many distant cities before this
did your lonely night speak to mine?
Do hundreds play you? Does only one?

Are there in all of the great cities
those who without you would have
long since lost themselves in the rivers?
And why does it always reach me?

Why am I always the neighbor of those
who force you from fear to sing
and to say out loud: life is heavier
than the weight of all things.

Rainer Maria Rilke, *The Book of Images,* 1991

The previous two chapters characterised the immigration profiles of Germany and Australia, highlighting the differences in historical development of the two countries which have also had an impact on the development of asylum policy. The status of newcomers has been discussed in light of the impact of post-war immigration trends, and in more contemporary terms, in relation to the question of the arrival of people seeking protection. This background offers the context for considering the most recent developments in these two societies of the admission or expulsion of asylum seekers and in particular of the involvement of NGOs in those processes.

As I argued through the previous chapters, the activities of NGOs engaged in human rights advocacy, are located *between* the state practices of (law and administration), and the concrete manifestations which state practices have on individual lives. NGOs are more likely to be in direct contact with asylum seekers than the bureaucrats, members of the judiciary and politicians who represent the state. The state gathers the statistical data relating to numbers applying for protection, mode of arrival, recognition rates, and cost of processing, while NGOs gather evidence of the impact of policy and processing procedures and of deportation and detention practices, on the lives of individuals through grass roots networks. These differences highlight in particular two tensions. First, between short and long-term planning and the responses of state and/or non-state agencies who deliver specific services and programmes. Second, the tension over what is perceived and communicated as being in the national interest of a state versus its international obligations. It is at the everyday level of 'practice' and social engagement, that the problems and fears associated with those seeking protection come to be articulated and reflected in administrative responses and legislative change.

The limit of public tolerance in relation to the arrival of refugees and asylum seekers though, is not primarily grounded in legal or administrative considerations, nor in normative considerations. Rather, tolerance at this (practical) level, is shaped by what is often a partial knowledge of an issue, as well as the first-hand, and often arbitrary encounters that occur in everyday life. An individual may have an affinity with, or sympathy for a particular asylum seeker whom they happen to know through a chance meeting or a particular network such as church organisation. At the same time, that individual may express strong resentment to the influx of asylum seekers and other foreigners who are seeking some form of inclusion or protection. There is an anomaly between personal encounters and loyalties which are unpredictable and the opinion and attitudes of a mass constituency of citizens toward 'others' as a group. How such an anomaly is utilised in public discourse can have a profound impact on public opinion toward marginalised groups.

In chapter four, I discussed the development of 'asylum politics' in Germany particularly after unification and in relation to the status of foreigners generally. Keeping in mind the developing social tensions over the influx of asylum seekers, I ask what strategies have NGOs adopted in tackling such issues and entering the debate? Indeed to what extent are NGOs able to influence the decision making processes over asylum policy? Are opportunity structures evident which allow NGOs to be proactive rather than reactive to policy and to administrative practices which affect those they represent? Addressing these questions will also reveal the place and role of NGOs more broadly in civil society. Are NGOs one of the vehicles of change and self-expression by citizens? Or, are NGOs an arm of the state bureaucracy and administration, located at a distance from the machinery of government, yet lacking independence or some boldness to counter the action of the state at particular moments?

In what follows I explore the NGOs who represent asylum seekers and immigrants, focusing on particular campaigns, strategies, events and responses which illustrate the variety of actions they initiate and participate in. The examples include various forms of civil disobedience, dissent and resistance such as the church sanctuary movement, as well as small-scale neighbourhood initiatives which aim at incremental change. I also explore the rise of violence against foreigners and asylum seekers and the NGO response to it. The discussions of representation and of practical protection, which follow, are applicable to both the German and Australian case studies. In concluding this chapter, I will consider the broader European Union (EU) responses to asylum seekers, as regional agreements are increasingly being sought to deal with the consequences of legal and illegal people movement. A regional approach is especially relevant for Germany as an important member of the EU in economic, political as well as strategic terms, having long been at the forefront of calls for EU-wide approaches to asylum seekers – a 'burden-sharing' approach.

## Representation in the public sphere: distilling different voices

The various points of friction and contention between the state, and the non-state sphere are associated with representation of various interests and viewpoints in a society and the communication of these interests or viewpoints on behalf of oneself or of a group. Max Weber situates representation in the political process of seeking legitimacy which would be binding over the action of others (1947; 416). Governments represent the interests of their constituency through consensual, as well as through coercive means. A second use of the concept of representation has been articulated in cultural theory where identity politics has utilised the concept of representation to denote various processes of socialisation and the social reproduction of cultural differences. In contemporary sociological literature representation is regularly characterised as an issue linked to self-determination, as in the case of indigenous peoples for instance. I use the term here with the first meaning in mind.

Representation of asylum seekers most often takes place through a third party, particularly in a host country, as an asylum seeker is rarely in the position of self-representation. This holds both in the legal process of a protection determination, and in terms of having an understanding of the local social and economic circumstances of a particular place. Moreover, as representation is inherently about relationships of power; seeking to influence others for self or group interests, asylum seekers are unlikely to be able to carry out their own representation. NGOs have the potential to unify groups of people from disparate backgrounds, and can defy territorial borders and allegiances, as they are not necessarily constrained to representing national interest in the way a state is. However, while it is possible to hypothesise about a model of non-government action instigating citizen action and responsibility, the model is firmly situated within a relationship *with* the state. A model of NGO as active participant is not meant to replace the state, or necessarily weaken the state, but to strengthen and enliven bonds with the base, or grass roots as well as with groups outside a nation-state. That is, NGOs need the state in order to function: they rely on the state and its institutions and infrastructure as partners as well as adversaries.[1] In the process of representation which refugee NGOs are engaged in, it can be said that representation is multi-layered, including:

1. The most evident *representation* is NGOs acting on behalf of the refugee in a continuing dialogue with the state, and various groups and networks in civil society, which are perceived as having an impact on policies and importantly attitudes which affect refugees.
2. The NGO represents itself; that is the membership and principles or mandate, in the social and political and cultural setting in which it is located. How this self representation is carried out will have an impact on funding sources and the ability to mobilise public support.
3. In the process of representing a moral issue, the NGO is representing the broader social group (nation) of which it is a member. This may often be an unstated and even unintended consequence of NGO action.
4. A related, but less visible feature of NGO representation is the potential of non-state actors as triggers for a wider re-engagement of citizens in the affairs of their polity.[2]

It is my assertion that in modern societies social movements and NGOs can be regarded as representatives of a much broader group than their own workers and membership base. Many citizens may be involved in issues at the periphery, perhaps in one-off actions such as participating in a demonstration, giving a donation, or some other form of tacit support for the aims of an organisation. This broad and indeterminate, perhaps fleeting support is something that movements and NGOs rely on, often in an unacknowledged way, when negotiating with and lobbying the state: the assertion stated or implied, that they represent a broad public of voters who are also concerned about the issues which the NGO is seeking to have some influence on.

---

[1] In elaborating the activities of the NGO sector on the issue of representing refugees, it is my intention to highlight the understanding of the receiver society which occurs through representation of the other. As Marcuse reminds us in his exposition of the meaning of tolerance, intellectuals can ' . . . break the concreteness of oppression in order to open the mental space in which this society can be recognized as what it is and does'(1956; 82). What tolerance is in a totalitarian democracy is quite another thing (ibid. 99). Applying such thinking to NGO action; we could expect the intervention of NGOs to render change of some kind, be it a different approach, a change in 'opinion' - or even an impact on policy.

[2] Certainly in the case of refugee advocacy, NGOs have in many instances invigorated citizens who were otherwise disengaged from direct action of even the softest form, letter writing campaigns for instance.

## Practical protection

In chapter two, I have argued that protection of those seeking asylum must be distinct from the general immigration intake, situating refugees and asylum seekers within a theory of needs with a universal logic, overriding particularist concerns which dominate the wider immigration issue in individual nation-states. The office of the UNHCR has recently published a report which recognises the growing need to differentiate between immigration and refugee flows in order to ensure adequate protection for persons at risk of persecution (UNHCR, 2000). This report focuses in particular on Europe, and reflects the unease of the UNHCR and many NGOs with developments in refugee protection in Western countries.

It has also been pointed out that substantive protection is given by states through granting either a permanent or temporary right to reside in a given territory and access to a range of social, economic and political rights during a period of residence. The granting of protection requires mechanisms which can trigger the reconciling of national (self) interest at the point where it intersects the internationally agreed upon interests of refugees and asylum seekers as stateless persons to whom the abstract 'global community' has an obligation An uneasy balance exists in relation to protection, from international to local settings.

Protection is the centre axis along a continuum which has national interest at one end and universal ideas of justice and human rights at the other. NGOs, both national and international, exert pressure at various points of the scale. It is the work of NGOs representing asylum seekers which ensures what I term 'practical protection'. In a myriad of ways NGOs and social movements find a variety of avenues and strategies which extend or heighten the possibilities of an asylum seeker reaching the 'place of judgement'. Needless to say, NGOs cannot grant protection. However, non-state actors do intervene in physical and symbolic actions which mediate the impact of state policies.

The framework for considering these actions were initially articulated in chapters one and two. The first of these theoretical issues to re-emerge is the question of rights and to whom they extend. Rights (such as the right to protection), are hollow concepts unless they are accompanied by the resources to substantiate the promise. Moreover, the capabilities argument, as articulated by Martha Nussbaum (2000; 98, 99), extends 'rights thinking' in the twofold sense that the language of capabilities overrides any dominant orientations. Moreover, thinking of capabilities remind us to search for the gaps between 'ought' and 'can': between an ideal and small-scale actions which are realistic and achievable at the local level. In some sense, 'capabilities' arguments, such as the one articulated by Nussbaum, takes the obligation thesis one step further, to argue that those with greater capabilities have perhaps an additional obligation to extend assistance to those with less.

In practical terms, NGOs rely ever more on public support for their work. Government funding to the non-government sector tends to be short-term and uncertain in both Germany and Australia, while public engagement to raise awareness of the role of NGOs and the recruitment of volunteers and of non-state funding has gathered momentum. Indeed, not only the NGO sector, but the state also calls for volunteers to carry out some service delivery roles in the area of refugee settlement. In all sectors, whether state or non-state, the use of volunteers has hidden costs and dangers as outlined in chapter two. The UNHCR, which had always worked collaboratively with aid and development NGOs working in refugee emergency situations, has also come to work more closely with NGOs in developed countries on the asylum issue. This has been particularly evident over the last decade, as asylum policies of Western countries have moved to restricting the rights of asylum seekers in measures of internal and external deterrence.[3] An important aspect of the development of the UNHCR's position on protection issues are the meetings of its Executive Committee (EXCOM).[4] Prior to the EXCOM meeting, an NGO consultation takes place, which has become an important forum for international and regional NGOs to exchange information and debate current issues. During this period, NGOs also lobby representatives of the UNHCR prior to the official EXCOM meeting. NGOs working independently and in partnership with the UNHCR have identified the emergent issues which require special attention in ensuring the protection of vulnerable groups. The protection of women and children is a particular case in point, where the special protection needs of women and girls has been highlighted by the ongoing efforts of NGOs. In some cases, governments have implemented programmes specifically aimed at refugee women and children.

However, as discussed in chapter two, the dilemma for a particular nation-state being asked for protection by a potential refugee revolves around striking a balance between the genuineness of an individual case; the reality of finite resources within a local political context; and the expanding number of requests for such protection. NGOs can be partners, protagonists or silent bystanders in this dilemma. While numerous factors shape the conditions which will effect the decision an NGO takes on its approach, the strategy, rationale and co-ordination within, as well as between refugee NGOs can be seen to have an cumulative effect over time, either draining their effectiveness or enhancing it. NGOs in this sense do face the difficult task of making decisions 'at the coal face', while bureaucrats have the leisure of distance from the impact of their work. Rarely if ever do the bureaucrats, politicians or indeed the judiciary have to explain directly to an asylum seeker why a claim for protection has been rejected, or why any monetary or legal assistance during a determination process has been denied. Rather, it is NGO workers who are often present with an asylum seeker when such news is received. Nevertheless, judicious and careful action in individual cases is paramount if NGOs are not to lose public

[3] In 1999, the UNHCR published a handbook for NGOs which outlines the development in protection issues, and legal and practical issues which affect the practical work of NGOs in assisting refugees, asylum seekers and displaced persons (UNHCR 1999).

[4] EXCOM meets in October of each year and comprises a selection of member states of the UN.

sympathy and thereby leverage with administrators and politicians. NGOs do face a very real burden in their work of having to master numerous 'domains' simultaneously if they are to be effective advocates of a particular group. Moreover, the load on NGO workers who have regular 'front-line' contact with the groups and individuals they are advocating for, cannot be underestimated. The interviews I conducted generally reflected an accumulative burden on NGO workers, leading to 'burn-out' of paid staff as well as volunteers. It was expressed to me repeatedly that this was particularly the case in view of the mounting restrictions to the legal and social rights of asylum seekers, together with a public mood reflected either in hostility or indifference to asylum seekers.

In terms of the response to those seeking protection in Germany, one of the key issues which has recurred at irregular intervals is the issue of xenophobia, and acts of violence toward foreigners. Chapter three has already analysed the change to the Basic Law in 1993, in part spurred on by a political reaction to violence against foreigners. I will now detail more specifically the pattern of violence toward foreigners over the last decade, arguing that though violent acts may only be perpetrated by a small number, the phenomenon of 'bystanders' – those who are present as witnesses, yet do nothing to prevent violence, is damaging in more subtle and pervasive ways. Moreover, the example of xenophobia and violence against foreigners, will extend into analysis of the actions of NGOs in advocating for the rights of asylum seekers, and more broadly for positive integration measures for immigrants.

## Street level violence

> On 22 September 1991, in a small Saxon town called Hoyerswerda in the territory of eastern Germany, foreigners, that is, guest workers and asylum seekers, were attacked by neo-Nazis and skinheads. While the attacks were condemned all over Germany for their violence and blatant xenophobia and racism, another issue loomed more dramatically. A Spiegel reporter sums it up. 'Hoyerswerda marked a turning point, less because a few dozen young xenophobes have given the go-ahead to fanaticism with steel balls and Molotov cocktails thrown at dormitories (sic) for asylum seekers and guest workers. Much worse: thousands of adult citizens, in spite of decade-long stereotypical East German education about 'People's Solidarity' accepted these criminal attacks silently, when they were not jubilantly welcoming it' (Peck 1995; 103).

Since the European autumn of 1991, a marked increase in violent attacks against 'foreigners', mainly refugees and asylum seekers, but also directed at long-standing residents of non-German ethnicity, have occurred in Germany. During 1991 more than 2400 assaults on foreigners and their property were reported, including many cases of arson which resulted in severe injuries and deaths

(Kanstroom 1993; 156).[5] However, it is not only the attacks themselves, but the public and political reaction to them which are significant.[6]

> More shocking than right-wing violence itself . . . is the 'recognisable syndrome of prejudices' that the violence is awakening in the broader population: the past as future. Resurgent national pride now takes the form of silent approval of the violent attacks against Turks and asylum seekers (ibid; 14).

Thus, during 1991 foreigners and the asylum issue became the second most important issue of public concern, after the issue of German unification. By the end of 1992, the 'problem of foreigners' was ranked the most significant issue of concern in West Germany and was ranked third in East Germany after unemployment and economic growth (Bade 1994b; 93). Chapter three has already indicated the various categorisations of newcomers to the Federal Republic in the period from the 1950s. However the absence of long-term integration measures, and a public discourse which largely failed to communicate adequately about the presence of immigrants, accumulated alongside the social and economic tensions of unification as triggers for xenophobia and violence.

It must be remembered, that far from being unique to Germany, anti-foreigner violence escalated across Europe through the 1990s from Italy, France and Sweden, to Britain and Russia. However, Germany does display some unique circumstances both historically and in more contemporary times in relation to immigrants living in Germany, which I have discussed in chapter three. Perhaps one of the key factors in the escalation of anti-foreigner violence in Germany can be traced to the asylum compromise of 1993, in conjunction with the disjointed political approach to immigration (Habermas 1994; 128-131). Numerous commentators have noted the ambivalence with which the German Government responded to the upsurge in violence against foreigners (Bade 1994, Kanstroom 1993, Ireland 1997).

In August 1991, Edmund Stoiber, the Bavarian head of state, who has long been prominent in the debate around asylum rights, spoke out about the change Germany was undergoing as a result of the influx of foreigners; particularly asylum seekers. He is quoted as describing the results of a multicultural Germany akin to a '*durchrasste Gesellschaft*', a 'mongrelised society' (Mattson 1995; 73).

---

[5] During 1992, 2,200 violent attacks on foreigners included 17 murders and many hundreds of serious injuries occurred. In August of 1992 an asylum seeker hostel in the northern port city of Rostock was set alight and triggered a new round of violence. In November of the same year three Turkish workers were killed in the western city of Mölln after a fire-bombing incident.

[6] In the compilation of a list of acts of violence from 1989-1994, Kurthen (et.al. 1997; 263-285), indicates that it is not only in Eatern German states that acts of violence took place at an increased rate in the early 1990s. Though clearly acts of violence were primarily targeted at foreigners or those who appeared to be foreigners, a significant proportion were also targeted at disabled people, homosexuals and Jews.

Stoiber later labelled the actions and rhetoric of the nationalist *Republikaner* party as a 'racist, xenophobic position'(ibid.), seemingly unaware of the contradiction and mixed message of his public pronouncements .

I would concur with the correlation Habermas draws between generalised societal reactions to foreigners, most starkly exemplified by the violent acts of far-right elements, and the symbolic politics entered into by senior figures in government. An accumulation of anxiety about foreigners eventually had the effect of the constitutional change in 1992/93, and ultimately gets the message across to: ' . . . even the dimmest of wits: the problem with the hatred of foreigners is the foreigners themselves' (Habermas 1994; 126). Further, from another analyst:

> There can be no doubt that politicians from all sides of the political spectrum intentionally or inadvertently used prejudicial rhetoric to pursue political strategies, but conservative politicians in particular repeatedly played to racist fears in Germany, slowly but surely generating an image of the foreign other as a parasite on the Germany body. This image dislodged itself from the arena of rational or even semirational discourse within right-wing extremist groups and, one could argue, within the general public, where it was subject only to further intensification, not to mediation (Mattson 1995; 73).

During the intense asylum debate of the early 1990s, slogans such as 'the boat is full', 'Germany for Germans', became prominent catch cries from supporters of far-right political parties, and eventually entered popular discourse.

The most immediate response to the violence of 1991 and 1992 were mass candlelight processions in various German cities, in which between 200,000 and 400,000 people took part. The first such rally took place in Munich in December 1992, followed by similar demonstrations in other cities (Bosswick 2000; 49). These were spontaneous actions, emerging from civil society, rather than organised by political parties (Habermas 1994; 140). However, these processions of solidarity were not interpreted favourably by all those concerned for the human rights of immigrants. While large rallies, demonstrations and processions such as the candlelight processions of the early 1990s, are symbolic of public sentiment and opinion, it can be argued that unless such demonstrations are sustained, or followed by longer-term, strategic actions to confirm the sentiment of a one-off rally or demonstration, they may be little more than a momentary act of solidarity.

> The candle processions after the racist attacks was nothing more than a gesture. It should have been followed up by more concerted action if so many people were convinced that the attacks were so bad. You could have expected that people would get more involved in positive initiatives, but that did not happen (Interview No. 25).

Through the 1990s acts of violence against foreigners continued in both East and West Germany. On January 18, 1996 a particularly notable hate-crime occurred in a refugee hostel in Lübeck, Schleswig-Holstein which was the scene of an arson attack. Ten people died in the fire that ensued; some thirty-eight were seriously injured. The hostel housed Arabs and Africans. This particular case rose to prominence not just because of the numbers killed and injured and the ferocity of the attack, but because a 20-year-old Lebanese refugee, who lived in the hostel with his family was charged with the crime. After two court cases, Safwan Eid has been cleared of the charges, but four white German suspects, known to the police for a variety of criminal and neo-Nazi activities have never been charged (Fekete 2000). By 1999 the incidence of violent attacks, and particularly anti-Semitic crime was on the rise again. The Council of Europe's Racism and Intolerance office, urged German authorities to take more action to combat acts of racism, intolerance and violence toward foreigners. A recent report by this office is particularly critical of the lack of effort by authorities to combat anti-Semitism, and urges greater efforts to integrate immigrant communities into the mainstream of German society. At the same time, a report by the Council of Europe's anti-racism committee says Germany currently exudes a climate of racism, anti-semitism and intolerance (The Associated Press, August 3, 2001). This climate has been fuelled by open as well as latent xenophobia and a lack of political will by successive governments to tackle racially motivated violence (Bosswick 2000, Arnswald et.al. 2000).

Heribert Prantl (1995), a prominent commentator on issues of German identity, in the post unification period, and on the development of an asylum 'problem', typifies contemporary attitudes to foreigners as explosive, akin to an incendiary device in the hands of a pyromaniac. Utilising a variety of case studies, he highlights a pattern of increasingly authoritarian tendencies in Germany - not just at the grass root, but in the centre of political power. The most potent example is the denial of rights to foreigners – even those who have lived in Germany for a long period. However, in myriad other ways, the discourse over the increased violence against foreigners, often stigmatising victims rather than the perpetrators, indicates an inversion in the popular discourse over the social 'problem' of foreigners. This is indicated by such characterisations as: 'If only *they* had not come to Germany', '*They* should have remained more silent', ' *They* should be less noticeable' (1995; 116).

During the year 2000 right-wing violence against foreigners escalated again, directed increasingly at Jews. Political leaders and senior members of the Jewish community called for action against racism and escalating hate crimes. In October, a demonstration against neo-Nazi groups took place in Düsseldorf. Paul Spiegel, head of the Central Council of Jews addressed the demonstrators, stating:

> We won't let this rabble take away our freedom. Jews and non-Jews have to unite to stop neo-Nazi terrorists forcing us off the streets again. When ranting skinheads can claim they are carrying out the will of the silent majority, then the silent majority is not without blame (Associated Press, October 28, 2000).

The problem which persists in relation to *foreigners* in Germany is the distance between private and public lives. In local neighbourhoods and in workplaces, Germans live and work alongside *foreigners* as neighbours, as colleagues, as friends. In social situations a person's citizenship status is not an issue. Similarly, workers pay taxes for the *public good* no matter the passport they hold. However in the public sphere, where debate is regularly conflated and simplified for mass consumption, the category *foreigner* is utilised as a weapon for causing division where it may not necessarily exist, as well as a shield to guard against the scrutiny of other social problems.

There are many reasons for people feeling dissatisfied and insecure. The fulfilment of human needs relates not just to the material conditions of life, but equally to the emotional and psychological pre-dispositions and attitudes which shape our responses to other people. Meeting the 'basic rights' of immigrants and refugees can readily be perceived in certain circumstances as excessive generosity when the needs of some local peoples have not been met. Far-right groups and political parties have been able to exploit such sentiment and to gather support with straightforward, often simplistic messages. Such messages as 'Germany for Germans, foreigners out', can be interpreted as being as much about the effects of economic deregulation and globalisation as about the presence of foreigners, but no doubt it is at the everyday level, where the targets of such sentiments are most visible, being culturally and racially distinct from the dominant group. Already by the mid 1980s commentators in Germany recognised the quite unambiguous link between attacks on foreigners and the heated public debate on asylum seekers, which turned by the late 1980s to a discourse on criminalisation and abuse of the asylum system, illegal entry, drug dealing and terrorist activities (Wolken in Bosswick 2000; 46).

## Asylum advocates and political action

The articulation and representation of interests in Germany is a complex web of groups and organisations with diverse constituents. Some interest groups have developed an organisational base with a specific focus on one area of policy, such as immigration. Because they represent distinct sub-groups, these organisations can be quite small (Dalton 1993; 236). However other organisations such as unions, churches and professional associations may encompass a large membership and work at least in part in the same policy area as issue-specific organisations. In the immigration and refugee area, a coalition of loose networks is crucial to the work of lobbying; enhancing the possibility of being seen to represent a significant enough base of citizens (voters) in order for those involved in legislative and administrative decision making to take notice of the network and the agenda they are articulating.

Throughout the 1970s and 1980s, various groups of German citizens proved to be outspoken and effective advocates for human rights, for the environment and the anti-nuclear movement, as well as for women's rights. Some of these movements became formalised in organisations such as the German Green Party (Bündnis 90/Die Grünen). As I have already discussed in chapter three, the NGO sector which represents the interests of immigrants, refugees and asylum seekers in Germany, is a vast network with long historical roots, particularly through the Catholic and Protestant churches and prominent lay welfare organisations. However, through the 1980s, other forms of immigrant organisations and representative bodies emerged. In addition, government at federal, *Länder* and local levels, recognised the need for a representative body or umbrella organisation to address immigrant integration. The first such government initiative took shape in Berlin with the establishment of the Commission of Foreigners' Affairs in 1981.[7] After the reunification of West and East Germany at the end of 1989, the question of living *with* foreigners gained new significance for Berlin which had been a divided city. Berlin became in a sense a national symbol for reunification. However East and West Berlin had quite different experiences of foreign populations living in their midst. At the time of reunification in East Berlin foreigners made up 1.6% of the total population, in the West of Berlin that figure was 14% (Press release of the Senatsverwaltung Für Gesundheit und Soziales, 8 August 1990).

Commissioners for Foreigners' Affairs (*Ausländerbeauftragte[r]*), now exist at federal, *Länder* (State) and local levels, and are responsible for implementing measures aimed at fostering a co-operative integration of foreigners, as well as various training and education measures for the German population and for specific service providers of the state, such as the police. The term *Ausländerbeauftragte(r)* is also used within organisations such as the churches to denote similar responsibilities. In Frankfurt am Main, the *Amt für multikulturelle Angelegenheiten,* was founded in 1990. By the mid 1990s Frankfurt had become the city with the highest percentage of foreigners; some 25 per cent of the population. Some of the work of *Ausländerbeauftragten* is targeted directly at asylum seekers. The various offices of Foreigners' Affairs have become a significant link between state and non-state organisations. The effectiveness of particular Commissioners varies between the *Länder,* as does the level of trust and co-operation with NGOs.

While the networks between NGOs are strong, with well-developed forms of collaboration, co-operation and information exchanges, the communication flows and relationships between NGOs and government are inconsistent and regularly strained, with long-standing distrust on both sides:

> Our [Berlin Refugee Council] connection with *Pro Asyl* is very important. I can pass on information to them which can be utilised at the federal level, or even be taken to the

---

[7] Barbara John was appointed as the first Commissioner in Berlin. The Commission offers a variety of services, advice and training on the integration of immigrants to both immigrants themselves and to the wider German society. Public relations and community awareness campaigns are a vital part of the Commissions work. The Office of the Commissioner for Foreigner's Affairs also regularly conducts opinion polls of Berlin citizens to gauge attitudes toward foreigners and their integration into the city.

> European parliament through ECRE. The bad thing is that with politicians the debate has almost stopped. They do not see us, nor Pro Asyl federally as partners, they are just not interested any more. This is a loss of democracy. The really bad thing is that among those who formulate and pass legislative changes, no one enters debates with us. It is not taken for granted for instance, that we can sit down with government at the same table (Interview No. 9).

It is far from clear, how a rapprochement between state and non-state actors can be achieved. When questioned on how NGOs could be more effective in their advocacy role on behalf of asylum seekers, Barbara John, the Berlin Commissioner for Foreigners' Affairs stated:

> They work with the heart and deeply felt convictions, but not always rationally. And I find one cannot do such work with too much emotion, or to pacify one's own convictions. Rather, it is important not to overly stress the Germans who must in the end pay for this work. NGOs tend to paint people as either 'good' or 'bad' in terms of human rights - but that exists only in fairy stories. You must remain rational and look after the interests of the tax payer too (Interview No. 4).

The federal Commissioner for Foreigners' Affairs, Cornelia Schmalz-Jacobsen, in addressing the same question stated:

> I would wish for more dialogue, a real dialogue (with NGOs). In Germany there is a mutual distrust between government and NGOs which does not exist in all Saxon countries. The government could not possibly do all the NGOs ask, but the government could foster more dialogue with the NGOs because there is very much expertise among NGOs (Interview No. 16).

In the political arena, it has particularly been the Green Party which has argued that Germany's official lack of immigration policy is detrimental to the overall development of German society, as well as to perceptions overseas. At an everyday level though, arguments about newcomers, citizenship rights, and models of inclusion, tend to become submerged in legal argument. For average citizens it is more commonly questions of how a local community is shaped, how resources are allocated, and whether decisions taken on a range of issues reflect mainstream concerns. Later in this chapter I will assess the impact of asylum seekers on local communities and analyses some responses and actions of NGOs.

NGOs in Germany are organised in quite distinct ways to their counterparts in Australia. Though the broad problems and issue which they address in the advocacy of asylum seekers bear similarities, the bureaucratic and administrative practices of the two countries diverge. In Germany, co-operation, information-sharing and constituency links exist between NGOs engaged in similar but not necessarily identical areas of concern. For instance, the union movement, the environment movement, and numerous human rights groups may join with refugee and asylum advocates on a regular basis, planning public actions and long-term strategies. Such co-operation enhances the capacity for advocacy and public recognition of NGOs who work in the area of refugee advocacy. Until the late 1990s any such collaborative initiatives were rare in the Australian case (Interview No. 55).

On a practical level, the decentralised response to meeting the housing and social needs of asylum seekers in Germany, has some distinct advantages as well as disadvantages; first, for asylum seekers, second, for their advocates (NGOs) and third, for the government authorities which have the responsibilities of administering the welfare of asylum seekers. In the first instance, the idea of 'burden sharing', which Germany has been a vocal advocate for on the European stage, is enacted within the German nation through decentralisation. Decentralisation also results in asylum seekers being more visible right across the nation, rather than only in large urban centres. This can have positive as well as negative outcomes for individual asylum seekers. First, the ethnic communities which an asylum seeker may have links to and be able to draw on for moral or other support during an application period, will often be located in specific urban centres. Being at a great distance from such groups or communities, as regularly happens through the German 'quota allocation' of asylum seekers to all *Länder,* can result in asylum seekers experiencing loneliness, lack of support networks and acute feelings of alienation in a strange environment. Asylum seekers often appear not only more visible, but also increasingly burdensome in smaller towns and rural districts than in urban centres where ethnically diverse populations are the norm. Though it is not within the scope of this research to explore in great detail the links between acts of violence on foreigners, and the living circumstances of asylum seekers in concentrated areas such as hostels or camps, such research is important to the formulation and re-formulation of policies not only for asylum seekers, but also for other groups of foreigners as well as for the local population living alongside such group housing. By comparison in Australia where no such decentralisation model operates, asylum seekers who live in the general community during their determination process suffer no particular social stigma that differentiates them from other immigrants and are able to draw on assistance from their own ethnic communities, as well as the wider population. However those asylum seekers who are subject to detention experience isolation in centres which are located in some the most remote regions of Australia.

I now draw on examples of particular initiatives and strategies which NGOs have drawn on in one-off actions, as well as in ongoing campaigns of advocating for the rights of asylum seekers to government and to the general public. In drawing on particular examples, I seek to highlight the way in which NGOs offer forms of practical assistance to asylum seekers.

## Everyday life

A recurring theme utilised by NGOs for well over a decade in advocating for the human rights of those seeking protection has been; 'the individual counts'. Pro Asyl have utilised this theme in national publicity campaigns to inform the German public of stories behind the statistics of asylum seekers; giving a human face to the individuals who are otherwise overlooked in administrative processes. In addition, many citizen initiatives in small towns, or particular suburbs of urban centres have developed projects which focus on the stories and living circumstances of individual asylum seekers. Such initiatives increased in number in response to the waves of violence against foreigners in the early 1990s. Local initiatives regularly rely on the leadership of one, or perhaps a handful of 'charismatic' figures or leaders. Such leaders tend to be involved in other human rights networks such as a local branch of Amnesty International, a local refugee council, or church organisation involved in assisting asylum seekers. Local initiatives commonly emerge in areas where a refugee hostel has been opened. Such initiatives tend to be exclusively voluntary, working alongside a state or church sponsored social worker, and providing such services as language tutoring, other educational assistance, or accompanying individual asylum seekers to hearings.[8] Local initiatives, staffed by volunteers, indicate a level of responsibility and ownership for what happens on the streets and in neighbourhoods. Collaboration between local initiatives, responds directly to the phenomenon of the 'silent bystander' which accompanied the rising xenophobia and violent actions of 1991 and beyond. The federal *Ausländerbeauftragte* until 1998, Cornelia Schmalz-Jacobsen, laments the role of bystanders in the ongoing efforts against racism and violent acts against foreigners:

> You cannot convince a real racist of an alternate view. The important thing is that not too many people stand at the sidelines. We have to say to them 'this affects you too, and what happens today to foreigners, can affect us all tomorrow' (Interview No. 16).

The well-established national NGOs, such as Caritas, Diakonie, the German Red Cross, Gesellschaft für Bedrohte Völker and the regional refugee councils of each of the *Länder* facilitate local initiatives through various forms of support; verbal and written advice, contacts with other relevant networks and social support. The dissemination of information which these national NGOs generate should not be underestimated. Particularly church-based organisations, as well as the German Red Cross are involved in international development work as well as social welfare and advocacy work within Germany. As a result, they have at their disposal accurate, up-to-date information, personal accounts and analysis from 'refugee-producing' countries which are distributed through networks within Germany.

[8] There are for instance, some fifty such small, neighbourhood initiatives attached to the Munich Refugee Council.

In large urban centres such as Berlin, Frankfurt, Munich or Hamburg, with relatively large numbers of foreigners, measures for integration and various resettlement services are well-established primarily through the auspices of the large NGOs, supported by state funding. What is lacking, is any central co-ordinating mechanism, body, or government bureaucracy such as DIMIA in the Australian case. German decentralisation results in a great variety of responses to asylum seekers in the different *Länder*. Such variation has a twin effect: first, processes of integration and resettlement are not well institutionalised and established as rights, but rather are open to challenge; and second, as a corollary of the first point, the work of local initiatives and the activity of citizens becomes more critical and relied on. It seems that the lack of co-ordinated, formal programmes for foreigner resettlement have resulted in greater responsibility being vested at the local level. In some local situations, an 'engaged' and active citizenry take on responsibilities, which in a more centralised system would be the domain of the state. The problem that arises is the question of sustainability and of obligation. Individual citizens who enter into such activities on a voluntary basis may withdraw their agency at any point and for a variety of reasons. The state on the other hand, cannot withdraw social support activities without risking constituency support.

The question of solidarity within local communities, extends beyond the issue of immigrants and their integration to other social issues, be it unemployment, homelessness and so on. Refugee NGOs generally acknowledge that in principle links between the needs of different marginalised groups exist; though just how priorities are to be set between these groups is not always clear. Finding volunteers who are willing to undertake various forms of work on behalf of asylum seekers does not seem to be a particularly difficult task.

> It is exactly where the problems are very great, that people want to show some solidarity and resistance, and also do not want to be seen as reacting for foreigners as other parts of German society in racist or xenophobic ways. It is here that individual contact with a refugee is important. Many people just do not know the facts of what happens to refugees. Many people just do not know that there are such things as detention centres, and that people in them are not criminals, in fact hardly anyone knows this. (Interview No. 14).

Local NGOs have sought to highlight to their local authorities and their respective state governments, the irrationality in economic and in humanitarian terms, of concentrated housing and other facilities for asylum seekers during the application period. Such 'concentration' in hostel or barrack-style accommodation has been shown to be both financially costly to the state and socially problematic in the 'ghettoisation' effect it has on asylum seekers. The financial cost of meeting the basic needs of asylum seekers during a determination process is commonly portrayed as an unfair burden on taxpayers. However, the living conditions and entitlements of asylum seekers are not necessarily understood by the general public.

A campaign in Munich in the mid 1990s sought to debunk some of the myths relating to the living circumstances of asylum seekers. A group of local organisations who worked with asylum seekers primarily as volunteers, together with the Munich Refugee Council, erected a shipping container in *Marienplatz*, the central shopping district of Munich, to demonstrate the living circumstances of asylum seekers. Containers were regularly used as hostel style accommodation. The containers were filled with the sorts of goods – food and clothing, which were made available for the asylum seekers to buy, most often with the use of coupons. The food and clothing were of inferior quality and it was not uncommon food items offered to have expired their use-by dates. Yet prices of these items were often higher than in regular shops (Interview No. 28). This campaign drew a significant response from the public of Munich. As well as such public actions, aimed at informing the public, local initiatives around Germany have instigated small public gatherings and forums with the specific purpose of introducing Germans to asylum seekers. Commonly called *Begegnungen*, such forums seek out those individuals and groups known to propagate hate talk and violence toward foreigners. Such groups and individuals are invited them to meet and hear the stories of their potential victims.

## Detention and deportation

Perhaps the most contentious aspect of asylum politics in Germany, and the area that has generated much reaction from advocacy NGOs in particular, has been the practice of detention and deportation of asylum seekers. This also encompasses the church sanctuary movement, which is active in the case of failed asylum seekers whose deportation is imminent. In the main, it has been church-based organisations which have been most vocal and active advocates against detention and deportation practices. Such a phenomenon at least partly explained by the relative independence of church organisations, whereby vocal public criticism of government policy is not uncommon.

No doubt, the journey to a country of asylum can be dangerous.[9] As is the case in all countries that deport asylum seekers, little is know of them after their deportation. NGOs utilise their international links to follow up cases of people who have been deported. It has been established by NGOs that in the last decade, at least three asylum seekers deported from Germany were killed in their country of origin after return. In addition, individuals have been documented as having been tortured or abused either by the military or the police after being returned to their country of origin; an unspecified number have disappeared without trace. Nine

[9] From the 1st of January 1993 until the 1st of January 1998, some 80 people died either on their way to Germany or at the border. A further 58 people committed suicide because of an imminent deportation and at least 95 asylum seekers attempted suicide, but failed, sustaining serious injuries.

asylum seekers died in Germany due to police brutality. Since 1993, some 39 individuals have died due to attacks on asylum hostels and accommodation centres and 319 suffered serious injuries (Kommittee für Grundrechte und Demokratie, 1998).

In Germany asylum seekers are detained in one of two ways: prior to deportation once their asylum application has been turned down, and at international airport in-transit facilities. The regional differences between German States which I have discussed so far, are highlighted also in relation to detention. The detention and removal of people deemed to be illegal falls to the individual state in which an individual resides. The federal government regulates the laws and policies which determine a person's status, while the *Länder* must enforce such regulations. Centralised documentation on detention in Germany is not as comprehensive or readily available as in the Australian case, due to the decentralisation of these responsibilities. The advocacy work of NGOs is thereby to some extent hampered by a lack of transparency.

In Berlin for example, where a large numbers of asylum seekers reside, the use of detention is subject to some NGO scrutiny, though access to detention facilities is difficult. The Green Party in Berlin, and particularly a small number of Green parliamentarians, have been pivotal in co-ordinating and communicating the developments in detention practices (Interview No. 10). The Greens organise the publication of a newsletter, 'ImmigrantInnen-und Flüchtlingspolitik', which includes reports, statistics, news items and other documents in the development of asylum policies. Such publications are distributed and utilised by a wide network of NGOs.

An initiative against detention practice; the 'Initiative gegen Abschiebehaft' (Organisation Against Deportation), began in Berlin under the auspices of the Berlin Refugee Council with the specific task of co-ordinating a campaign of information dispersal, legal representation and activism on the detention issue. A small core group of some seventy individuals, consisting of lawyers, students and other individuals meet on a regular basis to discuss individual cases, organise visits to detention facilities and plan public action. In the main, visits to detainees are restricted to pastoral care workers or health professionals. However through contacts with pastoral care workers this organisation has been able to gain access to detainees on a more regular basis, providing social support and legal advice, as well as attempting to intervene in deportations. In Germany as in Australia, the network of NGOs is also able to facilitate an exchange of information on detainees, their specific needs, legal representation and so on, leading to the possibility of some visits and representation while individuals are in detention. The network of NGOs are mindful though that they must act with due care and caution in defending those who are detained or deported. There is a recognition that a proportion of failed asylum seekers do not have a legitimate case for protection. However, as outlined in chapter three, the refugee definition is narrowly interpreted under German law, leaving many individuals vulnerable, outside the formal legal interpretation of refugee status, yet still needing some form of humanitarian protection. It is in such cases that NGOs seek to intervene.

The Jesuit Refugee Service (JRS) is active in the advocacy of asylum seekers in detention in Germany as well as in Australia. JRS Germany, and its international network of Jesuits and lay workers, has played an active role through the 1990s in lobbying politicians at the federal level on asylum policy (Interview No. 26). Though the JRS as an organisation is relatively small, it has effectively utilised a two-pronged strategy: 1) drawing effectively on the vast network of the Catholic church, and 2) utilising the public statements, writing and testimonials of high profile Jesuit priests who are widely respected in German society. JRS Germany have not only been active on the issue of detention practice, but also in advocating for the rights of 'illegals'; those whose asylum claim has been found to be 'manifestly unfounded', yet who cannot return to their country of origin. Networks of church and lay organisations and individuals provide information to so-called 'illegals' on where they can access free medical care, and have basic needs met. After legislative changes in November 1998, asylum seekers awaiting a determination became subject to severe restrictions on their rights and entitlements, with newly arrived asylum seekers facing detention. At this time the JRS acted as part of an NGO lobby which appealed to the Berlin Parliament.[10]

It is specifically the actions against deportation which have gained the most concentrated public attention. The deportation of individuals held in detention facilities often takes place with less than twenty-four hours notice. An action plan of NGO networks draws on individuals available to present themselves at a deportation port – usually an airport. Demonstrations include pamphlet drops to passengers boarding the deportees flight, informing them of the imminent deportation of an individual on their flight and what action they can take as passengers.[11]

In both Germany and Australia, the one issue of detention policy which has been the most controversial and been met by the strongest opposition by NGOs has been the detention of children. It is also the area most likely to yield a discretionary approach by administrators and bureaucrats. In Germany, children, including unaccompanied minors, have been subject to detention at the airport detention facility at Frankfurt am Main airport. The work of the German branch of the International Social Services (ISS), has highlighted the situation of unaccompanied minors (Interview No. 17). Both international and national NGOs have sought to draw public attention to the detention of families, including children (ECRE 1993).

---

[10] A new detention facility was set up in Berlin during 1999 (JRS Dispatches No, 46 and JRS *Servir*, No. 18)

[11] Often translated into a number of languages, these pamphlets ask passengers to draw the attention of the captain and crew to the involuntary and violent nature of the deportation, and to protest until the detainee is allowed to disembark from the plane prior to departure.

**The ethics of civil disobedience: the case of church sanctuary movements**

So-called 'illegals, or 'unauthorised arrivals' have been an issue of growing political and social concern across Western countries in the last decade. In countries of immigration such as Australia, with a universal visa system, those who are 'irregular' or 'undocumented' either at the point of arrival, or at some point after their arrival, are closely scrutinised and able to be accounted for, as will be discussed in the following chapter. In Germany, it is estimated that up to one million people are living with an 'illegal' status (Eichenhoffer 1999; 13). Local reactions to people living illegally in receiver societies are extremely mixed. We have already seen examples of violence against foreigners, acts which are flamed by the fears associated with those of illegal status taking jobs; of 'polluting' the social milieu by their presence; and an association with deviance. A small proportion of those who find themselves 'illegal' in Germany and under the threat of deportation are taken into the church sanctuary movement. Resistance to state practices takes many forms, from quiet acts of dissent, to open rebellion. The idea of giving sanctuary has its origin specifically in protecting individuals subject to either deportation or detention. It is an idea and a practice with a long history in religious organisations, choosing to shield those persecuted for various reasons.[12]

The phenomenon of church asylum, raises some confronting questions. This practice brings what are mostly peaceful, law-abiding citizens into stark conflict with the state. The decision to give an asylum seeker the protection of a church or parish, is an unambiguous statement that the state has failed in its obligation of protecting those fleeing political persecution (Just 1993). Little wonder then that church sanctuary has caused a great deal of friction between the federal and various *Länder* governments and the NGOs and church groups who have provided sanctuary. There have been a small number of cases where a period of sanctuary has allowed a legal appeal to take place, resulting in the formal granting of refugee status.

In Australia church sanctuary has not been actively practiced, though a sanctuary network was activated in relation to East Timorese asylum seekers as already discussed in chapter four. This network of activists also became engaged in opposition to policies of detention which became increasingly harsh by the late 1990s and into the twenty-first century. In 2001 and again in 2002, such a network has given sanctuary to asylum seekers who have escaped from detention facilities first from Villawood and later from the Woomera detention facility. The Australian

---

[12] Church asylum began to have an impact in Germany in the early 1990s. In the state of Bavaria between 1989 to November 1996, 33 church communities and convents have been asked to give asylum to individuals or families: they included Protestant, Catholic and Independent, so-called, 'free' churches. This is a phenomenon akin to citizen offering at least temporary protection, usually within a particular church parish or 'safe houses' affiliated with it.

government regards the harbouring of such escapees as acts against the state, which could attract a ten-year prison sentence. An analysis of detention practices in Australia follows in chapter seven.

Having so far discussed a cross-section of NGO activities, let us consider some of the constraints which limit the potential of NGOs. For instance, NGOs who undertake a defined areas of work such as the delivery of health or psycho-social services to refugees and asylum seekers, in the form of torture and trauma counselling, attract specific funding from local, state, or federal government. These types of organisations often have difficulty in engaging directly in advocacy activities. In such cases the inherently 'political activity' of advocacy can result in jeopardising funding and other forms of support from government agencies. However, a form of 'invisible political activity' is possible whereby a close relationship with other NGOs who do engage in direct advocacy can facilitate valuable front-line information, case studies, as well as qualitative and quantitative data being shared and able to be utilised by those with greater autonomy. Keck and Sikkink (1998) document the power which advocacy networks can generate within and between national polities through collaborative efforts. Many of the refugee NGO workers and advocates interviewed for this research have clarity of purpose, strategy and often a deep understanding of the social and political 'field' in which their work and action takes place. The political and cultural specificities of 'place' do result in distinct practices toward refugees and asylum seekers and therefore distinct responses of NGO practices which are imbued with a knowledge of the local context. We cannot assume that transposing the experiences of German NGOs into an Australian context, or vice versa will result in the same or similar outcomes. Nevertheless a number of factors are similar across the case studies, in relation particularly to those things which constrain and order the work of NGOs, they include:

1. The increasing difficulty of obtaining recurring funding, particularly from state sources.
2. The relative insignificance in terms of number of workers, of resources and of relative power to influence opinion makers and transmitters.
3. The often vast array of roles an NGO must take on, due to the increasing complexity of the law and administrative procedures that relate to asylum seekers.
4. Seeking the best strategies to remain relevant to the public, while minimising the chance of a 'backlash'.

## The 'harmonisation' of asylum policy in the EU: beyond a German problem?

Just as distinctions between German and Australian NGOs must be taken into account, regional pressures vary on the German and Australian governments in terms of administering asylum claims. For Germany, the impact of EU-wide approaches to asylum policy must be accounted for. In addition, bi-lateral and multi-lateral collaborations between governments on the movement of asylum seekers and on processing and determination systems have become more co-ordinated in the last decade.

The role of Germany within Europe is shaped both by the developments within the European Union as a whole, and by the future and stability of Eastern Europe. From the mid-1980s a heightened co-operation and 'harmonisation' of approaches and policies, and information swapping on immigration, particularly between OECD states has been evident (Overbeek 1995). The impetus for harmonisation and co-ordination of policy has coincided with an increase in numbers of asylum seekers arriving in Western countries, and with asylum seekers being increasingly representative of people from Third World countries. This stands in contrast to the period up to the early 1980s when the majority of asylum seekers looking for protecting in the West came from Eastern Europe.

Within the EU, the push for harmonisation comes above all, from the urge to lift the border controls between member states, opening movement within Europe, while at the same time tightening and extending control over entry from outside Europe.[13] Those who advocate for the rights of asylum seekers interpret the search for 'harmonisation' as a one-sided approach by governments to deter those seeking protection from entering a country. There is at the same time no 'harmonised' approach to address the question of who is in need of protection, nor a 'harmonised' approach to a procedure which could determine this (Kumin 1996; 6-7, Roth and Hanf 1998); individual states act in quite distinct ways which often relate more to domestic political pressures and public opinion than to the obligations of the international protection system. Bi-lateral and multi-lateral relations between states on the issue of border control, immigration and the movement of illegals had by the late 1980s developed into a highly integrated and sophisticated system of initiatives and information sharing.[14] In the area of

---

[13] This approach began with the Schengen Agreement of 1985, and the Dublin Convention of 1990. Through measures such as the 'safe country' and 'third country' policies, chain deportations became common by the mid 1990s with those seeking protection being sent from country to country, without being able to lodge a protection claim in any of the EU member states.

[14] The Schengen agreement allows passport free travel between EU member states, with the centralised Schengen Information System (SIS) where a database for persons 'non grata', for missing persons, and criminals, have widened security measures to the EU level. The more recent Amsterdam Treaty of 1997, is a reinforcement of 'soft' EU law, particularly in relation to immigration and asylum issues. That is, asylum is still almost exclusively a sovereign decision of the individual nations concerned, with little or no real power at the European level to enact decision contrary to national interest. Furthermore, the replacement of border controls by other means, such as security checks have been sub-contracted in many cases to private security firms. There is an increasing reliance on computerised checks of persons. Police work continues to target certain 'risk' groups, rather than working

migration and particularly unsolicited immigration, such collaborations tend toward a harmonisation of policies and administrative measures, diminishing the rights of asylum seekers. Throughout the 1990s, the phenomenon of people smuggling emerged as a security threat. Those individuals who are 'illegally traded' through trafficking and people smuggling networks; among them, economic migrants and asylum seekers, are viewed as fraudulent, cheats, even criminals, willing to pay thousands of dollars to penetrate the borders of Western nations. Advocates for the rights of forced migrants can be said to have the easy part of the bargain in upholding the rights of refugees and asylum seekers, while the state has the onerous task of arbitrating between individual cases, balancing humanitarian responsibility, national cohesion, and fiscal limitations. While many of the NGOs interviewed as part of this research acknowledge this dilemma, they see their role as continuing to challenge governments into just and accountable action.

Inter-governmental initiatives and co-operation directed specifically at security issues and the deterrence of asylum seekers have increased during the 1990s. The Intergovernmental Consultations on Asylum, Refugee and Migration Policies in Europe, North America and Australia (IGC), was initiated in 1985. Today the IGC operates as a multilateral consultation mechanism of information and policy ideas exchange between the governments of Australia, Belgium, Canada, Denmark, Finland, Germany, Italy, the Netherlands, Norway, Spain, Sweden, Switzerland, the U.K. and the United States of America. The European Council on Refugees and Exiles (ECRE) a non-government agency which represents a membership of NGOs from European countries aims to have a high profile at regional consultations on asylum policy.[15] Given the general lack of transparency that pertains to intergovernmental consultations, the presence of a body such as ECRE is highly valued by the NGO sector. ECRE provides a forum which allows NGOs to present a unified analysis of the key issues in refugee and asylum policy. This is done through the regular publication of documents and policy recommendations made by ECRE.

Policy co-ordination on immigration and asylum issues tends to take place inter-governmentally rather than communally (supranationally). This means that in relation to people movement, in the realm of security and defence policy, EU member states prefer to negotiate government to government. Thereby, while successful communal agreements between EU states on economic policy is reflected in the smooth transition to the single European currency (the Euro), the same cannot be said for asylum policy and other aspects of immigration policy. As

---

on all entries. In 1995 Germany had 701,000 names entered in its national SIS , of which over 600,000 were the names of immigrants.

[15] ECRE has a Secretariat based in London with a small staff, and a representative at the EU in Brussels. An Executive Committee has representatives from the major regions of Europe. Bi-annual meetings of the ECRE membership allow an information-exchange and consolidation of approaches.

O'Brien suggests there is a contradictory process evident in relation to economic issues and immigration:

> There, the need to improve the competitive position of European capital in the global rat race compels states to condone a large measure of 'irregular' or 'undocumented' - or whatever the currently favoured euphemism - immigration, and to devise some form of a common labour market policy. Further there is ample proof that policies devised to diminish illegal immigration in effect strengthen the development of a segmented labour market and hence the 'demand' for illegal migrant workers, because such a policy provides a fitting response to the growing need for 'non established' labour (in Overbeek 1995; 32).

Similarly, Habermas points out that European integration has led not only to economic interdependence but that the need for co-ordination in other policy fields; social policy and education has also grown (1992b). Moreover, in order to foster tolerance within the European Union, where multi-ethnic and multi-cultural groups can coexist in peace and co-operation, the limits of existing citizenship rules and the level of social, political and economic integration of immigrants in member states must be considered. It is outside the scope of this book however, to develop such analysis. It can be said that in general, the need for policy co-ordination at the supranational level has translated for citizens into a further distancing from decision making processes; that is, the gap between being affected by something and having the opportunity or will to participating in changing it, is ever growing (Habermas 1992b). I would continue the assessment of Habermas to argue that this distancing is at least in part displayed in the ambivalence and lack of political action which occurs on the asylum issue. As I have shown from both case studies, NGOs advocating for refugees and asylum seekers often experience little resonance with the public they attempt to engage.

As numerous analysts and commentators have argued, the response to asylum seekers around Europe has been synonymous with a fortress mentality, erecting a firewall against those seeking protection at the external perimeter of Europe along with a raft of legislative amendments in particular member states which led through the 1990s to such phenomenon as 'chain deportations' of asylum seekers in a revolving door between member states. The social and political tensions which have resulted from immigration in the new Europe, can be processed communicatively in a variety of ways. How issues are framed, and where the focus of attention is drawn; how long an issue is kept in the public spotlight, are all factors which form the background of policy development and resource allocation. A less obvious consequence of public debates is the potential to encourage political mobilisation and the flourishing of new social movements and citizen initiatives which identify and solve local problems. However the reality is far removed from such an idealised view. Rather, I would argue that at the EU level, as well as at other supra state levels, there is an ambiguity of interests, of approaches and of outcomes toward the asylum issue. It is still primarily at the level of the individual nation-state that decisions are taken which affect asylum seekers. Though EU collaborations have been expected to redistribute some of the immigrant load, primarily asylum seekers, through 'burden sharing', this has not happened. It has largely been the tightening of German asylum law and administrative procedures such as forced return, in addition to the restrictions of social and legal entitlements granted to asylum seekers that have resulted in a reduction in asylum applicants in Germany. In the late 1990s, the numbers of asylum applicants increased in Eastern European states.

Numerous authors have pointed to the relationship between the day-to-day living circumstances of foreigners and attitudes that develop toward them. The fact that asylum seekers are required to live together in hostels and other group accommodation, such as out of commission school halls or army installations which are no longer used for their original purpose, leads to a stigmatisation and stereotyping of such newcomers. The debate about accommodation is one in which refugee NGOs have participated at federal and at local levels. NGOs have gathered evidence of the cost savings which cash grants to asylum seekers to enable them to look after their own needs could make, rather than the 'in-kind' payments which are not only costly to organise and administrate, but are demeaning to the recipient, making them easy targets for abuse. Asylum seekers are provided with coupons rather than cash for food items and clothing. Presenting coupons in a shop immediately identifies an individual as an asylum seeker to the shop keeper and to fellow shoppers. Such examples of the everyday living circumstances of asylum seekers, are part of the broader emphasis and approach of Western governments toward 'unwanted' asylum seekers.

In the search for means of deterrence and legitimate physical expulsion, the approach of Western governments to the arrival of 'irregular' or 'illegal' arrivals seeking protection have converged over the last decade. Simultaneously, an unexpected convergence between transnational capital and human rights advocates on the issue of supporting more liberal, inclusive policies of immigration has occurred. While these two groups have very different reasons for advocating liberal policies toward immigration, the 'end-points' of their deliberations merge. Both parties have at least some influence in decisions taken by particular nation states, and both have some means to exert influence; be it economic power as in the case of transnational capital; or power by persuasion, represented by the human rights activists. In conclusion, the examples which I have discussed in this chapter can only claim to be generally representative of action toward asylum seekers. Nevertheless, I have illustrated some of the points of tension in the emerging debates regarding the arrival of asylum seekers in countries of the West, including the way in which their claims are administered, and the way in which integration into the receiver society, or expulsion from it is carried out. Ultimately some significant questions emerge for the receiver society. What consequences flow from the action described in this chapter? What transformations can we expect to the nation-state as social trust is eroded? Is the treatment of asylum seekers related to other groups within the nation-state, or can we 'bracket-off' the treatment of such 'outsiders' from that of other individuals?

Chapter 7

# Detention and state sanctioned violence in Australia

As part of the civilising process that marks modern societies, we expect to see the elimination of arbitrary violence from social life through the rule of law. One result of such social developments is that legitimate violence comes to be concentrated under the control of the state (Weber 1947). The state, through institutionalised mechanisms, guards not only the internal coherence of a society, but the perimeters of a national community (Bauman 1989; 27). We see many examples of such logic of the modern state through mechanisms of control and discipline. Even seemingly insignificant processes, repeated and formalised through hierarchies of expertise, sanction some actions and behaviour and punish others through complex social arrangements, laws and procedures (Foucault 1977). Both Foucault and Weber describe the use of enclosure as a form of discipline. We see this in the monastic rituals and observances of religious orders as well as in the organisation of prisons and other 'correctional' facilities.

Containment came to be utilised as a form of discipline, as in educational institutions and in factories, punishment or reform, in prisons and other correctional facilities, or as a form of quarantine, controlling the spread of infectious diseases. It came to be viewed culturally and implemented as forms of protection *from* those being contained, but potentially also protection *of* those being contained from the mob, or the masses outside. In modern societies, state sanctioned and organised forms of containment are utilised for those who have committed criminal offences, for those with serious infectious diseases and for those individuals who have a mental illness and are deemed a threat to their own safety or the safety of others. Otherwise modern societies, and in particular those which operate with democratic institutions, enshrine the freedom of the individual as a value of such significance that coercive measures of detention are rare. Detention usually takes place after a thorough process of independent adjudication on the individual grounds for detaining a person. Moreover, processes of appeal and review usually accompany guidelines for detention, as in the case of criminal detention.

As already stated, detention symbolises a cordoning off, or quarantining of certain individuals from the majority, or mainstream of a society to avert some perceived infection or harm to the majority by the minority. Saramango, in his novel *Blindness* (1997), explores the social and psychological consequences of forced encampment in the form of quarantining the victims of an outbreak of blindness. What begins as an administrative exercise of controlling those going blind, as the onset of blindness is thought to be contagious, escalates rapidly into a society-wide panic, as the number of blind begins to exceed those with sight. Paranoia, fear and the loss, or suspension of previous modes of social decency toward others, accompanies the increased incidence of blindness and the corresponding increase in those subject to detention. The loss of trust, first evident in those without sight, spreads to the seeing. Who will be next to lose their sight and require cordoning off from the mainstream? What will happen when the blind become the majority? How will they be able to be controlled and managed? The anxieties and questions raised in this fictionalised account of social distrust, accompanied by a marked loss of decency between people, are symbolic of developments in social and eventually political relationships soured by minor differences and misunderstandings. I maintain that the long-term and non-reviewable detention of asylum seekers which is practiced in Australia is a phenomenon, able to be maintained only through deeply-embedded misunderstandings in Australian society of those detained.

Detention is a policy decision and a strategic and administrative practice which is unambiguously about containment, separation and punishment. Imposed on individuals deemed 'anti-social', or as having breached a social code or law, detention reaffirms the security of the rest. Moreover, the association between detention and punishment, even in the case of asylum seekers, is not an arbitrary nor ambiguous association (Caloz-Tschopp 1997; 166). While the nexus between security and punishment is often hidden in official accounts of detention practice, and the rationale for such practices by governments, it becomes more visible through the testimony of those detained, requiring independent scrutiny of the media and non-state actors.

The rule of law and administrative levers demarcate the field of action in which asylum seekers and their advocates operate to achieve substantive protection. NGOs and various social movements have access to an autonomous field of action; the domain in which public awareness is reached and communication and actions take place. In turn, the application of, and the willing adherence to law and order are related to a familiarity and affinity with institutionalised values to the extent that these values are internalised by social actors (Habermas 1996; 67). Habermas shows that interests, values and motivations interpenetrate social orders;

> Social orders lend reality to normative patterns of behaviour by specifying values with regard to typical situations and by integrating values with given interest positions (Habermas 1996; 66).

Where institutional arrangements, and their legal enforcement broadly reflect societal norms and values, such arrangements will continue with little dissent. What then must occur in order for an institutional arrangement to be regarded as inappropriate? At what point can we expect a challenge to institutional arrangements? Moreover, in what cases should, or can international norms be able to penetrate the 'national logic' of a particular institutionalised arrangement?

Australia, as a 'country of immigration' has adopted various social and political strategies of incorporating newcomers as 'Australians' in relatively rapid processes, underpinned by the citizenship model of integration. As chapter four has indicated, it has not been migrants but rather Aboriginal Australians who became 'outsiders' after white settlement. White Australian conceptions of nation building recognised the need to utilise migrant labour and skills as well as the need to increase the population through further selective immigration. The prevailing model with regard to immigrants until the late 1970s remained an assimilationist one. In Australia, assimilation was not delineated within rigid, easily recognised cultural traits and traditions as in the case of Germany. Though many writers may point to the dominance of a form of Anglo culture, underscored by Protestant values, many other influences were detectable in Australian identity after white settlement.

So far we have seen evidence of a reasoned dialogue between state and non-state actors regarding the formulation and implementation of refugee policy. Friction and conflict exists as a constant in such relationships, as the state covers itself in the mantle of sovereignty and national interest, while non-state actors draw on human rights principles and moral arguments which supersede any one state. Nevertheless, some progress is made, information shared and passed on toward the improvement of policy and administration. In addition we have seen evidence of the state in both Germany and Australia acknowledging the specific knowledge and expertise of NGOs, and the consequent importance of a dialogue between the parties. Similarly, NGOs in both case studies indicate a degree of sympathy with the dilemmas which the state must address in the administration of refugee claimants, and in balancing the myriad of other interests within a state. The examples which are documented in this chapter however, show a contrary picture to the prevailing mood of 'cautious co-operation', evident in many of the state/non-state interactions discussed so far. The detention of asylum seekers has become the caesura of relations between the state and NGOs in Australia; a development which, while highly inflamed in recent years, has its origins a decade earlier with the introduction of mandatory detention by the Hawke Labor government.

## The uses of detention

As undocumented arrivals are not felons, the detention of these individuals beyond a reasonable time for health and security checks, highlights tensions for a democracy. The willingness to detain asylum seekers for long periods is symptomatic of a defensive political system. However, making stronger claims about the uses of detention is fraught with problems. Those actors who oppose detention practices in Australia; refugee NGOs and human rights organisations, also advocate for other groups of refugees, asylum seekers and immigrants more broadly who are not in detention, yet also face significant obstacles in their claims for protection and for integration into Australian society. In these cases, advocacy practice for one group must be evaluated in terms of consequences for other groups, as well as in terms of a general backlash either from the government, or the public. Moreover, the gathering of evidence on the detention issue is notoriously difficult. Regular access for NGOs, for health workers, researchers or journalists to detention facilities in Australia is difficult, at times impossible. When access is granted, it is usually strictly controlled, with time limits, lack of privacy and access granted to designated areas only.

Deportation is a regular practice by all states to remove those 'unlawfully' within the territorial areas of a specific state. In relation to persons claiming protection under the *Refugee Convention*, the concern expressed by such bodies as the UNHCR, is to ensure that individuals are not *refouled*: that genuine refugees are inadvertently sent back to the country of origin which persecuted them. The international legal norms that apply to detention outline the limits that should apply to such practices. The Geneva Convention (at Article 31.2) asks contracting states to only apply restrictions to the movements of refugees until their status is regularised, or they are accepted by another country. The Executive Committee of the UNHCR (EXCOM) has made numerous recommendations that detention only be used in limited cases until a person's identity is established. Particularly in recent years, as the detention of asylum seekers has become a more widespread practice, the UNHCR has become more vocal on the inappropriateness of detention for those seeking asylum, until all other alternatives have been exhausted (UNHCR 1999; 38-40). I will now evaluate the detention and deportation practices in Australia.

## Detention and removal of unauthorised arrivals in Australia

> It was a secret operation that would have done a totalitarian regime proud. But it happened in Australia, a country that so often speaks out against human rights abuses in the region. Let Leng Tang, 28, a legal migrant to Australia, farewelled his wife in the morning last Monday week and went off to scour Sydney's depressed western suburbs for a job. When he returned to Villawood migrant hostel that afternoon, he found that his bride of three months, Eng Hua Lim, had been one of 24 Cambodian boat people rounded up and ordered onto a Darwin-bound plane in readiness for deportation to war torn Cambodia.
>
> There had been no advance warning of the swoop by 17 immigration officers and security guards on Villawood . . . the chosen 24, including children and an octogenarian stroke victim, had been told to attend a morning meeting. There, they were handed a document telling them their applications for refugee status had been refused. They were each given a plastic bag and escorted, sobbing and wailing, back to their rooms to collect a maximum 20 kg of personal belongings before being driven 200m to be held incommunicado at the hostel's detention lockup to await transport to Sydney airport for the 3,100 km flight to Darwin (*Time*, June 3, 1991).

> The Immigration Minister, Mr Ruddock, last night blamed the detained parents of a seriously ill child for their son's predicament.
>
> Six-year-old Shayan Badraie has been diagnosed with an acute post-traumatic stress disorder. He does not speak and is regularly admitted to hospital because he refuses food and drink since seeing an inmate at Villawood attempt suicide by slashing his wrists several months ago. Earlier, at the Woomera centre, he saw inmates setting fire to themselves and guards using batons to quell a riot.
>
> He, his younger sister and Iranian parents have been in detention for 17 months. Their application for refugee status has been declined, and they are expected to be deported any day.
>
> But Mr Ruddock said yesterday that it was Shayan's parents, not the Government's mandatory detention policy, who were responsible for the child's illness. 'They have brought their child to Australia unlawfully, in the knowledge they would be detained when they got here. A lot of psychiatric conditions arise because you have a predisposition to them, and this can be triggered if your parents elect to bring you halfway around the world in order to make asylum claims.' (SMH, August 14, 2001; 2).

These two media reports on the detention and deportation approaches in Australia are separated by a ten-year period. During that period, an unwavering approach to individuals who arrive in Australia without valid documents and subsequently ask for protection has continued under the leadership of the consecutive Labor governments of Bob Hawke, 1983-1991, Paul Keating, 1991-1996, as well as the conservative Liberal/National coalition government of John Howard since 1996. People who enter Australia without authorisation either by an air or sea route and subsequently seek asylum, are subject to a policy of mandatory and non-reviewable detention until such time as they are either determined to be a refugee or deported. This approach continues despite the accumulation of empirical evidence by health practitioners, lawyers, journalists, national and international NGOs and government statutory authorities such as HREOC and the Australian Audit Office, indicating the serious concern which these practices have raised about the long term consequences for those detained. Such consequences are evident in three main areas; the mental health impact on those detained; the negative impact of detention policy and practice on Australia's reputation internationally; and in terms of the social self-image within Australia.

Though Table 6.1 (below), indicates that from 1995 to 1999 unauthorised air arrivals exceeded boat arrivals in each year, it has consistently been the arrival of boats carrying asylum seekers, that has generated anxiety, fear and distrust of these arrivals within Australia. As the table indicates, over-stayers, as persons who have entered Australia lawfully and overstayed the requirements of the visa issued them, far exceed the numbers of unauthorised arrivals. Over-stayers are predominantly tourists and students from Europe, Great Britain, and from the United States of America. This group receives little public scrutiny and can be said to cause no anxiety among the Australian public as 'illegals'.

**Table 6.1 Non-citizens in Australia without Authorisation**

| Year | Plane Arrivals | Boat Arrivals | Over-stayers |
|---|---|---|---|
| 2000/01 | 1,508 | 4,141 | 53,000 |
| 1999/00 | 1,695 | 4,175 | 53,000 |
| 1998/99 | 2.106 | 920 | 53,143 |
| 1997/98 | 1,550 | 157 | 51,000 |
| 1996/97 | 1,350 | 365 | 45,100 |
| 1995/96 | 663 | 589 | – |
| 1994/95 | 485 | 1,071 | – |
| 1993/94 | | 194 | – |
| 1992/92 | 2,448 arrivals | 194 | 81,164 |
| 1991/92 | by air from | 78 | – |
| 1990/91 | 1989 to 1993 | 158 | – |
| 1989/90 | | 224 | – |
| Total | 11,805 | 13,489 | n/a |

*Source:* DIMIA Factsheet 74

Chapter five briefly summarised the various waves of boat arrivals to Australia since the mid 1970s, which I return to now in more detail. The first significant arrival of boat people in the post World War II period, came in the early 1970s. This group were Vietnamese, having fled Vietnam after the fall of Saigon. This group were not subject to detention. Before 1989, those who arrived in Australia illegally had to rely on the discretion conferred on the Minister under the Migration Act 1958, to allow entry and to avert deportation (Cox and Glenn 1994; 289). Such assessments in the early 1980s made under discretionary powers tended to be inconsistent; a 'hit-or-miss affair' (Crock 1993; 30). Until the late 1980s the Australian Courts remained cautious with regard to border claimants. In 1989 the High Court in *Chan Yee Kin v Minister for Immigration and Ethnic Affairs* ([1989] 169 CLR 379), found that the bureaucracy had misinterpreted, or misapplied the criteria for determining refugee status as set down in international law. The ensuing years saw a strained relationship between the courts and the government, regarding the role of judicial review and the control mechanisms in migration decision making (Crock 1993; 32).

Cambodian boat people arrived in Australia from 1989 to 1992, fleeing the Pol Pot dictatorship. By October 1991, preparations of a detention facility at Port Hedland in the remote north-west of Western Australia had begun. Two developments were specific to the Cambodian boat arrivals, and subsequently brought about detention as a standard approach for all boat arrivals. First, the Australian Government had taken a leading role in the Paris Peace Agreements, to resolve problems within Cambodia which had led to a refugee exodus (Evans and Grant 1995). Gareth Evans, the then Foreign Minister, sought both a political and a humanitarian solution to the conflict. The Cambodian boat arrivals, seeking protection within Australia during the same period became inadvertently embroiled in foreign policy priorities competing with domestic considerations (Hamilton 1994). Second, the extension of permanent residency to Chinese students who had been in Australia before 20 July 1989 as a group, rather than the normal individual assessments required for those seeking protection, highlighted the arbitrary approach of the Australian state to people in need of protection.

Australia actively recruited overseas students through the 1980s. Many of these students were from the People's Republic of China. At the time of the 1989 student protest movement in China, and the subsequent violent suppression of it, some 20,000 PRC students were in Australia. Following the suppression in China, the then Prime Minister, Mr Hawke, promised sanctuary to these students. A special visa class was created, granting the PRC students temporary residence, which would expire at the end of June 1994. The consequences of this decision related not just to these PRC students, but resulted in a public focus on subsequent asylum applicants who had until that period mostly been immune from public scrutiny.[1] The Cambodian boat arrivals, most of whom arrived after the Chinese students, were most directly affected by this decision. Many commentators and activists lobbying for the Cambodian detainees, argued that political expediency took the place of the consistent application of legislation in assessing the protection needs and bona fides of individuals. Indeed, the generous treatment of the Chinese students was a singular and arbitrary decision, with negative ramifications for asylum seekers.

Subsequently, tensions rose between the Australian Government, the courts, and to a lesser extent the NGOs and human rights activists advocating the rights of refugees and asylum seekers. Several amendments to enforcement and review laws pertaining to refugees resulted (Crock 1998; 210). The *Migration Reform Act 1992,* was a response to the hefty criticism the Government had to field as a result of the issues arising from the practice of detention. The Act resulted in fundamental changes to decision making and review, focusing on a codified scheme, while leaving the possibility for ministerial discretion in place. Moreover, the *Migration Reform Act 1992* stipulates (under Part 2, Division 4B) mandatory detention (Crock 1993; 32). This amendment referred to all refugee claimants who had arrived after 19 December 1989. In other words, the government confirmed its detention practices in retrospective legislation.

Through the 1990s, the practice of mandatory and non-reviewable detention of boat arrivals continued. During this period, detention centres in Sydney and Melbourne increasingly housed air arrivals who were not in possession of travel documents and had engaged Australia's protection obligations. Port Hedland remained the primary detention centre for boat arrivals. The Sino-Vietnamese boat people, who came from 1994 to 1997, drew the majority of public attention. Many of these people were subject to the Comprehensive Plan of Action (CPA), drawn

---

[1] Many of the NGOs interviewed for this research, indicated that this particular, rather emotional decision by the then Prime Minister, Bob Hawke, had serious negative repercussions for other asylum seekers who sought to claim protection after this decision.

up as an international agreement to resettle or, if possible, repatriate Indo-Chinese refugees.

### *(a) Detention practices and their justification*

The primary official reason given for the detention regime in Australia is the maintenance of immigration control; that is, to 'uphold the universal visa requirement and to guard against unauthorised arrivals undermining the immigration program' (Mediansky 1998;126). However, there has also been an acknowledgement by DIMIA, as well as by individual politicians, that the practice of mandatory detention, is used as a deterrence to others who may arrive in this manner. This approach is contrary to the UNHCR recommendations on the justified application of detention of asylum seekers.[2] The question remains; why does Australia continue a policy of mandatory, and non-reviewable detention? Deterrence as a rationale is questionable, as unauthorised boat arrivals and air arrivals have continued to arrive over the last decade despite the detention regime. In commenting on the rationale for maintaining detention, Des Hogan, Refugee Co-ordinator for Amnesty International, Australia states:

> I think it's a control thing. Very much a part of the Australian psyche, I think. Coming here from the outside, it is quite interesting to see. The words anxiety, nervousness, fear; they seem to be fairly deeply engrained here (Interview No. 44).

Whatever the official and unofficial rationale for the continued practice of detention in often harsh and inhumane conditions in Australia, the growing body of evidence from government inquiries, from statutory bodies, international organisations and most recently from Australian health professionals, requires careful appraisal and consideration by both the government and by the Australian public who maintain an overwhelming support for the policies of the government.

It is noteworthy to consider the recognition rate of asylum applicants in Australia, which shows significant variation between those in detention and those permitted to live in the community. The recognition rates of protection claims in Australia averaged 14.6 per cent over the period 1990-99. In Germany the recognition rate over the same period was 7.6 per cent (see Table 2.1). Persons who seek refugee status from within the Australian community, in other words

---

[2] UNHCR's guidelines on the detention of asylum seekers, begins by stating that detention is inherently undesirable, particularly in the case of vulnerable groups such as single women and children, unaccompanied minors and those with particular medical or psychological needs. The guidelines assert that as a general principle the detention of asylum seekers should only be entered into in exceptional circumstances. The guidelines invoke Article 31 of the *Refugee Convention*, which asks contracting states not to apply restrictions to the movement of refugees and not to punish them on account of illegal entry.

who have arrived legally, have been less successful in their claims than those persons who are in immigration detention. However, average recognition rates fail to account for some significant detail in particular periods. During the fiscal year 1999-2000 for instance, 84 percent of primary applications were granted to people held in detention (mostly Iraqis and Afghanis), compared to 5 percent of applicants living in the community.

## A new rationale

In 1997 the Howard Government opened the running of Australia's immigration detention centres to public tendering. The tender was won by Australasian Correctional Management (ACM), a subsidiary of the American Wackenhut Corporation, better known for developing the idea of privately run prisons in the U.S. (MacCallum 2002; 28). As well as being responsible for the security of the detention centres, ACM is responsible for the delivery of social services, such as the accommodation, education, recreational, catering, health care, welfare and counselling to detainees, as well as the maintenance of the centres. Officers of DIMIA monitor the performance of ACM and the government retains ultimate responsibility for detention as set out in the Immigration Detention Standards which are part of the contractual agreement with ACM. One of the problems that has come to light from the privatisation of detention management, is the ability of the government to withhold information from the public on the grounds of commercial confidentiality agreements (Crock and Saul 2002; 82). Limited public scrutiny of detention practices and accountability procedures in relation to the treatment of detainees has resulted from privatised arrangements. While some access to the detention facilities in the urban centres of Sydney, Melbourne and Perth is possible for journalists and even the public, access to the remote centres of South Australia and Western Australia is closed to the public, with journalists only being admitted on formal tours.

**Table 6.2 The Cost of Detention**

| Year | Persons in Detention | Cost ($millions) | Cost per Detainee |
|---|---|---|---|
| 2000/01 | 7,993 | $104m | $13,011 |
| 1999/00 | 8,205 | $90.6m | $11,042 |
| 1998/99 | 3,574 | $22.6m | $ 6,323 |
| 1997/98 | 2,716 | $22.1m | $8,137 |
| 1996/97 | 2,460 | $24.1m | $9,797 |
| 1995/96 | 2,220 | $31.4m | $14,144 |
| 1994/95 | – | $14.5m | – |

*Source:* DIMIA

During 1999 new detention facilities were opened at the disused rocket base at Woomera and at the Curtin air base in the remote Kimberley town of Derby, as the existing detention centres could not accommodate the boat arrivals during that year. The attention given to the detention issue by the media has oscillated from periods of near silence, to periods of daily scrutiny across media outlets. The detention of Cambodians in the early 1990s, received consistent media attention for a limited period, which became part of the pressure resulting in the Senate inquiries of 1992 and 1994 (Kingston 1993; 8-14). The period from 1999 however, has been characterised by renewed and heightened media focus on the detention of asylum seekers. Some of this is due to the increase in numbers of boat arrivals. This alone however, is insufficient to explain the renewed interest in the detention issue, which had remained an issue of relatively minor public and political interest in the early to mid 1990s.

By 1999 regular protest activities within the Australian community, related to the treatment of asylum seekers in detention gathered momentum. Such protest activity drew on the existing human rights and refugee network, but also gathered support from new quarters: the *Refugee Action Collective* was pivotal in gathering grass-roots support, while *Australians for a Fair Australia* (an initiative including prominent public figures, academics and members of the public), utilised the media and public information campaigns, rather than direct action. New coalitions and networks of resistance to the Government treatment of asylum seekers gathered momentum during this period including student groups organised on university campuses and grass roots organisations which complimented and supported the existing network of NGOs engaged in asylum seeker advocacy.

Stories of riots and protests within detention centres and actions of self harm, including hunger strikes, the sewing-together of lips and suicide attempts were regular, almost daily news items through 2000 and 2001. Television footage during August 2000, depicted ACM staff, assisted by police from South Australia in full riot gear, with helmets, batons and shields, quelling a protest consisting of around eighty detainees at the Woomera detention centre. Ultimately, some 300 officers, using water cannon quelled the riot (Mares 2001; 35). Other accounts began to filter from detention centres of ACM officers using excessive force and in some cases beating detainees. Video footage from the Villawood detention centre showed detainees being assaulted and subsequently denied medical attention for their injuries (SMH August 2, 2001; 3).

In June 2001, the Australian Catholic Social Justice Council (ACSJC) characterised the treatment in detention centres as torture:

> At certain stages in their processing, asylum seekers in detention are not allowed contact with their families . . . Unlike those convicted of a criminal offence, asylum seekers do not know for how long they will be detained. In some immigration detention centres observations and musters involve waking asylum seekers at night or shining torches on them while they are sleeping (AAP June 26, 2001).

During the same period the World Council of Churches (WCC) indicated it was 'deeply troubled' about Australia's detention practices, particularly in light of the small numbers of unauthorised arrivals coming to Australia compared to other regions of the world (Reuters July 6, 2001).

Despite considerable public criticism of the mandatory detention system by human rights groups in Australia and internationally, the policy retained the support of the majority of Australians. A survey on Channel 9's *Sunday* programme,[3] for instance indicated that 78 per cent of Australians did not think asylum seekers were harshly dealt with (July 1, 2001).

Many asylum seekers held in immigration detention have expressed to legal and welfare representatives who visit them, a bewilderment at their detention – particularly when the period extends beyond what might be thought reasonable for health and security checks. This bewilderment turns at times to self blame, and can lead to self harm particularly where detention is combined with news of the rejection of a claim and deportation seems imminent (HREOC 1998; 238-42). Hunger strikes and suicide attempts are regular occurrences in Australia's detention facilities. The consequences of trauma experienced during detention will be discussed later.

## Re-traumatising refugees

Research conducted on the impact of detention on asylum seekers (Silove, McIntosh and Becker 1993, Silove and Steel 1998), indicates that detention has the potential to re-traumatise people from a refugee background, many of whom experienced torture and trauma in their country of origin. In these cases detention, particularly where its duration is not defined, leaves individuals susceptible to re-traumatisations. Torture and trauma counselling services have been reluctant to provide services to asylum seekers in detention due to the retraumatising they experience as a result of being detained for indefinite periods.

The impact of government policy on health, particularly the mental health of asylum seekers, has been of increasing concern to advocates. A recent report by Silove and Steel, *The Mental Health and Well-Being of On-Shore Asylum Seekers in Australia* (1998), has highlighted the retraumatisation and additional stress which the asylum process has on those living in the community and, in particular, the impact of detention on asylum seekers. The report stresses that even for those living the community, extreme anxiety is linked to delays in processing applications and poverty resulting from a lack of entitlements such as work permits, racial discrimination and conflict with immigration officials, fears of being sent home and separation from family (ibid.; 10-11).[4]

---

[3] A weekly current affairs programme on social and political developments.

[4] The report surveyed a group of Tamil asylum seekers in detention at Melbourne's Maribyrnong Detention Centre. Seventy two percent of these detainees reported having been

The most recent experiences of self harm by asylum seekers in detention, and the continuing concern over the physical and psychological development of children in detention, has refocused health professionals on their particular responsibility in relation to these individuals (Silove et. al. 2000; 608-9). By August 2001, the Australian Medical Association (AMA) had become involved in the detention issue, with the Federal President, Dr Karen Phelps speaking out against the health effects of detention (ABC Radio National, 13, August, 2001). Phelps had a personal meeting with the Minister for Immigration, voicing her concerns over the treatment of detainees.[5]

This however again returns us to the question of funding, as not only the cost of detention, which have already been detailed, but other consequences of detention become clear. As asylum seekers held in detention are granted TPVs, the states in which they are released are calling for extra funding from the federal government to deal with their needs. The South Australian Minister for Human Services, Dean Brown, has called for federal funding to cover the mental health services of ex-detainees who are in need of psychiatric treatment as a result of their detention experience (ABC, August 28, 2001).

## The action of NGOs

A coalition of Australian refugee NGOs have proposed an alternative detention model to DIMIA on a number of occasions, most recently through the Asylum Seekers' Interagency. While this model asserts the right of the Australian Government to practice mandatory detention of arrivals without a visa, it urges discretionary powers to be utilised which would allow claimants to live in the community while cases are being heard.

By the late 1990s, refugee NGOs were increasingly collaborating in lobbying and information dissemination processes aimed primarily at federal MPs of all the major political parties, as well as targeting the media. The Refugee Council of Australia (RCOA) has adopted a long-standing commitment to engaging the media at various levels in a positive informed portrayal of refugees and asylum seekers.[6]

---

tortured in their country of origin (ibid.; 29). The report poses the question of whether detention worsens the psychological symptoms of traumatised asylum seekers. On six measures, including; depression, suicidal ideation, post traumatic stress symptoms, anxiety, panic attack symptoms and physical symptoms, detainees were two to three times more likely to experience such adverse effects of detention compared to asylum seekers and resettlement refugees living in the community (Silove and Steel 1998; 30).

5 It must be borne in mind that doctors who have contact with detained asylum seekers are sworn to a confidentiality agreement by DIMIA.

6 The RCOA, as many other refugee and migrants organisations in Australia, has the twin role of representing both refugees who have come to Australia under the off-shore programme as well as asylum seekers. The first group requires representation primarily on

It seems that the tension identified by many NGO workers consistently across both case studies, revolves around the fine line of judgement as to the vigour with which a particular issue should be highlighted and argued out in the public domain. Once service delivery crosses over into advocacy action, such judgements as to how, where and in what way an issue is portrayed to the general public become important. NGOs have become more sophisticated and nuanced in their approach to identifying opportunities, and individuals with whom to engage. In short, the consequences of advocacy action need to be identified, particularly where such action enters the public domain and has the potential for some form of backlash for the groups being represented.

Many of the NGO advocates for refugees and asylum seekers in Australia have expressed the view that on an issue such as detention, politicians have an opportunity to lead public opinion and that they largely have failed to do so (Interview No. 35, No. 36, No. 39, No. 46, No. 50). Australian citizens remain relatively uninformed as to the distinctions between categories of immigrants. Certainly until the most recent public scrutiny of the detention issue after the opening of the Woomera facility in 1999, many Australians remained unaware that detention is a mandatory practice; who is subject to it; and under what conditions (Interview No. 41). The demonstrations, protests and violent outbreaks within detention centres and the various forms of self harm and suicide attempts even by children detainees have shocked the Australian public when they have been made public. However, such actions have tended to reinforce the cultural image of a barbarian 'other' as someone to be feared and ostracised, rather than included in the general community. The question then is how to deal with such a situation, and with the individuals affected by the legal and administrative measures of immigration detention. We see evidence of repeated recourse to various arguments and justifications which have their origin in legal procedures. Moreover, such procedures are in a sense embedded in some particularly Australian approaches to newcomers, already discussed in chapter four, which emphasise strict state control and a system of harsh penalties for uninvited arrivals; measures which are not only widely accepted but are indeed expected by the public. Inasmuch as legal procedures are open to regulation, change and the possibility of fallibility, processes must be in place which ensure that minorities have at least some chance of winning over a majority to the possibility of an alternative approach; establishing a revision of what are more usually *majority decision* (Habermas 1996; 179).

> Doubts about the legitimacy of majority decisions on matters with irreversible consequences are revealing . . . doubts are based on the view that the outnumbered

---

resettlement issues, while the second requires more broad-ranging representation on social and economic needs during a determination process, as well as the more contentious issues of the application of Australian law to protection claims.

minority give their consent to the empowerment of the majority only with the proviso that they themselves retain the opportunity in the future of winning over the majority with better arguments and thus of revising the previous decision (ibid.).

In the case under discussion here, the minority are the NGOs who advocate for the rights of asylum seekers and their relatively small group of supporters. The extent to which they have avenues open to air their grievances, with at least the possibility of legal or administrative reform in light of their arguments, tests institutional flexibility in the first instance and democratic procedure in the second. That is not to say that majority decisions undermine democratic rationality *per se*, but rather to remind us that minority arguments require at times an additional degree of receptiveness in order to be heard at all. The physical weight of a majority when accompanied by a corresponding level of noise, drowns out all other voices.

NGO representatives reflect that when they have spoken of detention in public forums and told of women and children being locked up, people have been horrified and surprised by individual stories (Interview No. 36). Some NGO representatives contend that it is broadly in the area of mental health that the detention policy has the greatest chance of being overturned. As we have seen from the discussion in chapter four, many of the people who are detained are ultimately recognised as refugees. Therefore there is legitimacy in the argument that the detrimental effects of detention will have a long-term negative impact on Australian society in the form of refugee residents who have been traumatised through detention in the first months or years in Australia.[7]

It is not an uncommon view, that the contemporary failure of Australian administrators and policy makers to adequately deal with asylum seekers could threaten the viability of the whole refugee programme (Nicholls 1998; 77). Some commentators point out that the *demonisation* of on-shore arrivals, carried out by successive Immigration Ministers, may ultimately prove to be detrimental to the refugee programme as a whole. Moreover, as Australia's immigration system is an integrated system, the lack of coherence in one section is likely to have negative effects on other elements of the system. It tends only to be immigration specialists; lawyers, politicians, some members of the media, and the workers and constituents of refugee NGOs, who are readily able to distinguish the different categories of migrants in any given yearly quota and moreover who understand the complexities of international obligations. Even the most ardent advocates for the rights of asylum seekers though, recognise the legitimacy and in fact the need for governments to arbitrate not only with great care, but with their citizens in mind on asylum claims. That is, if we accept that the granting of asylum requires resources, and that those resources are scarce, then it follows that only those in great need

[7] NGOs have instigated an ex-detainees support group in recognition of the special needs that ex-detainees face, once they have been granted refugee status, adjusting to life in the society that has detained them.

should qualify - those who indeed would suffer irreparably if returned. This argument was developed in light of the tensions between national and international obligations in chapter two. The undoubtedly difficult task for the institutions of government is to differentiate between claimants with speed and justice.

**Should detention continue?**

In the last ten years a number of government, non-government and international reports have investigated the practice of immigration detention in Australia and called for major reform to this practice. In March 1994, the Joint Standing Committee on Migration sought new submissions and published a report; *Asylum, Border Control and Detention.* This report recommended that asylum seekers who had arrived without travel documents should continue to be detained, but that Ministerial discretion could release them after six months. As Andrew Hamilton argues:

> The report also recommended that consideration be given to some more humanitarian treatment of imprisoned children. It [then] went beyond its brief to recommend further limitation of judicial review of decisions made about refugee status. Its substantial conclusions thus were totally opposed to the informed submissions offered to the committee (1994; 31).

Under the present immigration law, certain groups of people are eligible for release from detention on bridging visas. These include: children up to the age of 18, victims of torture and trauma and those over 75 years of age. However, individuals who belong to each of the groups listed are to be found in immigration detention in Australia, as their family members and, in the case of children, their primary care givers are in detention.[8]

On the 30th April, 1997, the United Nations Human Rights Committee found that Australia had practiced arbitrary detention which breached international human rights (specifically the International Covenant on Civil and Political Rights - the ICCPR), in the case of *A* – a Cambodian 'boat person' who had been detained at the Port Hedland facility for more than four years.

In a unanimous decision, the Committee found that the detention of *A* was arbitrary and in breach of articles 9(1) and 9(4) of the ICCPR. The Committee also determined that, pursuant to article 2(3), Australia must provide adequate compensation to *A* as a result of these provisions (Poynder 1997).

Following this decision, Amnesty International (AI) published a report on Australia's detention practices (AI 1998). In November 1998, AI brought an

---

[8] A child may be eligible for a bridging visa, but her mother and/or father is not, keeping parent(s) and child in detention until such time as they are either granted a protection visa (refugee status), or deported.

'Urgent Action' against Australia; the first such action since 1989. This urgent action concerned the imminent deportation of a Somali asylum seeker, Sadiq Shek Elmi. A communication with the UN Committee Against Torture in Geneva has been filed on his behalf. This, together with a concerted effort by NGOs, churches, the public and unions (a union refused to refuel the plane Sadiq Shek Elmi was to be deported on), has had the result of halting his immediate deportation from Perth airport.

In May of 1998, the Human Rights and Equal Opportunity Commission (HREOC)[9] tabled the report of an inquiry into the detention of unauthorised arrivals in Australia – 'Those who've come across the seas'. The impetus for the inquiry was complaints received by the Commission since 1989 by boat people, as well as by air arrivals who were in detention. The report finds that Australian immigration detention practices are in breach of international human rights standards in that they are mandatory and non-reviewable. The report is particularly critical of the detention of children and other vulnerable people, and of prolonged detention. Subsequent to noting its 'in-principle' objection to detention, the report is critical of the facilities and conditions of the detention centres.[10]

The report makes special mention of the practice of segregation, or 'incommunicado' detention of new arrivals at the Port Hedland facility (HREOC, 1998,131), whereby they are held separately from the main group of detainees, with no access to visitors such as lawyers and social workers. HREOC visited the facility in May 1997 and was advised by management at the centre that detainees could write to relatives overseas, but were not permitted to telephone or otherwise correspond with people in the Australian community (132). The complaints HREOC received listed average segregation in isolation cells for all cases as 33 days. The HREOC report also makes mention of a recently published report by the Australian National Audit Office, *The Management of Boat People*. This report notes that incommunicado detention may have been utilised as segregation to keep information from new arrivals regarding their rights to lodge a protection visa application and to legal advice:

> The 44 members of the *Teal* group not assisted to apply for protection visas by DIMIA were kept in separate detention at Port Hedland IRPC until 1 June 1996. Their protection visa applications were lodged one month after they were allowed to mix with detainees of longer standing at the IRPC (Australian National Audit Office, 1998,67).

---

[9] The Human Rights and Equal Opportunity Commission is an autonomous Federal Government Statutory Authority.

[10] The first recommendation of the HREOC report (R3.1) recommends that detention only be used as a last resort – on exceptional grounds. It urges that alternatives to detention be pursued. A further recommendation (R3.3) is that detention should be considered particularly undesirable for vulnerable individuals such as single women, children, unaccompanied minors, or those with special medical or psychological needs.

In June 2000, the Senate Legal and Constitutional References Committee of Australia's Parliament handed down a report into Australia's refugee and humanitarian determination process, *A Sanctuary Under Review*. This inquiry, is far-reaching in terms of the issues covered. It was triggered by two cases in particular which received a great deal of public attention and media scrutiny, not least due to the campaigning of NGOs. The first was the case of a Chinese woman who was deported to China while eight and a half months pregnant with her second child following the rejection of her claim for refugee status. It has been found that upon her return to China, the woman was forced to undergo an abortion. The second case is that of a Somali asylum seeker with a strong protection claim, who narrowly avoided deportation from Australia after the concerted effort of local NGOs, unions and church groups stopped his deportation through the intervention of the UN Committee Against Torture. The Committee's recommendations went well beyond a focus on these two cases.[11] The gathering weight of evidence from government, non-government and international reports and reviews of Australian detention and deportation practices, point to a disjunture between the totality of costs involved, compared with the relatively insignificant numbers of unauthorised arrivals to Australia; certainly in global perspective.

## The physical and symbolic production of social distance

Asylum seekers who are permitted to live in the community while a determination on their status is being made, are no more visible than other migrants, which in an immigration country such as Australia means that newcomers *per se* are not particularly distinguishable. Asylum seekers who live in the community are not required to live in specific housing areas such as hostels or other forms of dormitory accommodation as is the case in Germany. The average citizen cannot distinguish between a business migrant, a special skills entrant migrant, a family reunion migrant, a refugee under the humanitarian resettlement intake or an asylum seeker. This situation is in stark contrast to the majority of European countries who have no, or very limited immigration programmes, with the result that asylum seekers are visible and identifiable as such, rather than as more generalised migrants.

However, as I have argued previously, for those people claiming asylum who have arrived in Australia without travel documents, mandatory detention results in comprehensive invisibility. Though it is true that the number of people in immigration detention is small, this does not neutralise the treatment they receive, nor does it negate the large degree of public indifference. It is worthwhile to consider what this physical distance and incarceration does, first to the asylum seekers, and second to the citizen's view of herself. Immigration detention 'seals

---

[11] The entire report can be found at: www.aph.gov.au/senate/committee/legcon_ctte/refugees/index.htm

off' the asylum seeker from the community, enhancing the possibility of indifference. Whether such indifference is intentional or unintentional is a complex, multilayered question. When there is any public scrutiny of immigration detention, the fact of incarceration has the potential to inscribe a criminal identity to the asylum seeker, particularly in situations where little knowledge of asylum issues exists.

The detention of people claiming asylum, particularly when it extends beyond a reasonable time (UNHCR has long suggested detention beyond a three month period is unreasonable), can be said to be symptomatic of a social production of distance (Bauman 1989); a deliberative act which is not only a physical isolation, but a psychological one. In the EU, children are not detained for more than a few days, while in Australia the detention of their parents continues to be used as the rationale for detaining children for indefinite periods. Australia practices an administrative and physical distancing of individuals who have arrived without prior approval. The logic of these practices is founded on the notion that fraudulent claimants must be identifies. Should false claimants be kept out at all costs, even if the force of such a measure may engulf the chances of a genuine refugee? Should the host country turn a blind eye to some false claimants, focusing on offering protection to the refugee among them? What then of the issue of scarce resources; tangible resources in the form of monetary benefits and security; and the more abstract form of public good will toward newcomers, which false claimants draw on along with the genuine? These are the questions which continue to perplex countries of asylum. They deserve to be perplexing questions, particularly when we consider the consequences of denying protection to a refugee. Carens, drawing on the earlier logic developed by Rawls in *A Theory of Justice,* points out a useful distinction between perfect and imperfect procedures, which assists in searching for an answer to the above questions:

> A perfect procedure is one whose outcome is correct or just simply because it is the outcome of the procedure (assuming that the procedure itself has been properly constructed); there is no independent standard to what the outcome ought to be. A lottery is a good example. An imperfect procedure is one in which there is an independent standard of the appropriate outcome. A criminal trial is a good example. The desired outcome is to convict the guilty and acquit the innocent, but any given trial may or may not actually succeed in producing that outcome.
>
> Like a trial, a refugee determination process is an imperfect procedure. The purpose is to distinguish those who fit the definition from those who do not, but the process may or may not succeed in achieving that outcome in any given case. Just as two types of error can occur in a trial (acquitting the guilty and convicting the innocent), so two types of error can result from the refugee determination process (admitting the unqualified, rejecting the qualified) (Carens 1997,22).

The Australian state regularly and unapologetically utilises the idea of deterrence as justification for the continued practice of mandatory and non-reviewable detention of asylum seekers in Australia. Since the early 1990s this has been a bipartisan approach of the two major political parties; the Liberal/National coalition and the Labor Party. As we have seen in the German case, 'mode of arrival' can determine the likelihood of an individual seeking protection gaining access to a fair hearing. Developments are similar in the Australian case.

Most Western states, including Germany and Australia have implemented a raft on deterrence measures, with the aim of keeping at bay those who may seek to invoke protection obligations. The aim of these measures is not to search and identify those who may urgently need protection, but to deter *all* those seeking to enter the national territory, Such measures include, carrier sanctions, special visa requirements on nationals from refugee producing states, the placement of additional immigration officers at overseas ports, burden shifting arrangements with other states, and forced interdiction of refugees at frontiers as well as in international waters (Hathaway 1997). The Australian state, however, remains unique among Western countries in the vigour with which it pursues detention as a deterrence measure. Australia has also struck a regional agreement with Indonesia, overseen by the IOM whereby Indonesian authorities regularly intercept and detain 'irregular' migrants bound for Australia. The Australian government shares the cost of caring for the detainees in Indonesia with the IOM until such time as they can be voluntarily repatriated, or resettled in a safe third country. The majority of people detained in Indonesia under this initiative and intercepted on their way to Australia are Afghani and Iraqi.

As I have noted, the issue of boat people has received a level of media attention out of keeping with the numbers of such arrivals and the social and economic impact they have on Australian society. This trend has intensified in recent years as the application of detention policy on 'illegal' arrivals has become increasingly harsh. While it is difficult to find a handful of news or feature items focusing on refugees who have resettled in Australia, the issue of unauthorised arrivals and the controversy surrounding detention has received widespread media scrutiny, particularly since 1999. The concluding chapter will analyse and elaborate some of the recent media representation of asylum seekers.

## Some commonalties across the case studies

Most of the refugee NGO workers and advocates interviewed for this research have clarity of purpose, strategy and often a deep understanding of the social and political 'field' in which their work and action takes place. However a number of constraints which are similar across the case studies limit the work of NGOs. Such limits, often self-imposed limits, apply particularly to issues of the highest public controversy and scrutiny, including the detention and deportation of asylum seekers. Self imposed restraints reflect the accumulated experience of NGOs which in many cases anticipates reaction and backlash against asylum seekers in receiver communities. In such cases the strength of networks between NGOs is crucial, with those organisations who are relatively independent, in funding terms for instance, taking the most visible public action, including criticism of the state. Future actions and particularly the level of public campaigns are measured against perceived reaction by policy makers as well as the tenor of public opinion. The networks which NGOs are able to draw on enhance such reflexivity. On the other hand, more 'activist' and protest-oriented elements in the general non-state terrain, may act without consulting NGOs and other parties engaged on the same issue. In general, NGOs are regularly characterised by a lack of material and non-material resources; they often carry out a vast array of activities and roles; they must seek to remain relevant to changing public discourses and sensitive to the potential of a backlash.

**The survival of NGOs**

The multilayered processes of raising awareness, and finding appropriate avenues of communicating an understanding of the presence of asylum seekers are difficult tasks to co-ordinate and sustain at national let alone international levels. There are examples of successful international campaigning on human rights issues, such as those undertaken by Amnesty International on behalf of political prisoners. With regard to the more specific responses to refugees and asylum seekers, generated within particular nations, local connections are also vital in building an appropriate response which can eventually be reflected in the legislative and administrative processes that deal with refugees and asylum seekers. In other words, multiple strategies of engagement by NGOs can be expected to have a deeper and more sustained impact on the reception refugees face in a particular location than a single strategy such as international pressure. Ultimately, a multiple strategy approach is likely to provide more consistent results on an issue as sensitive to political vagaries as refugees and asylum seekers. This has been perhaps most evident in the over-use by successive governments of 'mode of arrival' to label asylum seekers as fraudulent, or even as terrorists, as was the case with the *Tampa* asylum seekers, even before a claim for protection has been lodged.

Numerous authors who analyse the contemporary refugee situation agree that asylum in a third country is only one part of what needs to be an integrated approach to people in refugee or 'refugee like' situations. Strategies for averting conflicts which lead to exodus (root causes), as well as strategies for peaceful return and reintegration post-conflict situations, are other elements of an integrated approach. In turn, the legal tools for refugee protection must be met with sufficient political will (Kumin 1996).

In view of the above discussion, what interactions and interventions can NGOs take? It is clear from the interviews conducted in both Germany and Australia, that in the main the refugee NGOs are a highly capable, informed sector, who remain cautious and guarded in their public activities for two main reasons. First, because refugee NGOs are a small grouping of actors, with limited resources and second, because of the sensitivity of the issue they advocate for. Timing and the choice of strategy employed are for refugee NGOs crucial themes in the approach to their work. Horizontal exchanges extending beyond national borders and encouraged through the widespread use of e-mail networks, are important for NGO activity. Access to up-to-date information and data, as well as to other practitioners, to researchers and academics, has been a vital new resource for NGOs as the role of the non-state sector has penetrated an increasing number of domains since 1989. The gap in capabilities between the state; with its large institutional organs of bureaucracy and administration supplying information to politicians and others involved in policy development; and the comparatively small NGO organisations, has been reduced by a flattening out of access to information technology. Gathering support, responses to particular decisions or actions and distributing information about rallies, demonstrations, protests and so on through global e-mail lists has expanded the potential membership base of NGOs and dramatically shortened the response time to campaigns.

The examples which I have discussed in this and the previous chapter, can only claim to be generally representative of a much larger reality of action towards asylum seekers, but are nevertheless illustrative of some of the points of tension in the developing debates regarding refugee arrivals in countries of the West and the way in which claims for protection are administered. Moreover, these examples indicate the way in which integration into the receiver society, or expulsion from it is carried out. The empirical detail of the detention of unauthorised arrivals who seek protection, reminds us again that control over territorial borders and membership rights, are among the few levers over which states retain ultimate sovereignty. The modern security state has rationalised modes of conduct towards citizens as *members* and toward newcomers as *outsiders* in administrative and bureaucratic techniques broken down into myriad component parts. From the development of policy, to the communication of it through media and finally through its implementation, first-hand and meaningful contact with the 'subjects' of policy is mostly absent. No individual player has more than a partial, fleeting or secondary contact with those upon whom policy impacts. This is especially the case with asylum seekers. The creation of social distance through bureaucratic techniques is a consequence of modern, highly differentiated and complex societies. Although it can cogently be argued that this social distance is not necessarily a negative feature in representative democracies, the vigorous mechanisms of allowing and indeed encouraging voices 'from below', could be beneficial for the process of democratising decision-making.

The example of the administration of detention policy in Australia highlights both a fixation with a rule bound approach, rather than the exercise of discretion, and a destabilising of the relationship between the state and NGOs. Despite years of effort, NGOs had little effect in penetrating the will of successive governments with the result of causing friction among NGOs themselves. Divergent approaches to an advocacy role have become particularly apparent with the case of detention, between those who take a conciliatory approach to state practices and those who are willing to make no compromises on fundamental principles. This chapter has analysed examples of direct and more hidden forms of control exercised on refugees and asylum seekers.

Violence is present in actions of the state in both overt and covert ways. The hidden acts of violence as well as the uses of 'symbolic violence', have great potency as a result of their often hidden, or 'veiled' quality. I argue that the idea of symbolic violence, as outlined in chapter two, is relevant to the accumulated evidence of state responses to asylum seekers, in visible as well as invisible practices, codes and dispensations. The substance of my hypothesis has been explored later in this chapter.

The social and physical distance from violence; both the observation of it and the physical impact, diminishes and blunts an interest in its consequences. The modern state has perfected techniques of creating and maintaining distance through administrative techniques, as well as through modes of communication, signifying status, value and desirability in a hierarchical schema, which accumulate to render asylum seekers mute. My analysis points to the likelihood of key events, as well as the less visible unitary approaches to an issue, as causing a deep tear in co-operative relationships between the parties to an issue, as well as more significantly, shifting policy direction onto a different gradient. I have drawn particularly on the issues of detention and deportation to illustrate my premise in this chapter. The practices of detention and deportation see the various agencies of the state; the police, military and security personnel, exerting various forms and degrees of coercion and violence on behalf of the state. It is no coincidence that such practices are carried out in border regions, extra-territorial zones such as international airports, and in the remotest areas within a country. Acts of 'symbolic violence' relate to the way foreigners are framed in public discourse, laying the cultural groundwork for possibilities of reaction toward such 'others'; reaction possible both at the macro level of state intervention in various forms of direct and indirect coercion and at the micro level of individual acts of violence on the street.

Chapter two painted in broad brush the way in which refugee policy relates first to immigration policy and second to the psychological space which newcomers as foreigners fill in public discourses on identity, place and belonging. The *conditions* for tolerance are shaped by policy and by institutionalised forms of regulation. Acts of tolerance are advanced through the exercise of choice in everyday encounters. Both the conditions for, and the actions toward, toleration need to be evident in a decent society. The state and NGOs fulfil different roles in the promotion of such conditions and actions. As the case studies have shown, tangible, everyday encounters with the 'other', are vital in achieving an informed view of newcomers, in this case, asylum seekers. However, the detention regime in place in Australia and the prevalence of violence towards foreigners in Germany, heightens the possibility of irrational fears developing, in turn displacing the ability for measured public debate on the issue of the 'other' and cultural difference.

Chapter 8

# Conclusion: Communication and the politics of asylum

**We walk towards a land**
We walk towards a land not of our flesh,
Not of our bones its chestnut trees,
Its stones unlike the curly goats
Of the Song of Songs.
We walk towards a land
That does not hang a special sun for us.
Mythic women clap:
A sea around us,
A sea upon us.
If wheat and water do not reach you,
Eat our love and drink our tears.
Black veils of mourning for the poets.
You have your victories and we have ours,
We have a country where we see
Only the invisible.

by Mahmoud Darwish
Translated from the Arabic by Rana Kabbani

The social and political construction of newcomers as strangers is a process which identifies and names what eventually become the popular public understandings of the various categories of the 'other'. To at least some degree, such public understandings demarcate the boundaries of what can be contested by advocates or third parties who are engaged on behalf of such newcomers. That is, the things that can be 'put on the table' as points of discussion, deliberation and negotiation must fit within general parameters of a particular society's normative framework, as well as the everyday social mores which distinguish societies and peoples. It goes without saying that if no one were considered a 'stranger', or in some way an outsider, measures for inclusion, or admission in the case of refugees, would not be necessary. In such a situation a state of 'perpetual peace', grounded on cosmopolitan values might be expected to prevail (Kant 1970, Nussbaum 1997).

This sentiment is expressed in the famous line of Terrence, 'I am a human being: I think nothing human alien to me' (Nussbaum ibid.; 33). In the less exalted world we inhabit, the categories and boundaries of who, or what is alien, are under continuous assessment, being contested and recontested. Who comes to be cast as a stranger cannot be assumed to be a straight-forward process: it is not necessarily the newest immigrant, or the one who cannot speak the native language. Among some, mostly unintended, consequences of globalisation of economies and of communications, is the production of new groups of outsiders; people who may previously have been 'within' a body politic. These 'new' outsiders, such as the long-term unemployed, while quite distinct from refugees and asylum seekers, nevertheless contribute to a cumulative effect which impacts on other groups of outsiders. Where the group of outsiders is, or is perceived to be expanding, the effect is one of de-solidarisation, a decline in sympathy and compassion, and a tightening of the 'circle of loyalty' by 'insiders' to a smaller group of fellow 'insiders' and only select newcomers, often based on subjective, ambiguous and shifting criteria.

The effect of various discourses on the popular perceptions of outsiders is an important issue here. Examples from both Germany and Australia illustrate the way in which the use of language and symbolic representations of asylum seekers can be powerfully utilised in shaping public opinion. Chapter two, in outlining the refugee system and its interaction with the broader immigration systems and logics in receiver societies, sketched some of the macro processes involved in deliberations over immigration. It becomes clear from the historical processes which resulted in the 1951 *Refugee Convention* and other aspects of international law, that the inviolability of the individual and the protection of fundamental human rights is at the core of a common humanity which assumes that all people, whether they are considered as 'insiders' or outsiders' of a particular territorial state, have equal moral worth.

This leads us to consider the various mediations that take place in social processes which filter and prioritise 'ways of seeing the world', and the people in it. In this book, I have considered the role of NGOs as one such mediator – though often a relatively powerless one. It can be argued that the accumulation of individual experiences and the way such experiences are filtered and communicated at the micro-social level, eventually lead to various legislative and administrative decisions on the macro level. Micro processes such as the individual experiences of the unemployed, the disabled, and various other minority groups, gather as a cluster of 'needs based' claims which inform administrative and legislative processes. However, the myriad of experiences and information gathered by NGOs can only be fed back into the policy making process if channels of internal communication between the state and non-state sector exist and are sufficiently nurtured. Moreover, the NGO sector; itself varied and diverse between front-line service delivery and advocacy-oriented work, must have adequate lines of communication such as horizontal and vertical exchanges, in order to foster adequate feed-back loops. Examples from both the German and Australian case studies related to the use of language and symbols in communicating about asylum seekers, indicate the impact such forms of communication can have. It is, needless to say, predominantly media discourse which is the significant mediating force which NGOs who are vigilant for opportunities to engage a wider public through the mass media search out.

## Telling tales about foreign bodies

In the introductory chapter of this book and in chapter two, I have already discussed in some detail the presence of the stranger as a permanent figure in modern societies, unsettling the certainties of our temporal and spatial worlds. Further, through the case studies detailed in chapters three through six, I have considered some aspects of the impact of policy and legislation on asylum seekers at the micro level, and particularly, various NGO responses to them, including grass-roots action. More specifically, the physical 'body' and the 'soul' of the refugee or asylum seeker deserve special attention. They are judged, assessed and viewed from numerous vantage points as an artefact in the sense that their physical bodies hold evidence of various political systems, or despotic regimes who fail to safeguard the basic rights of members. Our actions toward others both 'make' and 'unmake' the world we live in, just as we make ourselves known to one another through verbal and material artefacts which render our lived realities meaningful (Scarry 1985; 22). We receive images and information in a variety of ways and process them differently. The accumulation of received images becomes part of our individual and collective response repertoires - social responses, and in a more cumulative and comprehensive sense, political responses which eventually are transformed into the responses of both state and non-state institutions.

As I have argued earlier, violence is not only present in the various situations that have turned individuals into refugees, but violence remains a characteristic of the way people seeking protection are received and processed. How does the way we see such 'others' come to shape the response we make through our action or indeed our inaction? The reaction to unauthorised arrivals has regularly been accompanied by violent and fearful reactions within receiver societies. Violence has both tangible and symbolic forms, evident in the state response to asylum seekers: the use of water cannon and riot police in detention centres, the physical distance and harsh settings of immigration detention centres and most recently, the use of the military to push-off boat arrivals who have sought to invoke Australia's protection obligations. In Germany this phenomenon is characterised by the increasing impetus for 'external controls' not so much of German borders, but the borders of the EU as a whole, through a 'harmonisation' approach by EU members. Less directly, fear and even hatred is often generated through the modes of communication which governments utilise in the practice and administration of policies on a day-to-day basis. Though symbolic forms of violence and coercion may be less visible than overt acts of violence, symbolic forms may ultimately prove to be more damaging in the ability to penetrate ideas and attitudes. How then can we apply the ideas of symbolic systems to the tangible negotiations around refugees? Receiver societies are presented with the physical bodies of those seeking protection, and pass judgement on their stories through the testimony which the law requires.[1] At the same time that the law must consider each individual claim, the individual is but a representative of a group with no start or finish. Who indeed can predict the end of refugee movements and the need for protection? Will the favourable treatment of one claimant lead to an avalanche of claims? The legal institutions and the bureaucracy which apply legislation seek to implement 'general' rules to individuals in a non-arbitrary manner. In other words, the same general rules ought to apply to all who fall under a particular jurisdiction. The same set of laws and various disciplinary techniques apply to refugees and asylum seekers who are located in the same jurisdiction. What I want to emphasise here is the way in which the social and political construction of identities, in this case identity as stranger, come to penetrate the institutions of law and administration, and how 'impartiality' appears from the view of the refugee. This perspective also illuminates what it is that refugee NGOs are attempting to project in their advocacy functions: the impact of the 'cool', distant law and the impact of it on the 'hot', damaged 'body' and 'soul' of a refugee. At the same time, it has already been pointed out that because of the tangible and the symbolic violence which invades the process of becoming a refugee at every juncture, refugee policy is quite distinct from other areas addressing social needs. A person asking for protection experiences the process of making a claim, as making a *private* world, filled with *private* words *public*.[2] A person seeking protection must in a sense lay bare a personal history in a public confessional: first in a formal legal process, and less directly in various public settings such as NGO forums held to facilitate public awareness and to gather support, or in media interviews.

Foucault's analysis shows how the body and the soul have been subject to various forms of control and correction through constraint and training, utilising both *anatomic-metaphysical* and *techno-political* techniques (1977; 136). The *techno-political* register relates to armies, schools and hospitals – institutions of regulation, measurement and forms of empirical calculation. This second register relates to submission and 'use' (the useful body), whilst the *anatomic-metaphysical* register relates to functioning and explanation (the intelligible body). While all

[1] The marks and signposts a body carries with it and on it: the travel documents tucked in a top pocket, the family photos carried close at hand, the foreign currency, the marks of torture and mistreatment on torso, on feet, are part of the artefacts which remind us at once of the distinctions that mark 'outsiders', while simultaneously striking chords of common humanity, even self-identification.

[2] I take the idea of making *private* words *public* from Bourdieu's explanation of the anxiety a social scientist feels about revealing the confidential statements gathered through research; a process which relies heavily on trust between the researcher and the subject(s) of that research.

societies display some impositions of constraint and obligation on the body, the eighteenth century marked a turning point in the methods and the scale with which impositions came to be made. The techniques utilised in such large-scale impositions of control are in the modern era distinguished by a certain modality in that disciplining actions appear as if on an uninterrupted trajectory, where even constant coercion is normalised with the movement of time and space (Foucault 1977; 137). In other words, we either do not recognise forms of control and correction, or no longer regard them as problematic and in need of challenge.

We see a myriad of concrete examples of the various ways in which discipline comes to be imposed on the body and soul of the asylum seeker. Chapter six detailed state sanctioned and practiced violence by the modern use of *enclosure* in the form of detention of 'unauthorised' arrivals. Refugees and asylum seekers, particularly as they are cast into the linguistic pot of 'illegals' and associated with criminality as a result of their mode of arrival, are perceived as in some way contaminated and can come to be considered as a potential threat to the receiver society. They endanger its stability and order, transforming even the 'familiar' into uncertainty and 'strangeness'. This development can either be seen as a temporary distortion, resulting in a new configuration with its own order, or as a damaging process, weakening the receiver society, as well as harming individual asylum seekers. As various forms of judgement are crucial to the fate of an individual seeking protection, the issues of 'truth' and of trust between peoples emerges.

As genuine refugees come from experiences of the most brutal and blatant abuse of trust by their country of origin, the building of renewed trust in a receiver society, can be a long-term process. However, in order to be 'recognised' as a refugee, a legal determination necessitates the revelation of personal 'truths'. In part such 'truths' are carried on the body of refugees in the marks of torture and various forms of physical trauma. Nevertheless, even such evident marks must be talked about and described, often in great detail, as must the invisible marks contained in the soul. Biographies and the stories of flight must be retold, with even the most intimate details divulged.

> The confession has spread its effects far and wide. It plays a part in justice, medicine, education, family relationships, and love relations, in the most ordinary affairs of everyday life, and in the most solemn rites; one confesses one's crimes, one's sins, one's thoughts and desires, one's illnesses and troubles; one goes about telling, with the greatest precision, whatever is most difficult to tell. One confesses in public and in private, to one's parents, one's educators, one's doctor, to those one loves; one admits to oneself, in pleasure and in pain, things it would be impossible to tell to anyone else the things people write books about. One confesses – or is forced to confess. When it is not spontaneous or dictated by some internal imperative, the confession is wrung from a person by violence or threat; it is driven from its hiding place in the soul, or extracted from the body (Foucault 1978; 59).

The determination process in many cases, including in Australia and in Germany, has considerable resource limitations. NGOs are a vital intersection between the formal needs and requirements of the state, and the distress of an asylum seeker, who may have difficulty accessing or understanding the requirements of the bureaucracy and administration they encounter in their search for protection. In Germany the concept 'Glaubwürdigkeitsprüfung' (literally, a believability test), has a prominent position in the rationale of the federal office for adjudicating asylum claims (Weber 1998; 63). An asylum seeker is repeatedly tested, questioned and re-questioned to ascertain whether some fact or other is in keeping with the story she has told. One inaccuracy can jeopardise a claim and add to the list of 'fraudulent' or 'manifestly unfounded' claims. The official recognition rates of asylum claims are utilised to confirm the authenticity or otherwise of claimants in general. My interviews in both Australia and Germany revealed that NGO workers are regularly sceptical of official recognition rates. While no accurate or verifiable numbers are available on such claims, however it proved to be a consistent pattern that advocacy NGOs and legal representatives of asylum seekers, who had close and regular contact with individual asylum seekers, thus developing a relationship of trust often absent in official proceedings, claimed a regular disparity between an official account and the authenticity of refugee claims. Though this assertion is purely anecdotal, it suggests that genuine refugees are in some cases deported while still in need of protection (refoulement), and more often may enter the ranks of the 'illegals', living in receiver societies.

Refugee NGOs operating at the 'grass roots', in the delivery of services such as the provision of welfare, legal advice and so on, come into contact with asylum seekers at many stages of a determination process. Because of the nature of their work, NGOs often have insights, and build levels of trust where stories which may be too painful or culturally sensitive to reveal in a formal process, or to recount in the sterile written form required on protection application forms, are revealed. Refugees who have had particularly traumatic, or perhaps even violent experiences commonly need long periods of time to be able to recount their stories (Silove et.al. 2000). At the same time, during the 1990s the period within which an asylum seeker may lodge a claim have been shortened in many Western states, including in Germany and Australia; in some cases to a few weeks after an arrival.

As NGOs are exposed directly to individual stories and to the experiences of refugees, some quite particular challenges to their work are apparent. While we well know by now that constructing and recounting the authenticity of individual accounts through legal mechanisms is the means by which asylum seekers receive enduring protection, it is the way in which individual stories come to be represented publicly, as well as the accumulation of individual stories which has the potential to generate change.

Individual testimony is a concept which the German refugee NGOs utilised throughout the 1990s in their public information and media campaigns. Pro Asyl, adopted the slogan 'Der einzelfahl zählt' (the individual case counts), to signify the priority with which each asylum applicant ought to be treated. This was a strategy which more often than not worked effectively in enabling refugee stories to be inserted into the mainstream media with an urgency which abstract universal arguments about protection obligations and state responsibility could not achieve. However, this approach means that there is a premium on individual stories, of often the most emotive cases, still rendering the bulk of the asylum seeker 'caseload' to less favourable stereotyping in public descriptions. Refugee NGOs in Australia have come to approach the issue of media coverage cautiously, aware that they have little influence in shaping the trajectory of an issue once it in the 'public domain'.

### The media and public opinion

The power of communication and particularly of mass outlets of information in the contemporary world shape, redefine and reflect the social world. Advances in communications technology have extended the reach of media messages far beyond national borders or the control of any particular government. While the speed and accessibility of information through the world-wide-web has been an enormous boost to the capacity of NGOs to inform themselves, their constituents and partners across the world of new developments, the need for them to simultaneously access mainstream media has not diminished. While information may be available from a greater variety of sources and more instantly than ever before, news and current affairs has been concentrated through the syndication of major news networks. The same television pictures, radio 'sound bites' and 'wire' press stories are transmitted and printed to more locations than has previously been the case. CNN transmissions, Reuters and AAP 'wire' stories, and BBC World Service broadcasts, are digested, retransmitted and grafted with local content in a myriad of locations. The conflicts covered by the 'big media players' assume a significance because of the attention given to them, rather than the necessarily comparative seriousness of the conflicts relative to other 'like' conflicts which receive little or no media coverage.[3] To be sure, relationships between NGOs and the media, just as the contacts and relationships between individual politicians or political parties and the media are fluid and changing. How a particular story or event is framed and steered through various opinion forming processes is equally open and contentious. The German Federal Minister for Foreigner's Affairs under the Kohl government, laments the uneven interest the media shows toward foreigner issues: ' . . . they report when something goes wrong such as the burning of asylum homes. But for instance, when I held a conference . . . with some

---

[3] The Kosovo Crisis in 1999 and the Gulf War in 1991 are examples of saturation coverage by the big players in the Western media. In comparison, the ongoing war in Afghanistan prior to the terrorist bombing of the World Trade Centre in New York and the Pentagon in Washington on September 11 2001, or indeed the civil war in Sierra Leone received sporadic coverage.

prominent speakers, highlighting the positive contribution of guestworkers for Germany, no one from the media came' (Interview No. 16).

It has been, above all, a small number of senior journalists working in the 'quality press', that closely followed the developing issues of asylum politics in Germany. Such journalists also consider key contact with NGOs as important in presenting balanced accounts of asylum politics and the issues circulating such a sensitive issue. Through the early 1990s and particularly through the period of 1992/93, the issue of asylum seekers held great prominence in the German media, including print, radio and television. The public sphere was saturated with information and with the vigorous nature of the debate flowing from the arrival of asylum seekers. Questions of tolerance, the economy, job security and citizenship were the most prominent points of debate. Prominent politicians of all political parties entered the public debate; interviewed for television and radio 'talk shows' and writing 'opinion' pieces in prominent newspapers. There is no doubt that during 1992 and 1993 asylum seekers came to be viewed as one of the key social and political 'problems' for the Federal Republic. However, after the constitutional change to the Basic Law in 1993, the media eased the pedal from the issue of asylum. Christian Schneider, a journalist for the *Süddeutsche Zeitung* (SZ) has written about migration and asylum issues for many years along with his colleague Heribert Prantl. I asked him about the decline in media coverage of asylum issues after the 1993 Basic Law change:

> Up to last year [1995] we have reported asylum issues extensively. But what now seems to be the case is a sort of tiredness of the topic, even my colleagues say 'I just can't hear it any more'. We notice the reaction also in letters to the editor. Previously, when negative letters came they were anonymous, cheeky and insulting, but anonymous. Now they are even more insulting and provocative, but signed. The right-wing extremists dare to sign their name to these letters, and Prantl and I have had recent experience of telephone terror. We had to get silent [ex-directory] numbers after we wrote about asylum issues. That is the present climate (Interview No. 25).

In Australia, the level of media interest has also rarely been sustained for any length of time on the refugee issue. This is partly a result of the relatively small numbers of arrivals to Australia, as well as a consequence of the broad public acceptance of immigration in general, furthered through the multicultural policies of the 1970s and 1980s. The one issue which has been the focus of at times vigorous media debate, particularly from 1999 onwards, has been the detention of asylum seekers, as discussed in chapter seven.

Attention from the mass media can easily backfire on an issue such as refugees. Misconceptions and simplistic stereotyping of foreigners has the ability to undo years of collaborative effort in the public portrayal of a difficult issue such as the integration of newcomers. Experience in both Germany and Australia has led refugee NGOs to be wary of their dealings with the media. There is no doubt that the issue is highly sensitive to public opinion and conversely that public opinion is highly 'reactive' to debates about refugees and asylum seekers. This is evident at a number of different levels. Most directly, public sensitivities are 'pricked' or awakened, as refugees and asylum seekers are encountered in the everyday lives of citizens, where cultural and other differences are heightened in social interaction.

## The use and abuse of language

As I have previously discussed, a refugee story is told in a number of ways. The way such a story is told in turn can have significant repercussions for the receptiveness of host societies to refugees as well as to future policy outcomes. Commonly, refugee stories are told in one of two ways: first, through statistics and second, through the case studies of individual refugees. Both methods are employed to portray positive as well as negative images of refugees. News reports, government press releases and the official communications of international organisations such as the UNHCR, report and relay the scale of population movements, focusing on different areas of concern which reflect the interests and perspectives of the news generator as much as the interests of refugees. All actions, whether they are linguistic or non-linguistic, can be conceived as goal-oriented, in that an 'end' or outcome is sought which is thought to lead to understanding, though the paths utilised may be different (Habermas 1998b; 218). The perception formed of immigrants in a receiver society can alter substantially through the intervention or use of seemingly innocent factors.

Changes in the terms used to label various categories of migrants and foreigners have accompanied various developments in the composition of immigrant intakes, but they also reflect social attitudes and the thrust of official integration measures. As I have argued in chapter four, the German case, perhaps partly because of a more complex context, has many more linguistic variants of outsiders (non-Germans) than is evident in Australia. In Germany far-right groups have been able to gain some measure of credibility for hate campaigns aimed at foreigners, with simplistic cause and effect scenarios, blaming a myriad of social problems on 'foreigners'. Terms such as *Ausländer, Asylanten, Fremde, nicht Deutsche (*foreigner, asylum seeker, stranger, not German*)* have over time, come to be derogatory terms through an unsubstantiated association with high unemployment rates, crime, and social disharmony. Foreigners living in Germany have been subject to numerous other labels; including *Gastarbeiter* and the official term *Ausländische Arbeitnehmer* (foreign employees). In the early seventies, the term *Ausländische Mitbürger* (foreign fellow citizens) came into widespread use, introduced by those sympathetic to the concept of integration, including many of the NGOs considered in this study. However, the term stresses the foreign character of migrants, as well as highlighting the difference between citizens (Trähnhardt 1992; 173). During the early 1980s, the first large-scale numbers of non European – mainly 'third world' refugees – began arriving in Germany, whereas previously, primarily those fleeing the communist states of Europe had claimed asylum in Germany. At this time *Asylant* (asylum seeker) entered public speech, displacing *Flüchtling* (refugee) in common usage. Moreover, the stem word *Asyl* came to be coupled with other nouns in public speech associated with disaster and negative developments:

> . . . flood [*Flut*], river [*Strom*], mass [*Masse*], (asylum) was also joined to other words which simply cemented adverse public perception of the refugees: *Scheinasylant* [pseudo asylum-seeker], *Asylmissbrauch* [asylum misuse], *Wirtschaftsasylant* [economic asylum seeker] (Mattson 1995; 66).

Even the language utilised by NGOs continues to demarcate between people with the label *Ausländer*. NGOs regularly refer to *Ausländische Flüchtlinge*, differentiating between 'foreign refugees' and German refugees. Similarly many of the citizen initiatives I discussed in chapter six, aimed at facilitating local collaboration and co-operation between German citizens and immigrants, use the term *Ausländische Mitbürger* (foreign fellow citizens). Such labels are used in a taken-for-granted fashion which would be out of the question in Australia. In Australia, a citizen would not be regarded in public discourse or popular usage as foreign, or non-Australian.

The institutionalisation of multicultural policy in Australia, discussed in chapter five, has ensured a more cautious use of language describing foreigners. But again, the public discourse over asylum seekers, and in particular boat arrivals, has been the exception. The term 'queue jumpers' is used liberally to describe those who arrive without travel documents, juxtaposed against 'deserving refugees' in camps outside Australia, who patiently wait their turn to be selected for resettlement. Misleading as such language is to the situation of people fleeing persecution, this mode of communication seems to be highly effective as it reflects a long-standing Australian preoccupation with pre-determined and selective entry. An editorial in the prominent broadsheet daily, 'The Sydney Morning Herald', with the headline 'Queue jumping' states:

> There are no easy answers to the complex problems that go with refugees. But caught in a quandary over boat people, the Government has in effect chosen to punish people who are going through proper legal channels while allowing others to jump the queue (*SMH*, February 26, 2000).

We have seen with the illustration of the *Tampa* crisis, evidence of a minor and trivial occurrence gaining national, and ultimately international, significance in relation to the Australian government's treatment of asylum seekers. I will briefly recount the way in which this minor sea rescue became an international incident and the subsequent action taken by government. Throughout June and July of 2001, the Australian media was saturated with stories or riots, breakouts, suicide attempts and other forms of self-harm inside immigration detention centres. Allegations of physical and psychological abuse and mistreatment of detainees by staff also emerged. The Government was vigorously questioned about these developments, almost on a daily basis.

> Night after night, an ashen Philip Ruddock, the Immigration Minister, had been appearing on television in these weeks [leading up to the Tampa incident], to explain mass breakouts, suicides, nervous breakdowns, the presence of a catatonic boy and mass hunger strikes at the country's detention centres, including Villawood and Curtin.
>
> Howard was calling on the Senate to pass legislation to limit even further the access of asylum seekers to the courts. The annual boat season was under way and to prepare for their arrival, Ruddock had announced new detention centres at HMAS Coonawara in Darwin, the army camp at Singleton in NSW and at the El Alamein camp near Port Augusta in South Australia: Christmas Island was bursting: there would be 1,000 asylum seekers there once those on the deck of the Tampa landed.
>
> At some point after 9.40 on the night of August 26/27 someone made the decision that the Tampa was to be turned back to Indonesia by threatening the master with the full weight of the Migration Act. The Tampa was not to be thanked for rescuing the human cargo on the Palapa 1 but accused of facilitating their illegal voyage. Australia was taking the view that the Tampa was not on a search and rescue mission but conducting a people smuggling operation (SMH October 20-21, 2001; 40).

In the weeks following the *Tampa* crisis, the asylum debate was kept on the front page of national newspapers and the key item in television and radio broadcasts with another asylum seeker incident; the 'children overboard' affair (Marr & Wilkinson 2003, Weller 2002). The government claimed that children had been thrown overboard by their parents from boats making their way to Australian waters in early September 2001, in an attempt to intimidate the Australian government:

> The Government reported that children wearing lifejackets were thrown into the sea after the vessel was stopped by HMAS Adelaide off Christmas Island yesterday.
>
> Adults, also in lifejackets, jumped overboard in what Mr Ruddock described as 'disturbing . . . planned and premeditated' action with the 'intention of putting us under duress'.
>
> The incident keeps the border control issue on centre stage, after last week's forcible removal of people from HMAS Manoora onto Nauru (SMH October, 8, 2001: 1).

The Prime Minister John Howard, the Immigration Minister Philip Ruddock, and the Defence Minister, Peter Reith, made much of the 'children overboard' incident, particularly articulating repeatedly the bad moral character of people who threw their children into the sea as a form of intimidation. On the influential tailback radio show of host, Alan Jones, on October 7, Prime Minister Howard said: 'Quite frankly, Alan, I don't want in this country people who are prepared, if those reports are true, to throw their own children overboard. And that kind of emotional blackmail is very distressing' (Radio 2UE). Defence photographs were released, showing figures with life jackets floating in the ocean, though identifying information was removed from the photographs:

> For weeks the Government has maintained that children were thrown into the sea near Christmas Island on October 7 in an attempt to blackmail authorities into bringing them to the Australian mainland.
>
> It has made extensive political capital during the election campaign of assertions that its tough border protection policy was designed to keep out people who were so undesirable that they would deliberately put children at risk (SMH November 9, 2001; 1).

And on the morning of the Federal Election, the asylum seeker issue remained on the front page of all the country's major newspapers:

> Stories can be too good to be true. The tale of the Iraqi children thrown into the ocean off Christmas Island a couple of days after John Howard called the election was one such story. It always seemed too good to be true. Demonising boat people was nothing new. Church leaders claim it had been under way almost since the 1998 election.
>
> The Howard Government has linked them with terrorists, tarred them with the Taliban brush, christened them 'illegals' and denounced them as abusers of the Australian court system. It was only another detail in this grim portrait to say they were the sort of people who would put their children's' lives at risk to blackmail Australia into giving them asylum (SMH November 10-11, 2001; 27).

Though the political handling of the Tampa incident and the resulting 'push-off' policies which have been confirmed by legislation passed as part of the Migration Amendment Bill 2001, are clearly a new development in Australia's management of asylum seekers, the language of border protection, of 'queue-jumpers' and 'illegal aliens', is not altogether a new development.[4] Rather, in this, as in other approaches to 'on-shore' arrivals, a bi-partisan approach is evident in the Australian political system. Gerry Hand, the Minister for Immigration in the early 1990s in the Hawke Labor Government made regular public pronouncements about 'illegals' and 'queue jumpers', utilising derogatory labels as part of the legitimisation of tougher legislative and administrative approaches:

> In its zeal to protect the 'integrity' of our borders, the Federal Government has constructed one of the tightest and toughest immigration systems in he world. This system imposes a heavy burden on unauthorised boat arrivals . . . The system is strict and unyielding - deliberately so, to discourage further illegal boat entries . . . In almost

---

[4] From February 2002, evidence of the Senate inquiry into the 'Children overboard' affair emerged which indicated that senior Government officials, including advisors to the Prime Minister, knew a few days after the official photographs released by the Royal Australian Navy, depicting the incident were released in September, that they depicted a rescue rather than the result of children being thrown in the water. On February 19, 2002, the Prime Minister admitted that Peter Reith, the Defence Minister, told him three days before the election that there were doubts about the photos that were released of children thrown overboard (SMH February 20, 2002; 1).

> identical language, the Immigration Department's deputy secretary, Mr Wayne Gibbons, and the head of the department's protection and international division, Mr Ian Simington, refer to the threat facing Australian's northern borders as population movements in Asia gather momentum.
>
> Implicit in the comments is the fear that any loss of 'control' of the immigration program will not only lead to administrative chaos, but will also shake public confidence in immigration itself. This, above all, appears to be the driving force behind the government's tough stand on boat arrivals (SMH November 30, 1992).

Evidence shows that public opinion toward refugees and asylum seekers, shifts constantly and must be engaged and re-engaged with every new incursion on the rights of refugees. Such cyclical re-engagement is highly draining on the resources, both material and non-material, of NGOs. In addition, a lack of public awareness regarding asylum seekers, and why it is that they are seeking protection, results in a lack of public sympathy for this group, which in turn tempers the impact NGOs can have. However, there is a well established human rights based network of NGOs, particularly situated transnationally, as well as large church-based organisations, who have a strong human rights focus and are able to be utilised and mobilised on refugee issues by NGOs in local and regional settings.

I have recurringly argued that the 'security state' remains central in driving the political and social construction of refugees and in particular of asylum seekers as 'irregular' arrivals. Irregular (illegal) arrivals are perceived as a threat to the cohesion of the nation, while also providing a focus for resentment, readily exploited by politicians searching for simplistic ways of communicating about complex social problems to their constituents. For those countries, such as Australia, who accept a certain number of *Refugee Convention* status persons for resettlement, the emergence of a 'two-class' system is possible, and indeed has emerged in the last few years as indicated in chapters five and seven with the example of the Temporary Protection Visa (TPV). Those arriving spontaneously are more readily cast into a pot of 'non-authentic' or 'fraudulent' claims; or typecast as 'queue jumpers'. However, even those countries who do not set aside resettlement places, such as Germany and the majority of EU member states, have also continued along a path of putting increasingly harsh obstacles in the way of those seeking protection.

The issue of people smuggling and the illegal status of arrivals, has caused enormous tension, particularly as this form of entry is perceived as a security threat to the sovereign state, no matter the voracity of someone's cause for such entry; the strength of their claim is immediately negated by the illegality of their entry. In addition, refugee entry causes local anxiety due to the perceived change it causes in the receiver society, culturally and in terms of the resources needed to administer the claims of such entrants. However, I concur with Zolberg (1999), that despite the high levels of public anxiety, largely generated by the state itself through media networks, the state has not lost control of immigration in the 1990s, and indeed the categorisation of 'crisis' with regard to illegal entry in particular is much exaggerated. Numerous scholars across various disciplines remind us of the continuity between past and present population movements (Bade 2000, Joppke 1998, Hollifield 2000). Such continuity indicates that though the movement of people across borders has occurred in different 'waves' and for different reasons, some instigated from the source country, some from the country of destination, nevertheless the late twentieth century and the first years of the new century, have not witnessed what could be termed a crisis in the numbers of people moving across borders for temporary or permanent resettlement. Rather, it has been the response to, and interpretation of, newcomer arrivals by particular nation-states that amounts to a crisis.

> Citizens in democratic societies increasingly express disillusion with the formal political process at the same time as they disengage from political action in the form of collective groupings that express some form of resistance or challenge the state and its policies Though the collaborations and networks between various NGOs and social movements are often erratic and uncertain as I have indicated throughout this book, they do fill an important space in the social and political landscape at local, national and international levels.

I presume that a disillusionment with the political process, which needless to say is not found solely in the Federal Republic, has different, contrary, and mutually reinforcing causes. On one hand, citizens are unhappy because they see too few opportunities to be meaningfully engaged politically along the well-trodden paths of a nationalized party landscape; the non-activities of the local chapters of our political parties show how much unused energy is administered and laid to rest there. On the other hand, this wish for more democracy is intersected by the authoritarian wish to simplify an overly complex world by means of a simple recipe and strong men. The old stereotype of apolitically turning one's back on 'mere talk' [*Gerede*] and 'party squabbles' is receiving new impetus from fears about losses in income and status . . . Clearly politics has become overburdened by problems that are worldwide, and now also internally proliferating (Habermas 1997; 156-7).

The continuation of a system which extends political, social and economic rights only to members of a particular territory, is a system which can be maintained only through increasingly defensive measures, including communicative modes which constantly reinforce fear of strangers. As we have seen through the analysis of the German and Australian cases, Western democracies face a dilemma in relation to how best to respond to 'irregular' immigrants, setting in place legal and administrative measures to restrict the entry and the duration of stay of such arrivals, while at the same time being seen to be maintaining a 'fair' and open system in relation to obligations at the national and international level.

What emerges at this point from the comparative research of reactions to refugees in Germany and in Australia, is a convergence of the logic applied to the categorisations of asylum seekers, if not of strategies of deterrence. While the determination process of asylum claims ultimately appears as having more similarities than differences, the route taken during the process of evaluation and most importantly the public 'reasoning' utilised is quite distinct between Germany and Australia.

In summary, I have argued that asylum and refugee movements are issues of increasing significance for policy makers, and have become prominent issues not just in the area of political processes but also in the media. The movement of recruited, or selected, as well as unwanted people across national borders, heightens localised sentiments of being overburdened and swamped by foreigners and strangers; a sentiment exacerbated by the generalised insecurity that results above all from economic globalisation. The international environment in which nation-states are situated politically has changed dramatically in the period under consideration in this book, while the reception of immigrants in host countries continues to be delineated by some common threads including; the impact on the receiver society, and the relative cost and/or benefit of newcomers. Immigration is an area of government policy which is more likely to be symbolically potent and explosive than perhaps any other policy area, as it traverses the ideas of national consciousness, security, identity, as well as the economic and/or political realities of jobs and the redistribution of finite resources through health, education and welfare systems. The arguments against unlimited immigration, or 'open door policies', tend to focus on the limited resources of a particular nation, and the rights of those who are already members, over those who would wish to be included.

## Theoretical significance of the findings and contributions to research

This book has raised the problematic of reconciling local with global interests, in this case in relation to how states respond to refugees, and in particular the arrival of 'unauthorised', asylum seekers. In this way, we have seen the refugee question, acted upon quite distinctly in various local contexts. Local political factors may indeed have a greater bearing upon the outcome of a refugee's claims than international norms and they will certainly have the most significant impact on day-to-day living circumstances. The discussion of political obligation in chapter two, and how obligations can be 'grounded' or given substance, are perhaps most helpfully furnished with some normative tools for reconciling often contradictory interests by the 'new cosmopolitans' (Hollinger 2001).

Let us bear in mind, then, that the recurring theme throughout this book has been the gap between word and deed, between *ought* and *can*, leaving scores of people in vulnerable or harmful situations. Nonetheless, individual activists and NGOs continue to advocate the rights of those who are denied them, agitating in local, regional and international forums to close the gap between word and deed. As Ignatieff, commenting on the development of human rights, notes:

> The view from the ground may be discouraging, but a fifty-year retrospect lends ground for real hope. The existence of an international human rights law amounts to progress, even if the gap between statute and practice remains discouragingly large. Indeed, the key function of human rights language is to keep us aware of the gap between what we say and do. It is there to make trouble, and it will most certainly continue to do so (1999; 323).

With the dominance of globalised economies; with markets, money and communications able to leap borders and extend their influence and profitability, NGOs are well placed to take advantage of new opportunities because of their relative flexibility as well as their independence and broad constituency. NGOs, even when nationally based, have the potential of a global audience of people with an interest in those issues. International communications have also fostered an environment conducive to the increasing networks of human rights NGOs across borders. International networks may assist in providing leverage in local situations through networks and contacts with other states, inter-governmental or international organisations and NGOs in other countries. NGOs have the potential to be the gathering points, information-givers and gatherers and points of dissemination for spontaneous activity. They have the capacity to harness some local spontaneous energy and action, as they are connected to the local, and also have a less hierarchical decision-making structure than states. Though the experience of transnational refugee NGOs may be valuable, not only are German and Australian 'publics' distinct, but the constitution of civil society has historical and cultural variations. Therefore, a comparative case-study approach, such as the one adopted in this thesis, highlights important distinctions between countries and also between non-government activity in different locations. Local factors shape NGO actions as they do the receptiveness of the society to newcomers.

Apart from the other outcomes already discussed, the analysis of the empirical data, reveals that the work of human rights NGOs is a representation of a particularly society. Because of the absence of large scale and consistent citizen 'activation', willing to act on behalf of those who cannot represent themselves, the activities of the NGOs who are so engaged increases in significance. While it goes without saying that NGOs are never an adequate replacement for the functions of the state, their activities are not only complimentary to state activities, but provide a non-formal layer of 'checks and balances', necessary in robust democracies.

The small area of overlap in the literature on civil society, and the more practically focused NGO literature, is likely to benefit from the NGO activity considered in this book. In my research, and in particular the interviews I conducted, it has been the German refugee NGO sector who were particularly aware of the link between asylum seekers as a group with little rights and other groups within the national community who are alienated from full 'social citizenship' through long-term unemployment, discrimination due to disability, skin colour and gender.

What I have shown in the Australian case, is the continuation of a policy approach toward unauthorised arrivals which is out of step with the non-discriminatory ethos of Australia's immigration programme. This is evident in particular with the policy of mandatory detention. The political rhetoric of sovereignty, articulated most forcefully during the *Tampa* incident, is insufficient to legitimate what in effect have become policies which shift obligations to those potentially requiring protection, to neighbouring states.[5] However, though the period since 1999 may appear uncharacteristically harsh in the case of Australia, I have argued that the most recent developments do 'fit' a general trajectory of immigration control, whereby 'on-shore' asylum seekers face harsh treatment, which has been in place since the early 1990s. I have also argued that this policy has remained under-scrutinised and broadly accepted by the Australian public, due to a historically embedded acceptance of detention and separation of certain marginalised groups, deemed to be strangers such as Aboriginal people through settlements, missions and forced removal policies which remained in place well into the twentieth century.

The overview of the issue of forced migration through the prism of NGOs involved in advocacy reveals a number of key points. The desire of nation-states to control and to limit the entry and the duration of stay of refugees and especially 'uninvited' ones, has increased in the period of focus of this study; 1989 to 2003. Nation-states, particularly in the West, have become increasingly anxious about the arrival of refugees and asylum seekers and about their integration. While on the one hand this concern has been shown to be both legitimate and valid, it is also in some important ways a 'created' problem; influenced by the incomplete integration of previous waves of newcomers.

I have consistently argued that NGOs and social movements are an important part of the constitution of a national 'self-imaginary' and social solidarity, or indeed of an international affiliation of people who gather and form coalitions over a particular issue, in this case informed by human rights principles. As non-commercial interpreters and representative agents of a public will on specific issues they serve a significant public function. The role of the NGO sector and social movements, is particularly significant in the period I discuss, and indeed into the twenty-first century, as a counterpoint to the concentration of transnational corporations and media outlets in the framing and dissemination of the issues of concern to a particular society, or indeed of issues relevant to all peoples. The power of commercial media outlets in framing an issue, requires a counterpoint which NGOs can to some extent offer particularly through international networks. Ultimately, the NGOs working in the area of refugees are testing new ground for going forward and challenging their own societies and national governments, as well as international bodies about action toward refugees and asylum seekers. They are at once opinion-shapers, as well as being reflections of the society in which

---

[5] The cost of such 'shifting' seems often to be higher than dealing with the issue at a national level demonstrating the ideological and symbolic character of such decisions.

they work. The over-riding feature which characterises both case studies is the fragility of what NGOs working with and for asylum seekers are attempting to do in their work. Advocates cope with many domestic concerns, with budgetary constraints, and with a general 'de-solidarisation' of the broader citizenry.

## Suggestions for further research

A book length comparative study of this kind has limitations in terms of the extent to which issues can not be comprehensively analysed. The area of NGO advocacy within Western countries requires significant further research, particularly in view of the increasing propensity of governments to devolve particular welfare and community services to non-government agencies. As was discussed in chapter three, the trajectory of 'third way' politics has witnessed an erosion of the advocacy role of NGOs, as increasingly government funding is made available for service-delivery organisations who can demonstrate quantifiable outcomes in service-delivery, rather than the less tangible advocacy activities.

Though this book has not focused directly on the root causes of refugee movements and the causal factors which render citizens of particular nations as asylum seekers, searching for protection outside their own state; it nevertheless has remained a strong undercurrent to the book. As the ethical discourses on refugees and asylum seekers overlap with contingent and often urgent local needs of other groups, the search for 'durable' solutions is regularly hijacked by local political realities in a receiver state. The idea of 'durable solutions' needs to be connected more directly to the 'national interest' of refugee receiving states. In other words, refugees and those searching for protection need to be seen as a positive addition to a receiver society, rather than as a threat and a drain on resources.

There is agreement among many authors, non-government agencies and government representatives, that the granting of refugee status, with its attendant privileges such as residency and, after a qualifying period, full citizenship, must be deliberated upon with due caution, in order that protection is granted to 'genuine' cases. Such concern is motivated by a variety of stimuli. However, it is possible to make the general observations that such concern whether coming from government or non-government circles, is emblematic of a recognition that protection, linked with the resources of the receiver state, is a finite 'good' which ultimately is subject to measurement and quantification. Further research is needed into the economic justifications for particular asylum policies; Australia's detention policy being an example.

As I have argued, the non-government sector plays a significant role in identifying the key issues in deliberations over asylum seekers; in lobbying for solutions to particular situations; in engaging activities directed toward shaping public opinion; as well as in the day-to-day delivery of services for refugees and asylum seekers. This book has outlined both positive and negative aspects of such action in the NGO sector. The level of engagement between NGOs and the state must be under constant re-evaluation – testing motivations and loyalties. At a time when organisations in the 'third sector' are increasingly active, augmenting and in some cases replacing activities previously in the domain of the state, critical assessment of these activities and attention to the principles that underpin action are vital.

In focusing on the experiences of asylum seekers, filtered through the prism of NGOs who advocate for refugees and asylum seekers, an unintended link with other issues of significance in the receiver society arise. In Australia, the open sore of reconciliation between black and white Australians bears a strong symbolic relationship to how asylum seekers fare. The issues arising from Australia's detention policy, as analysed in chapter seven, remains the most controversial aspect of Australian policy toward refugees. In Germany, regular violent attacks on foreigners and on minority groups over the last decade, are an unsettling phenomenon, pointing to an overemphasis on foreigners as easy scapegoats for complex social and political problems.

No doubt asylum seekers pose a challenge to the particular country in which they arrive unannounced; a challenge both in substantive and in symbolic ways. We see that the arrival of asylum seekers seeking protection is a phenomenon with a global impact, rather than one affecting only certain destination states. At the same time, the drive for belonging, for social solidarity and connectedness is played out in various regional and localised claims, which need to be taken into account in relation to claims of transnational cosmopolitanism which are a feature of human rights NGOs. Ongoing processes of reconciling local claims and aspirations, are in tension with those that encompass the diversity of humanity. The search for appropriate mechanisms to reconcile tensions between local and global aspirations is part of the process of giving substance to the protection claims of asylum seekers and providing resettlement for those found to be refugees. While we witness rapid change in social, economic and political processes resulting from the phenomenon of globalisation, we also see at the national level an emphasis on security premised on a fear of outsiders; an emphasis which creates problems not only for marginalised groups such as asylum seekers, but ultimately also for the members of states which are enacting ever harsher measures of exclusion. In a world where states are intermeshed and interdependent, a fear of outsiders can only be alleviated in the long term by measures which balance various 'national interests' with a universal human rights agenda which values an individual before the imposition of borders, nationhood and citizenship.

# Appendix: Interviews

**GERMANY**

| | |
|---|---|
| **Interview No. 1:** | Spokesperson on Foreigners and Refugees, **Terres des Hommes - German Division, Osnabrück** |
| **Interview No. 2:** | Edit Czimer, spokesperson on Foreigners' concerns **Berliner Missionswerk** |
| **Interview No. 3:** | Bernd Günther SJ **Jesuit Refugee Service, Berlin** |
| **Interview No. 4:** | Barbara John, Ausländerbeauftragte **des Senats von Berlin** |
| **Interview No. 5:** | Hanns Thomä Venske, Ausländerbeauftragter **Evangelische Kirche, Berlin/Brandenburg** |
| **Interview No. 6:** | Dr Sepp Grässner, Director, **Service for Torture Victims, Berlin** |
| **Interview No. 7:** | Andrea Schwendner **Al-Muntanda, Diakonie Beratungstelle** |
| **Interview No. 8:** | Eckart Bartel (SPD), Foreigner and Migration Spokesperson **Parliament of Berlin** |
| **Interview No. 9:** | Frauke Hoyer, Director **Refugee Council, Berlin** |
| **Interview No. 10:** | Stefan Täubner SJ, **Jesuit Refugee Service, Berlin** |
| **Interview No. 11:** | Frau Kantemir and Herr Kosan State MPs Bündnis 90/the Greens **The Parliament of Berlin** |
| **Interview No. 12:** | Klaus Pritzkuleit, spokesperson **Evangelisches Kirchenamt** |
| **Interview No. 13:** | Peter Bartels, Spokesperson on asylum and refugee issues **Diakonisches Werk, Stuttgart** |
| **Interview No. 14:** | Hans-Dieter Schäfers, Refugee and Foreigner Division **Caritas Germany, Freiburg** |
| **Interview No. 15:** | Rosi Wolf-Almansreh, Director (Ausländerbeauftragte) **Amt für Multikulturelle Angelegenheiten, Frankfurt** |
| **Interview No. 16:** | Cornelia Schmalz-Jacobsen(FDP), Federal Parliament Ausländerbeauftragte **Federal Parliament, Bonn** |

**Interview No. 17:** Frau Jochenhövel-Schieke
**International Social Services, German division**
**Interview No. 18:** Herr Neikrowitz, Director, Social Services
**Airport Social Services, Frankfurt International Airport**
**Interview No. 19:** Judith Kumin, Director German Branch
**United Nations High Commissioner for Refugees**
**Interview No. 20:** Herbert Löffler, Asylum and Foreigner spokesperson
**Red Cross Germany, Bonn**
**Interview No. 21:** Herbert Leuninger, European Spokesperson
**Pro Asyl, Frankfurt**
**Interview No. 22:** Dr Scharifi, Dr Mehari, Founding Directors
**Psycho-Social Centre for Foreigners and Refugees, Frankfurt**
**Interview No. 23:** Frau Kammerlander
**Refugio, Munich**
**Interview No. 24:** Christian Schneider, Journalist
***Süddeutsche Zeitung*, Munich**
**Interview No. 25:** Jörg Alt SJ, Federal spokesperson
**Jesuit Refugee Service, German**
**Interview No. 26:** Michael Hainz SJ
**JRS, Munich**
**Interview No. 27:** Frau Bauer, Director
**Refugee Council, Munich**
**Interview No. 28:** Herr Fedke, Asylum spokesperson
**Caritas, Munich**
**Interview No. 29:** Reverend Schuster, Gedankenskirche
**Protestant Church, Munich**
**Interview No. 30:** Frau Schönhuber Kirchenasyl (church sanctuary movement),
**Pax Christi, Munich**

**AUSTRALIA**

**Interview No. 31:** Sr. Kath O'Conner
**Christians in Solidarity with East Timor (CISET)**
**Interview No. 32:** Frank Elvey
**Asylum Seekers Centre**
**Interview No. 33:** Loreto Conroy/ Gabrielle Cullen
**National Council of Churches, Australia**

**Interview No. 34:** David Bitel
**President - Refugee Council of Australia**

**Interview No. 35:** Ken Hastie
**Refugee and Asylum Seekers desk, Red Cross, NSW**

**Interview No. 36:** Nick Poynder
**Lawyer, Human Rights and Equal Opportunity Commission (HREOC)**

**Interview No. 37:** Margaret Piper, Director
**Australian Refugee Council**

**Interview No. 38:** Kerry Murphy
**Solicitor, O'Donnells, ex JRS Australia**

**Interview No. 39:** Louise Abbott
**Tracing Officer, Red Cross, NSW**

**Interview No. 40:** Eve Lester
**JRS, ex RACS, Victoria**

**Interview No. 41:** David Fair
**National Red Cross, ASAS co-ordinator**

**Interview No. 42:** Paris Aristotle
**Director, Victorian Foundation for Survivors of Torture**

**Interview No. 43:** Des Hogan, Refugee Desk
**Amnesty International**

**Interview No. 44:** Caroline Graydon
**Refugee and Immigration Legal Centre,Victoria**

**Interview No. 45:** Chris Sidoti
**Human Rights and Equal Opportunity Commissioner**

**Interview No. 46:** Jenny Bedlington, First Assistant Secretary
**Refugees and Humanitarian , DIMA**

**Interview No. 47:** Bob Illingworth, Compliance and Enforcement Strategies
**Border Control and Compliance, DIMA**

**Interview No. 48:** Steven Wolfson, Ellen Hansen - Legal Officer/ Media
**UNHCR, Australia**

**Interview No. 49:** Hermine Partamian
**Inner West Migrant Resource Centre**

**Interview No. 50:** Philippa McIntosh, Juliet Moore, (formerly co-ordinator and caseworker of RACS, NSW
**Members, Refugee Review Tribunal**

**Interview No. 51:** John Godfrey, Deputy Principal Member
**Refugee Review Tribunal**

**Interview No. 52:** Peter Wertheim
**President, Jewish Board of Deputies**

**Interview No. 53:** Margaret Cunningham, Director
**Service for the Treatment and Rehabilitation of Trauma and Torture Survivors – STARTTS**

# Bibliography


Adelman, Howard et. al. (1994), *Immigration and Refugee Policy Australia and Canada Compared,* Vol I and II, Melbourne Univerity Press, Carlton.

Agamben, Giorgio (1997), 'The Camp as the Nomos of the Modern' in de Vries, Hent and Weber, Samuel (eds.). *Violence, Identity and Self-Determination,* Stanford University Press, Stanford, pp. 106-118.

Aleinikoff, T. Alexander (1995). 'State-centred Refugee Law: From Resettlement to Containment' in Daniel, E. Valentine et. al.. (eds.). *Mistrusting Refugees*, University of California Press, Berkeley. pp. 257-278.

Almond, Gabriel A. and Verba, Sidney (1989), *The Civic Culture*: political attitudes and democracy in five nations, Sage, California.

Altvater, Elmar, Brunnengräber, Achim, et al. (eds.). (1997), *Vernetzt und verstrickt. Nicht-Regierungs-Oranisationen als gesellschaftliche Produktivkraft,* Westfälisches Dampfboot, Münster.

Amnesty International (1997), *The UN and refugees' human rights. A manual on how UN human rights mechanisms can protect the rights of refugees*, Amnesty International, London.

Anderson, Benedict (1991), *Imagined Communities*, Reflection on the Origin and Spread of Nationalism, Verso, London.

Appadurai, Arjun (1996), *Modernity at Large. Cultural Dimensions of Globalization*, University of Minnesota Press, Minneapolis.

——————— (1990), 'Disjuncture and Difference in the Global Cultural Economy', *Theory, Culture and Society*, **7**, pp. 295-310.

Appiah, Kwame, Anthony (1998), 'Cosmopolitan Patriots', Pheng, & Robbins, Bruce (eds.). *Cosmopolitics. Thinking and Feeling Beyond the Nation*, University of Minnesota Press, Minneapolis, pp. 91-116.

Arendt, Hannah (1967), *The Origins of Totalitarianism*, George Allen & Unwin, London.

——————— (1958), *The Human Condition*, University of Chicago Press, Chicago.

Arato, Andrew and Cohen, Jean (1988). 'Civil Society and Social Theory', *Thesis Eleven*, **21** pp. 40-64.

Arnswald, Ulrich et al. (2000), *Sind Die deutschen Ausländerfeindlich?,* Pendo, Zürich.*Ausländerrecht: einschließlich Asylrecht* (1988), Bearbeitet von Winfried Kissrow,Verlag W. Kohlhammer, Stuttgart.

Australian National Audit Office (1998), *The Management of Boat People*, Commonwealth of Australia, Canberra.

Bade, Klaus J. (2000), *Europa in Bewegung. Migration vom späten 18. Jahrhundert biszur Gegewart*, Verlag C.H. Beck München.

——————— (1997), 'From Emigration to Immigration: The German Experience in the Nineteenth and Twentieth Centuries' in Bade, Klaus & Weiner, Myron, (eds.). *Migration Past, Migration Future*, Berghahn Books, Providence, pp. 1-38.

———— (1996), *Migration –Ethnizität– Konflikt: Systemfragen und Fallstudien*, Universitätsverlag Rasch, Osnabrück.
———— (1994a), *Ausländer Aussiedler Asyl*, Verlag C.H. Beck, Munich.
———— (1994b), 'Immigration and Social Peace in United Germany', *Daedalus*, pp. 85-106
———— (1987), *Population, Labour and Migration in 19th-and 20th-CenturyGermany*, Berg, Leamington Spa.
Balfour, Michael (1992), *Germany. The Tides of Power*, Routledge, London.
Barry, Brian and Goodin, Robert E (1992), *Free Movement. Ethical issues in the transnational migration of people and of money*, Harvester, Wheatsheaf, New York.
Barwig et al. (1994), *Asyl nach der Änderung des Grundgesetzes. Entwicklungen in Deutschland und Europa*, Nomos Verlagsgesellschaft, Baden-Baden.
Bauböck, Rainer (1994), *Transnational Citizenship. Membership and Rights inInternational Migration*, Edward Elgar, England.
———— (2000), 'Social and Cultural Integration in Civil Society' McKinnon, Catriona and Hampshcr-Monk, Iain, *The Demands of Citizenship*, Continuum, London, pp. 91-119.
Bauman, Zygmunt (1999), *In Search of Politics*, Polity Press, Cambridge.
———— (1995), 'Making and Unmaking of Strangers' *Thesis Eleven*, **43**, pp. 3-16.
———— (1989), *Modernity and the Holocaust*, Polity Press, Cambridge.
Beck, Ulrich (2000), 'What is Globalization?' in Held, David and McGrew, Anthony eds. *The Global Transformations Reader. An Introduction to the Globalization Debate*, Polity, Cambridge, pp. 99-103.
———— (1999), 'Democracy Beyond the Nation State. A Cosmopolitan Manifesto' *Dissent*, Winter, pp. 53-55.
———— (1996), 'How Neighbors Become Jews: The Political Construction of the Stranger in an age of Reflexive Modernity', *Constellations*, Vol. 2., **3**, pp. 378-396.
Beetham, David (1999), *Democracy and Human Rights*, Polity Press, Cambridge.
Benhabib, Seyla (1992), *Situating the Self. Gender, Community and Postmodernism in Contemporary Ethics*, Routledge, New York.
Benjamin, Walter (1978), *Reflections. Essays, Aphorisms, Autobiographical Writings*, Peter Demetz (ed.) Schocken Books, New York.
Berger, Suzanne (1981), *Organizing interests in Western Europe. Pluralism, corporatism, and the transformation of politics*, Cambridge University Press, Cambridge.
Bhabha Jacqueline and Shutter, Sue (1994), *Women's Movement: women under immigration, nationality and refugee law*, Trentham Books, London.
Blair, Tony and Schröder, Gerhard (2000), 'The Third Way/Die Neue Mitte' , annotated by Joanne Barkan, *Dissent* Spring, pp. 51-65.
Bohman, James and Lutz-Bachmann, Matthias (eds.) (1997), *Perpetual Peace. Essays on Kant's Cosmopolitan Idea*, Massachusetts Institute of Technology.
Bosswick, Wolfgang (2000), 'Development of Asylum Policy in Germany', *Journal of Refugee Studies*, Vol. 13, **1**, pp. 43-60.
Bourdieu, Pierre et al. (1999), *The Weight of the World. Social Suffering in Contemporary Society*, translated by Priscilla Ferguson et al. Polity Press, Cambridge.

Bourdieu, Pierre (1991), *Language and Symbolic Power,* Polity Press, Cambridge, translated by Gino Raymond and Matthew Adamson.

——— (1990), *The Logic of Practice,* translated by Richard Nice, Polity Press, Cambridge.

——— (1977), *Outline of a Theory of Practice,* translated by Richard Nice, Cambridge University Press,, Cambridge.

Brochman, Grete and Hammar, Tomas (1999), *Mechanisms of Immigration Control: A Comparative Analysis of European Regulation Policies,* Berg, Oxford.

Brown, Chris (1998), 'International Social Justice', in Boucher David, and Kelly, Paul (eds.) *Social Justice. From Hume to Walzer,* Routledge, London.

Bryant, Christopher (1997), 'Citizenship, national identity and the accommodation of difference: reflections on the German, French, Dutch and British cases', *new community* **23** (2) pp. 157-172.

Brubaker, Rogers (1994), 'Are Immigration Control Efforts Really Failing?' in Cornelius, Wayne A. et al. (eds.) *Controlling Immigration. A Global Perspective,* Stanford University Press, California, pp. 227-231.

——— (1992), *Citizenship and Nationhood in France and Germany,* Harvard University Press, Cambridge.

Brunnengräber, Achim and Walk, Heike (1997), 'Die Erweiterung der Netzwerktheorien: Nicht-Regierungs-Organisationen verquickt mit Markt und Staat' in Altvater, Elmar, Brunnengräber, Achim, et al. (eds.) *Vernetzt und verstrickt. Nicht-Regierungs-Oranisationen als gesellschaftliche Produktivkraft,* Westfälisches Dampfboot, Muenster, pp. 65-84.

Caloz-Tschopp, Marie-Claire (1997), 'On the Detention of Aliens: The Impact on Democratic Rights', *Journal of Refugee Studies,* **10** (2) pp.165-180.

Carens, Joseph (1997), 'The Philosopher and the Policymaker. Two Perspectives on the Ethics of Immigration with Special Attention to he Problem of Restricting Asylum', in Hailbronner, Kay et. al. (eds.). *Immigration Admissions. The Search for Workable Policies in Germany and The United States,* Berghahn Books, Providence, pp. 3-50.

——— (1992), 'Migration and morality: A liberal egalitarian perspective' in Barry Brian and Goodin Robert (eds.). *Free Movement. Ethical Issues in the transnational migration of people and of money,* Harvester Wheatsheaf, New York. pp.25-47,

——— (1987), 'Aliens and Citizens: The Case for Open Borders', *Review of Politics,* **49** (2) pp. 251-73,

Castles, Stephen (1996), 'Immigration and Multiculturalism in Australia' in Bade, Klaus J. Migration, Ethnizität, *Konflikt: Systemfragen und Fallstudien,* Universitätsverlag Rasch, Osnabrück. pp. 251-272

——— (1995), 'How nation-states respond to immigration and ethnic diversity', *new community* **21** (3) pp. 293-308.

——— (1994), 'Democracy and Multicultural Citizenship. Australian debates and their Relevance for Western Europe', in Bauböck, Rainer (ed*). From Aliens to Citizens. Redefining the Status of Immigrants in Europe,* Avebury, England.

Castles, Stephen & Miller, Mark J. (1993), *The Age of Migration. International Population Movements in the Modern World,* Macmillan, London.

Castles, Stephen et. al. (1988*), Mistaken Identity. Multiculturalism and the Demise of Nationalism in Australia,* Pluto Press, Sydney.

Cohen, Jean and Arato, Andrew (1992), *Civil Society and Political Theory*, MIT Press, Massachusetts.

Cohen, Jean (1999), 'Trust, voluntary association and workable democracy' in Warren, Mark. E. (ed). *Democracy and Trust*, Cambridge University Press, Cambridge, pp. 208-248.

―――――― (1985), 'Strategy or Identity: New Theoretical Paradigms and Contemporary Social Movements' *Social Research*, **52** (4) pp. 663-716.

Cohen, Roberta and Deng, Francis M. (1998*). Masses in Flight. The Global Crisis of Internal Displacement,* The Brookings Institution, Washington.

Collins, Jock and Henry, Francis (1994). 'Racism, Ethnicity and Immigration', in Adelman, Howard et al.(eds.*) Immigration and Refugee Policy. Australia and Canada Compared,* Vol. II, Melbourne University Press, Melbourne, pp. 515-548.

Collins, Jock (1988), *Migrant Hands in a Distant Land. Australia's Post-war Immigration*, Pluto Press, Sydney.

Cox, David R. and Amelsvoort, Alfred Van (1994*), The Wellbeing of Asylum seekers in Australia. A study of policies and practice with identification and discussion of the key issues*, Centre for Regional Social Development, Latrobe University.

Cox, David, and Glenn, Patrick (1994), 'Illegal Immigration and Refugee Claims' in Adelman, Howard et. al. (eds.*). Immigration and Refugee Policy. Australia and Canada Compared,* Volume I, Melbourne University Press, Carlton. pp. 283-308.

Cremer, Hans-Joachim (1998), 'Internal Controls and Actual Removals of Deportable Aliens: The Current Legal Situation in the Federal Republic of Germany, pp. 45-116. in Hailbronner, et al. (eds.*) Immigration Controls. The search for Workable Policies in Germany and the United States*, Berghahn Books, Providence.

Crock, Mary (1998), *Immigration and Refugee Law in Australia,* The Federation Press, Sydney.

―――――― (1993), 'A Legal perspective on the Evolution of Mandatory Detention' in Crock Mary, (ed*). Protection or Punishment. The Detention of Asylum Seekers in Australia,* The Federation Press Sydney, pp. 25-40.

Crock, Mary and Saul, Ben (2002), *Future Seekers. Refugees and the Law in Australia*, The Federation Press, Annandale.

Dahrendorf, Ralf (1965), *Society and Democracy in Germany*, Weidenfeld And Nicolson, London.

Dalton, Russell J. (1993), *Politics in Germany*, Harper Collins, New York.

―――――― (1988), *Citizen Politics in Western Democracies. Public Opinion and Political Parties in the United States, Great Britain, West Germany*, and France, Chatham house, New Jersey.

Daniel, Valentine E. and Knudsen John (1995), *Mistrusting Refugees*, University of California Press, Berkeley.

Davidson, Alastair (1997*), From Subject to Citizen. Australian Citizenship in the Twentieth Century,* Cambridge University Press, Melbourne.

Day, Lincoln H. (1991), *Australia's Obligation to Refugees. Working Papers in Demography*, ANU Research School of Social Sciences.

Degeling, Pieter and Colebatch, Hal (1997), 'Structure and action as constructs in the practice of public administration' in Hill, Michael (ed). The Policy Process. A Reader, second edition, Prentice Hall, London, pp. 353-363.

Department of Immigration and Multicultural Affairs, Humanitarian Settlement (2000), *Community Support for Refugees*, Discussion Paper, July.

——— (1997), *Refugee and humanitarian issues: Australia's response*, October.

Douglas, Mary (1966), *Purity and Danger, An analysis of concepts of pollution and taboo*, Routledge and Kegan Paul, London.

Dowty, Alan (1987), *Closed Borders. The Contemporary Assault on Freedom of Movement*, Yale University Press, New Haven.

Driver, Stephen and Martell Luke (1997), New Labour's communitarianism, *Critical Social Policy*, **52** (17) pp. 27-46.

Dummet, Michael (2001), *On Immigration and Refugees*, Routledge, London.

Durkheim, Emile (1965), *The Elementary Forms of the Religious Life*, New York, The Frees Press, Translated by Joseph Ward Swain, 2nd. ed.

Dworkin, Ronald (1978), *Taking Rights Seriously*, Harvard University Press, Cambridge.

Eichenhofer, Eberhard (1999), *Migration und Illegalität*, Universitätsverlag Rasch, Osnabrück.

European Council of Refugees and Exiles (1998), *Report 1996/7*.

——— (1993), *Working Paper on Airport Procedures in Europe*, London.

Eriksen, Erik and Weigárd, Jarle (2000), 'The end of Citizenship?' in McKinnon, Catriona and Hampsher-Monk, Iain (eds.). *The Demands of Citizenship*, Continuum, London, pp. 13-34.

Evans, Gareth and Grant B. (1995), *Australia's Foreign Relations in the World of the 1990s*, Melbourne University Press, Melbourne.

Faist, Thomas (1998), 'Transnational Social Spaces out of International Migration: Evolution, Significance and Future Prospects', *Archive Européenne Sociologique* **39** pp. 213-47.

Federal Race Discrimination Commissioner (1997), *Fact the Facts. Some Questions and Answers about Immigration, Refugees and Indigenous Affairs*, AGPS, Canberra.

Fekete, Liz (2000), 'How the German press stoked the Lübeck fires' *Race & Class*, **41** pp. 19-41.

Ferris, Elizabeth G. (1993). *Beyond Borders. Refugees, Migrants and Human Rights in the Post-Cold War Era*, WCC Publications, Geneva.

——— (1989). 'The Churches, Refugees, and Politics', in Loescher, Gil and Monahan, Laila (eds.). *Refugees and International Relations*, Oxford University Press, Oxford, pp. 159-178.

Fisher, William F. (1997), 'DOING GOOD? The Politics and Antipolitics of NGO Practices', *Annual Review of Anthropology*, **26** pp. 439-64.

Foster, Robert J. (1991), 'Making National Culture in the Global Ecumene', *Annual Review of Anthropology*, **20** pp.235-260.

Foucault, Michel (1978), *The History of Sexuality*, Vol. 1, Random House, New York.

——————— (1977), *Discipline and Punish. The Birth of the Prison*, Penguin Books. London.

Forment, Carlos A. (1996), 'Peripheral Peoples and Narrative Identities: Arendtian Reflections on Late Modernity' in Benhabib, Seyla (ed.). *Democracy and Difference*, pp. 314-330, Princeton University Press, New Jersey.

Forsythe, David P. (2000), *Human Rights in International Relations*, Cambridge University Press, Cambridge.

Fraser, Nancy (1997), *Justice Interrupts. Critical Reflections on the "Postsocialist" Condition*, Routledge, New York.

Fraser, Nancy & Gordon, Linda (1994), 'Reclaiming Social Citizenship: Beyond the Ideology of Contract Versus Charity' in James, Paul, *Critical Politics. From the Personal to the Global*, Arena Publications, Melbourne, pp. 59-75.

Freeman, Gary P. & Jupp, James. (1992), *Nations of Immigrants. Australia, the United States, and International Migration*, Oxford University Press , Melbourne.

Fulbrook, Mary (1990), *A Concise History of Germany*, Cambridge University Press, Cambridge.

Galbally, Frank (1978), *Review of Post-arrival Programs and Services for Migrants*, AGPS, Canberra.

Garton Ash, Timothy (1994),. *In Europe's Name. Germany and the Divided Continent*, Vintage, Great Britain.

Geißler, Hainer (1996), 'Bürger, Nation, Republik – Europa und die Multikulturelle Gesellschaft', in Bade (ed.) *Die multikulturelle Herausforderung.Menschen über Grenzen – Grenzen über Menschen*, Beck'sche Reihe, München. pp 125-146.

Gellner, Ernest (1994a), *Encounters with Nationalism*, Blackwell, Oxford.

——————— (1994b), *Conditions of Liberty. Civil Society and its Rivals*, Penguin, London.

——————— (1983), *Nations and Nationalism*, Blackwell, Oxford.

Gewirth, Alan (1982), *Human Rights. Essays on Justification and Application*, The University of Chicago Press, Chicago.

Gibney, Mark (1988), *Open Borders? Closed Societies. The Ethical and Political Issues*, Greenwood Press, New York.

Giddens, Anthony (1998), *The Third Way. The Renewal of Social Democracy*, Polity Press, Cambridge.

——————— (1979), *Central Problems in Social Theory. Action, Structure and Contradiction in Social Analysis*, MacMillan Press, London.

Gilroy, Paul (2000), *Between Camps. Nations, Cultures and the Allure of Race*, Penguin Books, London.

Global Consultations on International Protection (2001), *Refugee Protection and Migration Control: Perspectives from UNHCR and IOM*, EC/GC/01/11.

Godbout, Jacques T. (1998), *The World of the Gift*, McGill-Queen's University Press, Montreal & Kingston, Translated by Donald Winkler.

Goetz Klaus. H. (1996), 'The Federal Constitutional Court' in Smith, Gordon et. al. (eds.). *Developments in German Politics*, Macmillan press, London, pp. 96-116.

Goodin, Robert E. (1996), *The Refugee in International Law*, Clarendon, Oxford.

———— (1988). 'What Is So Special about Our Fellow Countrymen? *Ethics*, **98** pp 663-86.

Goodwin-Gill, Guy S. (2001), 'Asylum 2001 – A Convention and a Purpose', *International Journal of Refugee Law*, **13** (1/2) pp 1-15.

———— (1996), *The Refugee in International Law*, Clarendon, Oxford.

Grass, Guenther (1993), 'The Condition of Germany', *Dissent*, Spring, pp 178-88.

Gunther, Bernd SJ (1998), 'Blind Faith. Seeking asylum in a country committed to deterring immigrants' *the mustard seed,* Winter, pp. 24-26

Gutman, Amy (1994), *Multiculturalism, Examining the Politics of Recognition,* Princeton University Press, New Jersey.

Habermas, Jürgen (1998a). *The Inclusion of the Other. Studies in Political Theory*, in Cronin, Ciaran, and Del Greiff (eds.), Pablo, the MIT Press,

———— (1998b). *On the Pragmatics of Communication*, Maeve Cooke (ed.), Polity Press, Cambridge, Massachusetts.

———— (1997). *A Berlin Republic: Writings on Germany,* translated by Steven Rendall, University of Nebraska Press, Lincoln.

———— (1996a). *Between Facts and Norms. Contributions to a Discourse Theory of Law and Democracy,* (translated by William Rehg), Polity Press, Cambridge.

———— (1996b). 'Three Normative Models of Democracy' in Benhabib, Seyla (ed.). *Democracy and Difference,* pp. 21 - 30, Princeton University Press, New Jersey.

———— (1994). *The Past as Future*, Translated & edited by Max Pensky, Polity Press, Cambridge.

———— (1992) .'Citizenship and National Identity: Some reflections on the Future of Europe', *Praxis International*, **12** ( 1). pp 1-19.

———— (1985). 'Civil Disobedience: Litmus test for the Democratic Constitutional State' *Berkley Journal of Sociology*, **30**, pp. 95-116.

Hage, Ghassan (1998). *White Nation. Fantasies of White supremacy in a multicultural society*, Pluto Press, Annandale.

Hailbrooner, Kay (1998), 'New Techniques for Rendering Asylum Manageable' in Hailbronner, Kay, Martin, David and Motumura, Hiroshi (eds.) *Immigration Controls. The search for Workable policies in Germany and the United States,* Berghahn Books, United States, pp. 159-202.

Halliday, Fred (2000), 'Global Governance: Prospects and Problems' in Held, David and McGrew, Anthony (eds.). *The Global Transformations Reader. An Introduction to the Globalization Debate*, Polity Press, Cambridge, pp. 431-441.

Hall, Stuart (1990), 'Cultural Identity and Diaspora' in Rutherford,J.(ed). *Identity Community, Culture, Difference,* Lawrence & Wishart, London, pp. 222-237.

Hamilton, Andrew (1994), 'The Caroline Chisholm Series: 2', *Eureka Street*, **4** (3) April.

Hammer, Tomas (1990), *Democracy and the Nation State: Aliens, Denizens and Citizens in a World of International Migration,* Avebury, Aldershot.

Harris, Stuart and Weinfeld, Morton (1994), 'Refugees and Other Migrants, International Instruments and Future Options and Dilemmas' in Adelman, Howard et. al. *Immigration and Refugee Policy. Australian and Canada Compared,* in 2 Volumes, Melbourne University Press, Carlton, pp. 309-334.

Hathaway, James. C (1991), 'Reconceiving Refugee Law as Human Rights Protection', *Journal of Refugee Studies*, **4** (2) pp. 113-31.

———— (1997), *Reconceiving International Refugee Law*, Martinus Nijhoff Publishers, The Hague.

Hawkins, Freda (1989), *Critical Years in Immigration: Canada and Australia Compared*, New South Wales University Press, Kensington.

Hegel, G.W.F (1991), *Elements of the Philosophy of Right*, Cambridge University Press, Cambridge.

Held, David (1995), *Democracy and the Global Order. From the Modern State to Cosmopolitan Governance*, Polity Press, Cambridge UK.

Held, David and McGrew, Anthony (2000), *The Global Transformations Reader. An Introduction to the Globalization Debate*, Polity, Cambridge.

Heller, Agnes (1999), *A theory of Modernity*, Blackwell, Massachusetts.

———— (1988), 'On Being Satisfied in a Dissatisfied Society' I and II, in Heller and Feher, *The Postmodern Political Condition*, Columbia University Press, Columbia, pp. 14-43.

Höfling-Semnar, Bettina (1995), *Flucht und deutsche Asylpolitik. Von der Krise des Asylrechts zur Perfektionierung der Zugangsverhidnerung*. Westfäflisches Dampfboot, Münster.

Hof, B. (1992), 'Arbeitskrüftebefard der Wirtschaft, Arbeitsmarktchancen für Zuwanderer, in Friedrich-Ebert-Stiftung (Hrsg.)., *Zuwanderungspolitik der Zukunft, Rehe Gesprächskreis Arbeit und Soziales*, B p7-22. Bonn.

Hollifield, James F. (2000), 'The Politics of International Migration. How Can We "Bring the State Back In"?, in Brettell, Caroline B. and Hollifield, James F. (eds.). *Migration Theory. Talking across Disciplines*, Routledge, New York, pp. 137-186.

———— (1999), 'Ideas, Institutions, and Civil society. On the Limits of Immigration Control in Liberal Democracies', *IMIS-Beiträge*, University Osnabrück, **10** pp 57-90.

———— (1996), 'The Migration Crisis in Western Europe: the Search for a National Model' in Bade, Klaus (ed.) *Migration, Ethnizität Konflikt*, UniversitUatsverlag Osnabrück, Osnabrück, pp. 367-430.

Hollinger, David A. (2001), 'Not Universalists, Not Pluralists: The New Cosmopolitans Find Their Own Way', *Constellations*,. **8**. (2) pp. 236-248.

Honig, Bonnie (1993), *Political Theory and the Displacement of Politics*, Cornell University Press, Ithaca.

Honneth, Axel (1997), 'Is Universalism a Moral Trap? The Presuppositions and Limits of a Politics of Human Rights' in Bohman, James, and Lutz-Bachmann, Matthias, *Perpetual Peace. Essays on Kant's Cosmopolitan Ideal*, the MIT press, Massachusetts, pp. 155-178.

———— (1995), 'The other of justice: Habermas and the ethical challenge of postmodernism' in White, Stephen K. (ed.) *The Cambridge Companion to Habermas*, Cambridge University Press, Cambridge, pp. 289-324.

———— (1992), 'Moral Development and Social Struggle: Hegel's Early Social-Philosophical Doctrines' in Honneth et al. (eds.) *Cultural-Political Interventions in the Unfinished Project of Enlightenment*, the MIT Press, Massachusetts, pp. 197-219.

Hooghe, Liesbet and Marks, Gary (1999), 'The Making of a Polity: The Struggle over European Integration' in Kitschelt et al. (eds.) *Continuity and Change in Contemporary Capitalism,* Cambridge University Press, Cambridge. pp. 70-97.

Hudock, Ann. C. (1999), *NGOs and Civil Society. Democracy by Proxy?,* Polity Press, Cambridge.

Hudson, Bob (1997), 'Michael Lipsky and street level bureaucracy' in Hill, Michael, *The Policy Process. A Reader,* Prentice Hall/ Harvester Wheatsheaf, Hertfordshire, pp. 393-404.

Hughes, Jane and Liebaut, Fabrice (1998), *Detention of Asylum seekers in Europe: Analysis and Perspectives,* Martinus Nijhoff, Denmark.

Human Rights and Equal Opportunity Commission (1998), *Those who've come across the seas: detention of unauthorised arrivals,* Commonwealth of Australia.

Husband, Charles (1991), 'Multiculturalism as Official Policy in Australia', in Nile, Richard (ed.) *Immigration and the Politics of Ethnicity and Race in Australia and Britain,* Bureau of Immigration Research, Carlton, pp. 118-127.

Ignaticff, Michael (2001),.*Human Rights as Politics and Idolatry,* edited and introduced by Amy Gutman, Princeton University press, Princeton.

———— (1999), 'Human Rights', Hesse, Carla and Post, Robert (eds.), *Human Rights in Political Transitions: Gettysburg to Bosnia,* Zone Books, New York, pp. 313-324.

———— (1998), *The Warrior's Honor. Ethnic War and the Modern Conscience,* Chatto and Windus, London.

———— (1984), *The Needs Of Strangers,* Vintage, Great Britain.

———— (1993), *Blood and Belonging.* Journeys into the New Nationalism, Vintage, London.

Inglis, Christine et al. (1994), 'An Overview of Australian and Canadian Migration Patterns and Policies', in Adelman et. al. (eds.). *Immigration and Refugee Policy. Australia and Canada Compared,* Melbourne University press, Carlton, pp 3-30.

Ireland, Patrick R. (1997), 'Socialism, Unification Policy and the Rise of Racism in Eastern Germany' *International Migration Review,* **31** (3) pp. 541-568.

Jakubowicz, Andrew (1984), 'Ethnicity, multiculturalism and neo-conservatism', in Bottomley, Gill & De Lepervanche, Marie, *Ethnicity, Class and Gender in Australia,* George Allen & Unwin, Sydney pp. 28-48.

Jarausch, Konrad H. (ed.) (1997), *After Unity. Reconfiguring German Identities,* Berghahn Books, Providence.

Jayasuriya, Laksiri (1997). Immigration and Multiculturalism in Australia, School of Social Work and Social Administration, University of Western Australia.

Jayasuriya, Laksiri (1991), 'Multiculturalism and Pluralism in Australia', in Nile, Richard (ed). *Immigration and the Politics of Ethnicity and Race in Australia and Britain,* Bureau of Immigration Research, Carlton. pp. 81-97.

Joint Standing Committee on Migration (1994), *Asylum, Border Control and Detention,* The Parliament of the Commonwealth of Australia.

———— (1992), *Australia's Refugee and Humanitarian System: Achieving a Balance Between refuge and Control,* The Parliament of the Commonwealth of Australia.

Joly, Daniéle (1996), *Haven or Hell? Asylum Policies and Refugees in Europe,* Macmillan Press, London.

———— (1992), *Refugees. Asylum in Europe?* Minority Rights Publications, London.

Joppke, Christian and Lukes Steven (1999), *Multicultural Questions*, Oxford University Press, Oxford.

Joppke, Christian (1999), *Immigration and the Nation-State.* The United States, Germany, and Great Britain, Oxford University Press, Oxford.

———— (1998). 'Why Liberal States accept Unwanted Immigration' *World Politics,* **50** (2) pp. 266-293.

———— (1997), 'Asylum and State Sovereignty: A Comparison of the United States, Germany, and Britain' *Comparative Political Studies,* **30** (3) pp. 259-298.

Jupp, James and Kabala Marie (1993), *The Politics of Australian Immigration,* AGPS, Canberra.

Jupp, James (1994), *Exile or Refuge? The Settlement of Refugee, Humanitarian and Displaced Immigrants*, AGPS, Canberra.

———— (1991), *Australian Retrospectives. Immigration*, Sydney University Press, Melbourne.

Just, Wolf-Dieter. (1993), *Asyl von Unten. Kirchenasyl und ziviler Ungehorsam - Ein Ratgeber,* Rowohlt, Hamburg.

Kanstroom, Daniel (1993), 'Wer sind Wir Wieder? Laws of Asylum, Immigration, and Citizenship in the Struggle for the Soul of the New Germany, *The Yale Journal of International Law.* **18** (1) pp. 155-211

Kant, Immanuel (1991), *The Metaphysics of Morals,* (trans. by Mary Gregor), Cambridge University Press Cambridge

———— (1991), *Political Writings*, edited by Hand Reiss, Cambridge University Press, Cambridge.

Katzenstein, Peter J. (1987), *Policy and Politics in West Germany. The Growth of a Semisovereign State,* Temple University Press, Philadelphia.

Keck and Sikkink (1998), *Activists Beyond Borders. Advocacy Networks in International Politics,* Cornell University Press, Ithaca.

Keely, Charles,B. & Stanton Russell, Sharon (1994), 'Responses of Industrial Countries to Asylum-Seekers', *Journal of International Affairs*, **47** (2) pp. 399-417.

Keely, Charles B. (1996). 'How nation-States Create and Respond to Refugee Flows', *International Migration Review,* **4** pp. 1046-1066.

Kingston, Margo (1993), 'Politics and Public Opinion' in Crock Mary, (ed). *Protection or Punishment. The Detention of Asylum Seekers in Australia,* The Federation Press Sydney, pp. 8-14.

Kohn, Hans (1967), *The Idea of Nationalism,* 2nd edition, Collier-Macmillann, New York.

Kommitee für Grundrechte und Demokratie (1998), *Menschenrechte ohne Asyl in Deutschland*, Sensbachtal.

Koser, Khalid (2000), 'Germany: protection for refugees or protection from refugees?' in van Selm, J. (ed.) *Kosovo's Refugees in the European Union*, Pinter, London, pp. 24-42.

———————— (1996). 'European migration report: recent asylum migration in Europe' *New Community*, **22** (2) pp. 151-158.

Krais, Jürgen and Tausch, Christian (1995), *Asylrecht und Asylverfahren*, Deutscher Taschenbuch Verlag, Munich.

Kulluk, Fahrünnisa E. (1996), 'The political discourse on quota immigration in Germany', *New Community*, **22** (2), pp. 301-320.

Kumin, Judith (1996), 'Harmonization of refugee law: Can the protection gap be closed?, unpublished paper given to the *International Baar Association*, Berlin, 23 October.

———————— (1995), 'Asylum in Europe: Sharing or shifting the Burden?', *World Refugee Survey* 1995, UNHCR

Kunz, E. (1988), *Displaced Persons: Calwell's New Australians*, ANU Press, Sydney.

Kurthen, Hermann et al.(1997), *Antisemitism and Xenophobia in Germany after Unification*, Oxford University Press, Oxford.

———————— (1995), 'Germany at the Crossroads: National Identity and the Challenges of Immigration' International *Migration Review*, **4**, pp. 914-938.

Kymlicka, Will (1995), *Multicultural Citizenship. A Liberal Theory of Minority Rights*. Clarendon Press Oxford.

———————— (1995), *The Rights of Minority Cultures*, Oxford University Press Oxford.

Lack, John, & Tempelton, Jacqueline (1995), *Bold Experiment. A Documentary History of Australian Immigration since 1945*. Oxford University Press Melbourne.

Leuninger, Herbert (1995), 'Vom Rechtssubjekt zum Objekt des Staates. Das neue Asylrecht als Entrechtung des Flüchtlings' in. Basso-sekretariat, Berlin (eds.) *Festung Europa Auf der Anklagebank*, Westfälisches Dampfboot, pp. 74-81.

———————— (1993), 'Flüchtlinge werden zu Sündenböcken gemacht', in Sommer J. (ed.) *Asyl. Fremde in der Festung Europa*. Benziger, Zürich, pp. 37-46.

Lipschutz, Ronnie D. (1992), 'Reconstructing World Politics: The Emergence of Global Civil Society', Millennium: *Journal of International Studies* **21** (3) pp. 389-420.

Locke, John (1960), *Two Treatises of Government*, Cambridge University Press, Cambridge.

Loescher, Gil and Monahan, Laila (1989), *Refugees and International Relations*, Oxford University Press, Oxford.

Loescher, Gil (1997), 'Protection and Humanitarian Action in the Post-Cold War Era, *Migration Policy in Global Perspective Series*: Working Paper #11 The International Center for Migration, Ethnicity and Citizenship, New School for Social Research, New York.

———————— (1994), 'The International Refugee Regime: Stretched to the Limit?' *Journal of International Affairs*, **47** (2) pp. 351-377.

———————— (1993). *Beyond Charity. International Co-operation and the Global Refugee Crisis*, Oxford University Press, New York.

MacCallum, Mungo (2002), 'Girt by Sea. Australia, the Refugees and the Politics of Fear', *Quarterly Essay*, **5**, pp. 1-73.

MacIntyre, Alasdair (1985), *After Virtue, A study in Moral Theory*, 2nd edition, Duckworth, London.

McMaster, Donald (2001), *Asylum Seekers. Australia's Response to Refugees,* Melbourne University Press, Carlton.

Mansbridge, Jane (1996), 'Using Power/Fighting Power: The Polity' in Benhabib, Seyla (ed.). *Democracy and Difference*, pp. 46-66, Princeton University Press, New Jersey.

Mansouri, Fethi and Bagdas, Melek (2002), *Politics of Social Exclusion: Refugees on Temporary protection Visas in Victoria*, Deakin University, Geelong.

Manz, Beatriz (1995), 'Fostering Trust in a Climate of Fear' in Valentine, Daniel E. and Knudsen John (eds.). *Mistrusting Refugees*, University of California Press, Berkeley, pp. 151-167.

Marcuse, Herbert (1965), 'Repressive Tolerance', in *A Critique of Pure Tolerance*, Beacon Press, Boston, pp. 80-123.

Mares, Peter (2001), *Borderline. Australia's treatment of refugees and asylum seekers,* University of New South Wales Press, Sydney.

Margalit, Avishai (1997), 'The Moral Psychology of Nationalism' in McKim, Robert and McMahan Jeff (eds.). *The Morality of Nationalism*, Oxford University Press, New York, pp. 74-87.

———— (1996), *The Decent Society*, Harvard University Press, Massachusetts.

Markus, Maria (2001), 'Decent Society and/or Civil Society?1', *Social Research,* **68** (4), pp. 954-973.

———— (1995). 'Civil Society and the Politicisation of Needs', in Gavroglu K. et. al (eds.). *Science, Politics and Social Practice*, Kluwer Academic Publishers, The Netherlands, pp. 161-179.

Marr, David and Wilkinson, Marian (2003), Dark Victory, Allen and Unwin, Crows Nest.

Marrus, Michael R. (1985), *The Unwanted. European Refugees in the Twentieth Century,* Oxford University Press, New York.

Marrus, Michael R. and Bramwell, Anna C. (1988), *Refugees in the Age of Total War,* Unwin Hyman, London.

Marshall, Barbara (1996), *British and German Refugee Policies in the European Context,* Discussion Paper 63, Royal Institute of International Affairs, London.

Marshall, T.H. (1950), *Citizenship and Social Class, and Other Essays,* Cambridge University Press, Cambridge.

Mattson, Michelle (1995), 'Refugees in Germany: Invasion or Invention? *New German Critique*, **64**, pp. 61-86.

Martin, Philip (1994), 'Germany: 'Reluctant Land of Immigrants', in Cornelius et al. (eds.) *Controlling Immigration. A Global Perspective*, pp.189-226.

Martin, Jean (1978), *The Migrant Presence. Australian Responses 1947-1977,* (Research Report for the National Population Inquiry), George Allen & Unwin, Sydney.

———— (1965), *Refugee Settlers: A Study of Displaced Persons in Australia*, ANU, Canberra.

Mauss, Marcel (1990), *The Gift: Forms and Function of Exchange in Archaic Societies,* Routledge, New York.

May, Larry & Kohn, Jerome (1996), *Hannah Arendt. Twenty Years Later,* The MIT Press, Cambridge.

Mediansky, Fedor (1998), 'Detention of Asylum Seekers: The Australian Perspective', in Hughes, Jane and Liebaut, Fabrice (eds.). *Detention of Asylum seekers in Europe: Analysis and Perspectives,* Martinus Nijhoff, Denmark, pp. 125-139.

Mehrländer, Ursula (1994), 'The Development of Post-War Migration and Refugee Policy' in Spencer, Sarah (ed.) *Immigration as an Economic Asset: the German Experience,* Trentham Books, London. pp. 1-14.

——— (1993), 'Federal Republic of Germany: Sociological Aspects of Migration Policy' in Kubat D. (ed.) *The Politics of Migration Policies: Settlement and Integration The First World into the 1990s,* Center for Migration Studies, New York.

——— (1974), Soziale Aspekte der Ausländerbeschäftigung, Bonn, Bad Godsberg.

Meier-Braun, Karl-Heinz (1995), '40 Jahre "Gastarbeiter" und Ausländerpolitik in Deutschland' in Aus Politik und Zeitgeschichte B35/95, *Bundeszentrale für politische Bildung*, Bonn, pp. 14-22.

Melucci, Alberto (1989), *Nomads of the Present. Social Movements and Individual Needs in Contemporary Society,* Century Hutchinson, London.

——— (1996), *Challenging Codes. Collective action in the information age,* Cambridge University Press, Cambridge.

——— (1992), 'Challenging Codes: Framing and Ambivalence in the Ideology of Social Movements', *Thesis Eleven*] **31**, pp. 131-142.

——— (1988), 'Social Movements and the Democratisation of Everyday Life', in Keane,J.(ed). *Civil Society and the State,* Verso, London, pp. 245-260.

Messner, Dirk (1997), 'Netzwerktheorien: Die Suche nach Ursachen und Auswegen aus der Krise staalicher Teuerungsfähigkeit' in Altvater, Elmar, Brunnengräber, Achim, et. al. (eds.).*Vernetzt und verstrickt. Nicht-Regierungs-Oranisationen als gesellschaftliche Produktivkraft,* Westfälisches Dampfboot, Muenster, pp. 27-64.

Modood, Tariq and Werbner, Pnina (ed.) (1997), *The Politics of Multiculturalism in the New Europe: Racism, Identity and Community,* Zed Books, London.

Müller, Johannes (1996), *Flüchltinge und Asyl. Politisch handeln aus christlicher Verantwortung,* Verlag Josef Knecht, Frankfurt a.M.

Münch, Richard (1996), 'German Nation and German Identity', in Heurlin, Bertel (ed). *Germany in Europe in the Nineties,* Macmillan Press, London, pp. 13-43.

Münch, Ursula (1993), *Asylpolitik in der Bundesrepublik Deutschland. Entwicklung und Alternativen,* Leske + Budrich.

Münz, Rainer (1994), 'European East-West Migration, 1945-1992', *International Migration Review,* **28** (33), pp. 520-538.

Münz, Rainer and Ulrich, Ralf (1997), 'Changing Patterns of Immigration to Germany' in Bade, Klaus and Weiner, Myron (eds.) *Migration Past, Migration Future. Germany and the United States,* Berghahn Books, Providence, pp. 65-119.

Muus, Philip (ed.) (1997), *Exclusion and Inclusion of Refugees in contemporary Europe,* ERCOMER, Utrecht.

Neuman, Gerald (1993), 'Buffer Zones Against Refugees: Dublin, Schengen, and the German Asylum Amendment', *Virginia Journal of International Law,* **33** (3), pp. 503-526.

Nicholls (1998) 'Unsettling Admissions: Asylum Seekers in *Australia' Journal of Refugee Studies* **11**(2), pp. 61-79.

Noiriel Gérard (1994), *Die Tyrannei des Nationalen. Sozialgeschichte des Asylrechts in Europa* (German Edition), zu Klampen, Lüneberg.

Nussbaum, Martha C. (2000), *Women and Human Development. the Capabilities Approach*, Cambridge University Press, Cambridge.

—————— (1997), 'Kant and Cosmopolitanism', in Bohman, James, and Lutz-Bachmann, Matthias, *Perpetual Peace. Essays on Kant's Cosmopolitan Ideal,* the MIT press, Massachussetts. pp. 25-58.

O'Brien, Peter (1988), 'Continuity and Change in Germany's Treatment of Non-Germans', *International Migration Review*, **22** (3), pp. 109-134

Offe, Claus (1992), 'Bindings, Shackles, Brakes: On Self-Limitation Strategies, in Honneth, A., McCarthy, T.,Offe, C & Wellmer,A. (eds.). *Cultural-Political Interventions in the Unfinished Project of Enlightenment*, MIT Press, Massachusetts, pp. 63-94.

—————— (1981), 'The attribution of public status to interest groups: observation on the West German case', in Berger, Suzanne (ed.)., *Organizing interests in Western Europe. Pluralism, corporatism, and the transformation of politics*, Cambridge University Press, Cambridge. pp. 123-158.

O'Neill, Onara (2000), *Bounds of Justice*, Cambridge University Press, Cambridge.

—————— (1986), *Faces of Hunger. An Essay on Poverty, Justice and Development,* Allen & Unwin, London.

Overbeek, Henk (1995), 'Towards a new international migration regime: globalization, migration and the internationalization of the state', in Miles, Robert, and Thränhardt, Dietrich (eds.). *Migration and European Integration. The Dynamics of Inclusion and Exclusion,* Pinter, London, pp. 15-36.

Padgett, Stephen (2000), *Organizing democracy in eastern Germany. Interest groups in post-communist society,* Cambridge University Press, Cambridge.

Pateman Carole (1985), *The Problem of Political Obligation. A Critique of Liberal Theory*, Polity Press, Oxford.

Peck, Jeffrey et al. (1997), 'Natives, Strangers and Foreigners: Constituting Germans by Constructing Others', in Jarausch, Konrad H. (ed.) *After Unity. Reconfiguring German Identities,* Berghahn Books, Providence, pp. 61-102.

Pensky, Max (1995), 'Universalism and the situated critic', in White, Stephen (ed.). *The Cambridge Companion to Habermas,* Cambridge University Press, Cambridge, pp. 67-96.

Pfaff, V (1994), 'Die Entkernung des Asylgrundrechts' in Pro Asyl (ed.) *Tag des Flüchtlings,* 30 September, pp. 6-11.

Phillips, Anne (1996), 'Dealing with Difference: A Politics of Ideas, or a Politics of Presence?' in Benhabib, Seyla (ed.). *Democracy and Difference*, pp. 139-152, Princeton University Press, New Jersey.

Pickering, Sharon et.al. (2003), *'We're working with people here' The impact of the TPV regime on refugee settlement service provision in NSW*, unpublished report, Charles Sturt University.

Piper, Margaret (1994), 'The Role of NGOs in Refugee *Protection' Old Problems, New Directions,* unpublished paper, Proceedings of the Conference on Refugee Protection, Australian Council of Churches, Sydney.

Pitkin, Hanna, Fenichel (1998), *The Attack of the Blob. Hannah Arendt's Concept of the Social,* The University of Chicago Press, Chicago.

Plaut, Gunther (1995), *Asylum. A Moral Dilemma*, Praeger, Westport Conneticut.

Pogge, Thomas W. (1992), 'Cosmopolitanism and Sovereignty' *Ethics* **103**, pp. 48-75.

Poole, Ross (1999), *Nation and Identity*, Routledge, London.

Poynder, Nick (1995), 'Recent Implications of the Refugee Convention in Australia and the Law of Accommodation to International Human Rights Treaties. Have We Gone Too Far?, *Australian Journal of Human Rights*, **2** (1), pp. 76-90.

Prantl, Heribert (1995), *Deutschland leicht entflammbar. Ermittlungen gegen die Bonner Politik,* Fischer Taschenbuch Verlag, Frankfurt am Main.

Pusey, Michael (1991), *Economic Rationalism in Canberra. A Nation Building State Changes its Mind,* Cambridge University Press, Cambridge.

Putnam, Robert (1993), *Making democracy work: civic traditions in modern Italy,* Princeton University Press, Princeton.

Radtke, Frank-Olaf (1998), 'Lob der Gleich-Gültigkeit. Die Konstruktion des Fremden im Diskurs des Multikulturalismus', in Bielefeld, Ulrich (ed.) *Das Eigene und das Fremde. Neuer Rassismus in der alten Welt?* Hamburger Edition, Insitut für Sozialforschung, Hamburg, pp. 79-96.

Räthzel, Nora (1995), 'Aussiedler and Ausländer: Transforming German National Identity, in *Social Identities*, **1** (2)., August, pp. 263-282.

Rawls, John (1999),.*The Law of Peoples. With "The Idea of Public Reason Revisited"*, Harvard University Press, Massachusetts.

———— (1993), *Political Liberalism*, Columbia University Press, New York.

———— (1972), *A Theory of Justice*, Oxford University Press, Oxford.

Refugee Review Tribunal (1994), *Annual Report 1993/4*, Australian Government Publishing Service.

Renan, Ernest (1994), 'Qu'est-ce qu'une nation?' in Hutchinson, John and Smith, Anthony D (eds.). *Nationalism*, Oxford University press, Oxford, pp. 17-18.

Reynolds, Henry (2001), *The question of genocide in Australia's history. An indelible stain?*, Viking, Ringwood.

Richmond, Anthony (1988), 'Sociological Theories of International Migration: The Case of Refugees', *Current Sociology*, **36**(2), pp. 7-5.

Rittstieg, Helmut & Rowe, Gerard (1992), *Einwanderung als gesellschafliche herausforderung. Inhalt und rechtliche Grundlagen einer neuen Politik. Eine Untersuchung im Auftrag des Amtes für multikulturelle* Angelegenheiten der Stadt Frankfurt am Main, Nomos Verlagsgesellschaft, Baden-Baden.

Risse, Thomas and Sikkink, Kathryn (1999), 'The socialization of international human rights norms into domestic practices: introduction' in Risse, Thomas, Ropp, Stephen C. and Sikkink, Kathryn, *The Power of Human Rights. International Norms and Domestic Change,* Cambridge University Press, Cambridge, pp. 1-38.

Risse, Thomas and Ropp, Stephen (1999), 'International human rights norms and domestic change: conclusions' in Risse, Thomas, Ropp, Stephen C. and Sikkink, Kathryn, *The Power of Human Rights. International Norms and Domestic Change*, Cambridge University Press, Cambridge, pp. 234-278.

Rorty, Richard (1998), 'Justice as a Larger Loyalty', in Cheah, Pheng, & Robbins, Bruce (eds.) *Cosmopolitics. Thinking and Feeling Beyond the Nation*, University of Minnesota Press, Minneapolis, pp. 45-58.

Rosenau, James N. (2000), .'Governance in a Globalizing World' in Held, David and McGrew, Anthony (eds.) *The Global Transformations Reader. An Introduction to the Globalization Debate*, Polity Press, Cambridge, pp. 181-190.

Roth, Claudia and Hanf, Petra (1998), 'Restriktiv - effektiv - undemokratisch: Freizügigkeit, Asyl und Einwanderung im neuen EU- Vertrag' in Fischer, Martina (ed). *Fluchtpunkt Europa. Migration und Multikultur*, Suhrkamp, Fankfurt am Main, pp. 201-210.

Rubio-Marin, Ruth (2000), *Immigration as a Democratic Challenge. Citizenship and Inclusion in Germany and the United States*, Cambridge University Press, Cambridge.

Sandel, Michael (1998), *Liberalism and the Limits of Justice*, second edition, Cambridge University Press, Cambridge.

——— (1984), *Liberalism and its Critics*, Basil Blackwell, Oxford.

Santel, Bernhard (1995), 'Loss of control: the build-up of a European migration and asylum regime', in Miles, Robert, and Thränhardt, Dietrich (eds.). *Migration and European Integration. The Dynamics of Inclusion and Exclusion*, Pinter, London, pp. 75-91.

Salamon, I. M. (1994), 'The rise of the nonprofit sector', *Foreign Affairs*, **73**(4), 109-22.

Saramago, José (1997), *Blindness*, translated by Juan Sager, The Harvill Press, London.

Sassen, Saskia (1998), *Globalization and its Discontents*, The New Press, New York.

Scarry, Elaine (1999), 'The Difficulty of Imagining Other Persons' Hesse, Carla and Post, Robert (eds.), *Human Rights in Political Transitions*: Gettysburg to Bosnia, Zone Books, New York, pp. 277-312.

——— (1985), The Body in Pain. The making and Unmaking of the World, Oxford University Press, Oxford.

Schmitt-Beck, Rüdiger (1992), 'A myth insitutionalized. Theory and research on social movements in Germany', *European Journal of Political Research*, **21**, pp. 357-383.

Schubarth, Wilfried (1997), 'Xenophobia among East German Youth' in Kurthen, Hermann et. al. (eds.).*Antisemitism and Xenophobia in Germany after Unification*, Oxford University Press, Oxford, pp. 143-158.

Schweitzer, Carl-Christoph et al (1995), *Politics and Government in Germany, 1944-1994. Basic Documents*, Berghahn Books, Providence.

Senders, Stefan (1996), 'Laws of Belonging: Legal Dimensions of National Inclusion in Germany', *New German Critique*, **67**, pp. 147-176.

Seligman, Adam B. (1992),. *The Idea of Civil Society*, The Free Press, New York.

Shue, Henry (1988), 'Mediating Duties', *Ethics*, **98**, pp. 687-704.

——— (1980), *Basic Rights. Subsistence, Affluence, and U.S. Foreign Policy*, Princeton University Press, New Jersey.

Sikkink, Kathryn (1993), 'Human rights, principled issue-networks, and sovereignty in Latin America, *International Organization* **47**(3), pp. 411-41.

Silove, Derrick et al. (2000), 'Policies of Deterrence and the Mental Health of Asylum Seekers' *Journal of the American Medical Association*, **284**(5), pp. 604 - 611.

Silove, Derrick and Steel Zachary (1998), *The Mental Health and Well-Being of On-Shore Asylum Seekers in Australia*, Psychiatry and Teaching Unity, University of New South Wales.

Silove, Derrick et al. (1993), *Retraumatisation of Asylum-Seekers*, unpublished paper.

Smith, Anthony D. (1998), *Nationalism and Modernism. A critical survey of recent theories of nations and nationalism*, Routledge, London.

Soysal, Yasemin Nuhoglu (1994), *Limits of Citizenship. Migrants and Postnational Membership in Europe*, The University of Chicago, Chicago.

Spencer, Sarah (1994), *Immigration as an Economic Asset. The German Experience*, Trentham Books, Staffordshire.

Storey, Andy (1998), 'The ethics of immigration controls: issues for development NGOs' in Eade, Deborah (ed). *Development and Rights*, Oxfam, Oxford, pp. 114-127.

Storey Hugo (1995), 'Human Rights and the New Europe: Experience and Experiment', in Beetham, David (ed.) *Politics and Human Rights*, Blackwell, Oxford.

Strange, Susan (1996), *The Retreat of the State. The diffusion of power in the world economy*, Cambridge University Press, Cambridge.

Tabonni, Simonetta (1995), 'The Stranger and Modernity: From Equality of Rights to Recognition of Difference' *Thesis Eleven*, **43**, pp. 16-27.

Tam, Henry (1998),. *Communitarianism. A new Agenda for Politics and Citizenship*, New York University Press, New York.

Tamir, Yael (1993), Liberal Nationalism, Princeton University Press, Princeton.

Tarrow, Sidney (1998), *Power in Movement. Social Movements and Contentious Politics*, 2nd edition, Cambridge University Press, Cambridge.

Taylor, John (1998), *Body Horror. Photojournalism, Catastrophe and War*, Manchester University Press, Manchester.

Taylor, Charles (1996), 'A World Consensus on Human Rights?' *Dissent*, Summer, pp. 15-21.

——————— (1994), 'The Politics of Recognition', in Gutmann, Amy (ed). *Multiculturalism. Examining the Politics of Recognition*, Princeton University Press, Princeton, pp. 25-74.

Taylor, Savitry (2000), 'Should unauthorised arrivals in Australia have free access to advice and assistance?' *Australian Journal of Human Rights*, **6**(1), pp. 34-58.

Tazreiter, Claudia (2002), 'History, Memory and the stranger in the practice of detention in Australia' *Journal of Australian Studies*, **72**, pp. 3-12.

Thorburn, Joanne (1996), 'Root Cause Approaches to Forced Migration: Part of a Comprehensive Strategy? A European Perspective', *Journal of Refugee Studies*, B(2), pp. 119-135.

Thränhardt, Dietrich (1996a), 'European migration from East to West', *new community* **22**(2), April, pp. 227-242.

——————— (1996b), *Germany's Immigration Policies and Politics*, unpublished paper.

——————— (1995a), *Die Lebenslage der ausländischen Bevölkerung in der Bundesrepublik Deutschland. Bundeszentrale für politische Bildung*, Bonn.

———— (1995b), *Die Reform der Einbürgerung in Deutschland' in Einwanderungs konzeption für die Bundesrepublik Deutschland*, Friedrich Ebert Stiftung.

———— (1992), 'Germany - An Undeclared Immigration Country' in Thränhardt, Dietrich (ed.) *Europe - A new Immigration Continent. Policies and Politics in comparative Perspective*, Lit Verlag, Münster, pp. 167- 194.

Touraine, Alain (1988), *Return of the Actor. Social Theory in Postindustrial Society*, University of Minnesota Press, Minneapolis.

Turner, Bryan S. (1990), 'Outline of a Theory of Citizenship', *Sociology*, **24**, pp. 189-217.

United Nations High Commissioner for Refugees (2000). *The State of the World's Refugees. Fifty Years of Humanitarian Action*, Oxford University Press, Oxford.

———— (2000), *Reconciling Migration Control And Refugee Protection In The European Union: A UNHCR Perspective*, Geneva, October.

———— (1999), *Protection Refugees. A Field Guide for NGOs*, United Nations Publications.

———— (1997), *The State of the World's Refugees. A Humanitarian Agenda*, Oxford University Press, Oxford.

———— (1995), *The State of the World's Refugees. In Search of Solutions*. Oxford University Press, Oxford.

———— (1993), *The State of the World's Refugees. The Challenge of Protection*, Oxford. University Press, Oxford.

United Nations General Assembly (2000), *Executive Committee of the High Commissioner's Programme* (Fifty-first session) A/AC. 96/9307, July, Note on International Protection.

UNHCR/IOM (2001), 'Refugee Protection and Migration Control: Perspectives from UNHCR and IOM', *Global Consultations on International Protection*, May, EG/GC/01/11

UNHCR/ A. Hollman (2001), *Refugees by Numbers*.

Van der Veer, Peter (1997), 'The Victim's Tale: Memory and Forgetting in the Story of Violence', in De Vries, Hent and Weber, Samuel, *Violence, Identity, and Self-Determination*, Stanford University Press, Stanford, pp. 186-200.

Vasta, Ellie (1996), 'Dialectics of domination: Racism and multiculturalism' in Vasta Ellie and Castles Stephen (eds.). *The Teeth are Smiling; The persistence of racism in multicultural Australia*, Allen & Unwin, St Leonards, pp./46-72.

Vertovec, Steven (1996), 'Berlin Multikulti: Germany, 'foreigners' and 'world-openness' *new community* **22**(3) pp. 381-399.

Viviani, Nancy (1996), *The Indochinese in Australia, 1975-1995: From Burnt Boats to Barbecues*, Oxford University Press.

———— (1984), *The Long Journey: Vietnamese Migration and Settlement in Australia*, Melbourne University Press.

Wagner, Wolf (1996), *Kulturschock Deuschland*, Rotbuch Verlag, Hamburg.

Wahl, Peter (1997), 'Mythos und RealitUat internationaler Zivilgesellschaft. Zu den Perspektiven globaler Vernetzung von Nicht-Regierungs-Organistionen' in Altvater, Elmar, Brunnengraeber, Achim, et al. (eds.) *Vernetzt und verstrickt.Nicht-Regierungs-Oranisationen als gesellschaftliche Produktivkraft*, Westfälisches Dampfboot, Münster, pp. 293-314.

Waldron, Jeremy (1996), 'Minority Cultures and the Cosmopolitan Alternative' in Kymlicka, Will (ed). *The Rights of Minority Cultures*, Oxford University Press, Oxford pp. 93-122.

Wallraff, Günter (2000), 'Die Intoleranz des anderen zu dulden ist nichts anderes als Freiheit' in Arnswald, Ulrich et al. (eds.) *Sind Die Deutschen Ausländerfeindlich?*, Pendo, Zürich, pp. 137-144.

——— (1988), *Ganz unten. Mit einer Dokumentation der Folgen*, 2nd edition, Kiepenheuer & Witsch, Köln.

Walzer, Michael (1991), 'The Idea of Civil Society', *Dissent*, 1991, Spring, pp. 293-304.

——— (1983), *Spheres of Justice. A Defence of Pluralism and Equality*, Martin Robertson, Oxford.

Weber, Max (1947), *The Theory of Social and Economic Organization*, The Free Press, New York, Translated by A.M. Henderson and Talcott Parsons.

——— (1946), 'Politics as a Vocation', in Gerth, H.H. & Mills, C. Wright, *From Max Weber, Essays in Sociology*, Oxford University Press, New York, pp. 77-128.

Wcbcr, Ralf (1998), *Extremtraumatisierte Flüchtling in Deutschland. Asylrecht und Asylverfahren*, Campus, Verlag, Frankfurt.

Weller, Patrick (2002), *Don't Tell the Prime Minister*, Scribe Publications, Melbourne.

Wolf, Christa (1997), *Parting from Phantoms. Selected Writings, 1990-1994*, University of Chicago Press, Chicago.

Wolin, Sheldon (1996), 'Fugitive Democracy' in Benhabib, Seyla (ed.). *Democracy and Difference*, pp. 31-45, Princeton University Press, New Jersey.

Young, Iris Marion (1998), 'Polity and Group Difference: A Critique of the ideal of Universal Citizenship', in Shafir, Gershon. (ed.). *The Citizenship Debates*, University of Minnesota Press, Minneapolis. pp 263-290.

Zolberg, Aristide et al. (1989), *Escape from Violence. Conflict and the Refugee Crisis in the Developing World*, Oxford University Press, New York.

Zolberg, Aristide R. (1999), 'Matters of State: Theorizing Immigration Policy'. in Massey Douglas (ed.). *Becoming American, American Becoming*, Russell Sage, New York.

# Index